HISTORY OF THE CHANNEL ISLANDS

Also by Raoul Lemprière

PORTRAIT OF THE CHANNEL ISLANDS

HISTORY OF
THE
CHANNEL
ISLANDS

RAOUL LEMPRIÈRE

Robert Hale & Company · Publishers

© *Raoul Lemprière 1974*
First published in Great Britain 1974

ISBN 0 7091 4252 8

Robert Hale & Company
63 Old Brompton Road
London S.W.7

PRINTED IN GREAT BRITAIN
BY EBENEZER BAYLIS & SON LIMITED
THE TRINITY PRESS, WORCESTER, AND LONDON

Contents

Illustrations

MAPS

Acknowledgements

I would thank the following for assistance in the preparation of this book:

Jersey: Miss I. Croad; Mr Raymond Falle, Local History Librarian and Miss L. M. Jurd, Reference Library Assistant, Jersey Public Libraries; Mr T. G. Hutt; Mr R. H. Mayne, a Vice-President of the Société Jersiaise; Mr H. T. Porter; Dr J. T. Renouf, Curator of the Museum of the Société Jersiaise; Mrs Joan Stevens, President of the Société Jersiaise.

Guernsey: Mr C. H. de Sausmarez, M.B.E.; Miss R. de Sausmarez; Mr C. D. Eley, Chief Officer of the Guernsey Police; Mr R.W. J. Payne, Hon. Secretary of the Société Guernesiaise; Mr J. C. H. Sheppard, Chief Librarian of the Guille-Allès Library; Mr J. M. Y. Trotter, Librarian of the Priaulx Library; Mr R. H. Videlo, Her Majesty's Greffier.

Alderney: Mr P. W. Radice, Clerk of the States.
Sark: Mr H. Carré, Greffier.

Oxford: Mr Robin Peedell, Assistant-Librarian, Brasenose College; Mr J. R. Maddicott, Librarian and Archivist, Exeter College.

Poole: Mr R. F. Hawker, D.S.O., O.B.E., Borough Engineer and Surveyor; Mr H. F. V. Johnstone, Reference Librarian, Poole Public Libraries.

Windsor: Mr Derek Shawe, D.F.C., Chapter Clerk, St George's Chapel.
Salem, Mass.: Mrs Charles A. Potter, Librarian, James Duncan Phillips Library, Essex Institute.

I would also thank my wife for her constant help and encouragement throughout the writing of this book, and, in particular, for typing the manuscript.

The photographs of present-day Guernsey are reproduced by permission of Mr Carel Toms. The photographs of the Golden Torque and the German prisoners leaving Jersey in 1945 are reproduced by permission of the Société Jersiaise. The photograph of Princess Margaret in Jersey in 1959 is reproduced by permission of the *Jersey Evening Post*. The remainder of the photographs, with the exception of those of St Martin's Church, Castle Cornet, Market Place (1838), High Street and Elizabeth College, Guernsey, are of items in the author's collection and were taken by Mr D. J. Le Brocq and Mr C. R. Le Clercq of Jersey, for whose co-operation and interest I am obliged.

St Helier   RAOUL LEMPRIÈRE

To
BRIGITTE

Preface

I summon up remembrance of things past.
William Shakespeare (1564–1616)

The Channel Islands, situated off the west coast of Normandy, are divided into the two bailiwicks of Jersey and Guernsey. The Bailiwick of Jersey comprises the island of that name (45 square miles) and two small reefs of islets known respectively as the Ecréhous and the Minquiers. The Ecréhous lie off the north-east coast of Jersey, approximately half-way between the island and France. The three main islets of the group are Maître Ile, Marmotière and Blanc Ile. The Minquiers cover a large area and lie off the south coast of Jersey, less than half-way between the island and France. The main islets are Maîtresse Ile and Les Maisons. The Bailiwick of Guernsey comprises the island of that name (24 square miles), Alderney, Sark, Herm and Jethou. The prevailing wind is south-west and the Gulf Stream causes the islands' climate to be warmer than it otherwise would be. All the principal islands are inhabited, both Jersey and Guernsey being densely populated.

The Channel Islands, despite a high degree of development in both Jersey and Guernsey and the many thousands of visitors who visit all of them each year, still retain much natural beauty, especially in coastal scenery. There is a family resemblance between all the group, arising from a common geographical location and a common history and development, but each has its distinctive character. Some place-names are shared by several of the islands and sometimes with Normandy as well. Granite is found in all the islands and has been used in building for centuries. The two main towns in the group, St Helier and St Peter Port, are entirely dissimilar, the former being principally built on a low-lying flat area and the latter on a series of hills and slopes.

Jersey lying slightly to the east and apart from the other islands is sophisticated, full of life and vitality, appealing to wealthy residents, tourists and bankers, at the same time retaining a strong, if declining,

agricultural element. Guernsey, the hub of the other islands, is less sophisticated, has a strong agricultural element, some wealthy residents and
bankers and fewer tourists. Alderney, windswept and bleak when the sky
darkens and the wind blows and the sea is whipped into a fury, is independent, free and easy, appealing to residents and tourists who wish to
'get away from it all'. Sark, beautiful and tranquil, attracting those who
seek quietness and solitude, is a place where time pauses even if it does not
quite stand still. Little Herm, favoured for its shell beach, on a fine warm
summer's day, is compared with a South Sea island by those who have
never seen one.

The Channel Islands are highly populated. At the census held in 1971
Jersey had a population of 69,329, Guernsey 50,436, Alderney 1,690, Sark
and Brechou 582, Herm and Jethou 105. Until the beginning of the
nineteenth century the population consisted of the native inhabitants who
were predominantly, although not exclusively, of Norman descent and
a few non-natives. Nowadays a high proportion of the population
consists of non-natives or persons of non-native descent.

Down the centuries the Channel Islands have achieved a high degree of
autonomy and have developed a distinctive form of government,
judiciary and civil administration.

Both bailiwicks have a lieutenant-governor, who represents the Crown.
The four principal islands each has a civil head—in Jersey and Guernsey
called 'the Bailiff', in Alderney 'the President' and in Sark 'La Dame'.
They each have a legislature—in Jersey, Guernsey and Alderney called
'the States' and in Sark 'the Chief Pleas'. They have their own courts—
Jersey and Guernsey each having a Court of Appeal, 'Royal Court' and
subsidiary courts, Alderney 'the Court' and Sark 'the Seneschal's Court'.

The Channel Islands have had a long and eventful history.

About 933 the islands became part of the Duchy of Normandy. Since
1066, when Duke William II of Normandy became King William I of
England, they have been associated with only a few short breaks, with the
Crown of England. Vestiges of the islands' Norman origins survive in
place-names, surnames, language, laws and customs.

After 1204 the Channel Islands followed the fortunes of England (later
Great Britain) and the islanders were constant in their loyalty to her. This
loyalty was rewarded by the grant of privileges, which were extended and
confirmed by successive sovereigns. Having won these privileges the
islanders were jealous of them and ever vigilant to maintain them
undiminished.

Being remote from England's protective arm the islands suffered
severely from French attacks and were only saved from further devasta-
tions by the intervention of Pope Sixtus IV who in 1481 by Monition,
confirmed in 1483 by a Bull, conferred upon them at the instance of

King Edward V and with French approval, the privilege of neutrality in time of war.

The fact that the Channel Islands are islands and not part of the mainland of Europe has had a great influence on their history. If they had been part of the mainland undoubtedly they would have become part of France and shared her fortunes. As it was in the centuries following the grant of the privilege of neutrality they escaped, in large measure, much of the agony of the civil and religious conflicts which feature so prominently in the history of both England and France.

The islands often served as places of refuge—probably for the Gauls fleeing before the Roman invaders, and certainly for French Protestants after the Reformation and at the time of the Revocation of the Edict of Nantes, for English Royalists at the time of the Civil War, for French Royalists at the time of the Revolution and for French and other continental revolutionaries in the mid-nineteenth century. And during this century they have become tax havens catering for a different kind of refugee.

Life has not always been easy for the Channel Islanders. Their principal natural resources have been their own talents, particularly their ability to adapt themselves to changing circumstances. When one source of revenue stopped, they soon found another to take its place. Those who were unable to find a living at home emigrated either to England or in later centuries to more distant lands, often with great success.

The pages which follow tell the history of the Channel Islands for more than a thousand years. It is not the story of a great nation, of mighty battles and outstanding events, but rather that of the people—some of whom gained great distinction—of a few small islands in the English Channel plodding along the high road of history. It is the story of a battle for survival against French attacks, religious strife, nepotism, commercial disasters, disease, hunger and want and all the other troubles to which man is heir. There were years of peace, occasions for public and private rejoicing and times of prosperity compensating in some measure for the dangers and difficulties, the failures and disasters. The history of the islands is still being made and the islanders of today are ever ready to meet the challenge of the future, as were those of yesteryear.

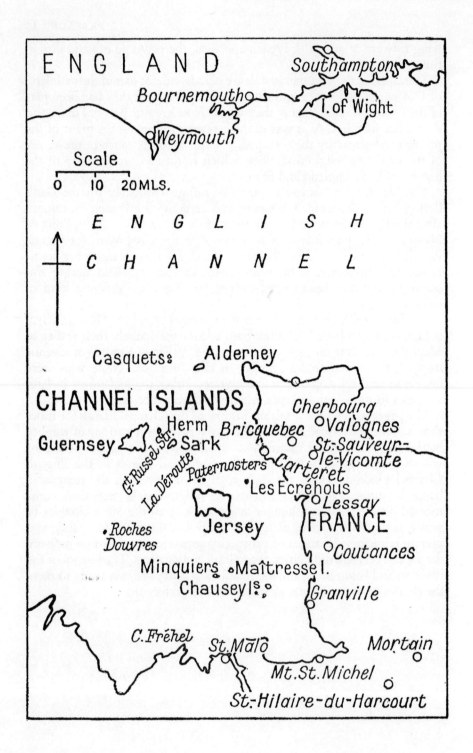

CHAPTER ONE

The Islands Emerge into History—Early Times to 933

... if we turn round to gaze at the remote past, we can barely catch sight of it, so imperceptible has it become.

Marcel Proust (1871-1922)

The foot of man first trod the soil of the Channel Islands even before they were detached from the mainland of Europe, as is evidenced by archaeological remains from La Cotte de St Brelade, a remarkable cave in Jersey, which has been excavated almost continuously since 1894 and has yielded the crania of three rhinoceroses and the remains of at least five mammoths. There are numerous other achaeological sites throughout all the islands dating from very early times to historic times; many other such sites have been destroyed down the centuries. La Hougue Bie in Jersey is a splendid dolmen dating from between 3000 and 2500 B.C. and said to be one of the finest memorials of its kind in western Europe. Le Déhus Dolmen in Guernsey is another important site.

One of the islands' outstanding archaeological treasures is the gold torque, discovered about three feet below ground level by workmen digging the foundation for new houses at the corner of Lewis Street, St Helier, in 1889. It "is made from a four-flanged stem of gold of cruciform section, twisted to give all the glisten of spiral curves: each end terminates in a solid rod of slightly conical shape, bent back to form a hook". Its overall length, excluding the turn back of the terminal hooks, is 141.2 centimetres, its width is 1.5 centimetres, and its weight is 746 grammes. The torque dates from the late Bronze Age. It now belongs to La Société Jersiaise.

The Guernsey churches, St Martin's and Castel, each has a prehistoric sculpture in its churchyard. At St Martin's the figure is known as the 'Grandmother of the Cemetery'. It is a rectangular stone pillar terminating in a carved female head and shoulders serving as a gatepost between the two gates of the churchyard. The sculpture probably dates from the sixth century. The prehistoric sculpture at Castel is carved far more crudely than 'the Grandmother', and there has been only a very elementary attempt to carve a female head and shoulders. The sculpture probably dates from the second or third century. In the churchyard of St Saviour's in the same island there is a stone gatepost at the entrance from Les Buttes, upon which are carved two crosses, one at the front and one at the back. It is believed that this stone is a christianized menhir.

The Channel Islands formed part of Gaul, and when that province, later to become France, was subjugated by the Romans under Julius Caesar between the years 58 and 50 B.C., the islands became part of the Roman Empire. The evidence would seem to indicate that there was no regular occupation of the islands, although from time to time Roman coins have been unearthed. It is said that the Romans knew Jersey as 'Caesarea', Guernsey as 'Sarnia' and Alderney as 'Riduna'. This statement arises from an interpretation placed on the itinerary, attributed to the Roman Emperor Marcus Aurelius Antoninus, but whether it is correct or not is a matter for conjecture. As in Britain, Roman power ultimately ebbed away.

The nunnery in Alderney is thought by some to have its origins in a Roman fort of the fourth century. It stands by the seashore on the western side of Longy Bay and consists of a curtain wall, some 17 feet high, enclosing a rectangular area and the building now used as a dwelling.

At Le Pinacle, St Ouen, Jersey, are the remains of a small building erected in Roman times.

A number of hoards of Armorican coins have been found in Jersey, the most notable being that comprising more than 10,000 unearthed at La Marquanderie, St Brelade, in 1935. It is believed that the hoards found at Le Câtel, Little Caesarea and La Marquanderie were buried by refugees from Gaul at the time of the Roman invasion.

How it was that Christianity was first brought to the Channel Islands will never be known. Poingdestre, a Jersey historian writing towards the end of the seventeenth century, put it very well when he wrote:

As for Christian Religion it is not easy to marcke precisely the time of its first beginning in these Islands: for questionlesse it came not in all at once, by a Generall Conversion, noe more than in other parts.

Jersey and Guernsey have been divided into twelve and ten parishes respectively for a very considerable time. Owing to the lack of any documentary evidence, it is difficult to assess how ancient these divisions are. The opinion has been expressed that the five central parishes of Jersey— St Saviour, St John, St Mary, St Peter and St Lawrence—date back to around 475. Physical evidence in the form of an inscribed and decorated stone, said to have come originally from a Roman villa, would indicate that a church or chapel existed on the site of St Lawrence's Church, Jersey, possibly as long ago as the beginning of the seventh century. Similar evidence would indicate that a church or chapel existed on the site of the Vale Church, Guernsey, as early as the seventh or eighth century. The presence of these buildings might indicate the existence of parishes at that time. In this context it must also be borne in mind that in nearby Coutances a bishopric had been established at least as early as the sixth century and that in Sark St Maglorius's monastery was established in the same century. Some, if not all, of the other parish churches in Jersey and Guernsey could be nearly as ancient as St Lawrence's and the Vale, although they are undocumented until some centuries later.

Two saints who are particularly associated with the Channel Islands are St Helier and St Maglorius.

Helier is a shadowy saint who is said to have lived in the sixth century and to have been a native of Tongres (Limburg). Legend has it that he became a hermit in Jersey where he was murdered by heathens, reputedly in the year 555. His saint's day is the 16th July.

There is a legend that Helier expressed the wish to be buried at Bréville, a village near Granville in Normandy, and that when he died his body was placed in a stone coffin which the sea carried to a little inlet on the coast close by the village. From there the parishioners carried the coffin with great solemnity to their village, where they eventually dropped it owing to its great weight. At the spot where the coffin hit the ground water appeared and a well was established. The well, surmounted by a five-foot statue of St Helier, is to be found in the north-east corner of the churchyard of the parish church; another statue of the saint is built into the reredos of the church, while in the presbytery is an old tapestry depicting St Helier wearing a mitre and holding a staff.

Maglorius, who is known in the Channel Islands as Mannelier, was born in Wales in the late fifth or early sixth century, and was educated in the monastery of St Illtyd (the Knight) at Llantwit Major. He was a kinsman of St Samson, who was also educated there, and with him he travelled to Brittany where they became abbots of two monastries, Samson of that at Dol and Maglorius of that at Lemmeur. Samson was Bishop of Dol (about 552–558) and after his death was succeeded by Maglorius. The latter is said to have built a monastery in Sark where he died about 586.

In Jersey a parish church and an abbey were dedicated to St Helier and a chapel to St Maglorius in St Saviour. In Guernsey a parish church was dedicated to St Samson.

There is a tradition that St Gervold visited Jersey in or shortly after 800. The account of his supposed visit to the island, then known as Angia, is contained in the Chronicle of the Abbey of St Wandrille at Fontenelle near Caudebec-en-Caux, Normandy, and reads thus,

Of the abbot Gervold in peril on the sea, but suddenly snatched therefrom by the aid of the Holy Father.

Another miracle, also, which was performed on Gervold, father of this Abbey, must be told. Now this Abbot, by command of Charles Augustus, was carrying out a certain mission in an island which is called Angia, inhabited by a race of Britons, and lies near the country of Constantine, and at that time was under a chieftain named Anouuarith. Having satisfactorily carried out his work, and achieved the objects which had been set him, a favourable wind blowing he [Gervold] took to the sea on his return journey, when suddenly a west wind began to blow most strongly, and a dreadful crashing of the sea arose insomuch that the globes of the waves and the vast masses of water seemed higher than tall trees.

And when all who were with him in the boat were in utter despair, and there was no hope of survival, and all men's faces were like masks of death, at length the said venerable Abbot, remembering what relics of St Wand-regisil he had with him, embraced and kissed them fervently; and his other companions, and the sailors of the boat, in tears with the most constant prayers, begged for Christ's mercy and the prayers of their said Holy Patron; and made vows to God Almighty and his blessed confessor himself, promising to fulfil them if by their aid they should be deemed worthy to be rescued from such a crisis. Whereupon, by the merits and intercession of the same most holy father, the savage perils were divinely commanded to cease, and an amazing calm was immediately restored, and the tempest of the sea dispersed. And with happy voyage, all praising God together, and rendering thanks of all kinds for their rescue to God omnipotent and to St Wandregisil, they came to the haven where they would be.

Thus God omnipotent, who once harkened to the stricken Jonah in the belly of a whale, saved the said venerable father with his companions through the intercession of his venerable confessor. Wherefore all who were there at the time, and those to whom this story came, praised Christ the Son of God, who by the merits of his servant Wandregisil performed such a miracle.

The Vikings made their appearance about the ninth century, when they swept down from Scandinavia in their long boats along the northern coasts of Europe. At first they came to ravage and burn and carried off their booty to their northern fastnesses. In time, however, they started to settle in various places, one of which was that part of Gaul, now known as

Normandy—the land of the Norsemen or Normans. The chief of this settlement was Rollo.

Rollo spent the first ten years of the tenth century with his Vikings, who were probably predominantly Danish, fighting battles in the Seine Valley with varying degrees of success. He ultimately established himself so strongly in northern France that the Franks had no alternative but to accept the existence of him and his followers as an accomplished fact. In 911, by the Treaty of St Clair-sur-Epte, Rollo was recognized as Duke of Normandy by Charles the Simple, King of the West Franks, in return for acknowledging the King as his suzerain and agreeing to protect Normandy from attacks by other groups of Vikings. Rollo kept his side of the arrangement and supported the King. He maintained law and order and caused the land to be settled and cultivated. In 912 he became a Christian.

The Duchy of Normandy eventually covered the area of the Archdiocese of Rouen, Rouen itself being the capital. The duchy was subdivided into three *vicomtés* each of which was governed by a *vicomte*.

The ancient procedure of the *Clameur de Haro*, which is still invoked from time to time in the Channel Islands, is said to have originated as a plea to Rollo for swift and certain justice. The word *Haro* is supposed to be a corruption of 'O Rollo!' Even today an appeal for help to the mighty Rollo has the effect of an immediate injunction restraining a person from committing an alleged wrong until the appropriate court has been able to give judgement on the matter.

Once Christianity had been adopted by the Normans, there were no more enthusiastic churchbuilders to be found. As the years passed so a large number of churches and monasteries were established throughout Normandy.

The Channel Islands were added to the duchy about 933. However, it would appear that some years passed before they became fully integrated with the mainland part of the duchy. Whatever form of government, laws and way of life the islands had previously possessed were entirely swept away when the Normans conquered them.

CHAPTER TWO

Part of Normandy—933–1204

On 14th October 1066 Duke William II of Normandy
won the Battle of Hastings, and ever since, except
for a few short breaks, the Channel Islands have been
associated with the Crown of England.

Duke William I, nicknamed 'Longsword' (933–942), of Normandy
added the Channel Islands to his Duchy in about 933. He was succeeded
in turn by Duke Richard I, 'the Fearless' (942–996), Duke Richard II,
'the Good' (996–1026), Duke Richard III (1026–28), Duke Robert I, 'the
Devil' or 'Magnificent' (1028–35), and Duke William II, 'the Bastard'
or 'the Conqueror' (1035–87), who was to become King William I of
England.

In 1020 Duke Richard II divided Guernsey from north-east to south-
west and granted the eastern half, comprising the parishes of St Sampson,
St Andrew, St Peter Port, St Martin, the Forest and Torteval, to Néel de
St Sauveur, Viscount of the Cotentin; the western, comprising the
Vingtaine de l'Épine and the parishes of Castel, St Saviour and St Peter-
in-the-Wood, he granted to Anquetil, Viscount of the Bessin.

The Fief du Cotentin reverted to Duke William II in 1048 as a result
of Néel's being involved in a revolt against the duke's authority. After a
lapse of twenty years the fief was restored to Néel, but he was not reinstated in the office of viscount. The fief reverted once more to the duke,
this time Geoffrey of Anjou, when Roger de St Sauveur died 1137–38
without heirs. It has ever since been known as the Fief Le Roi, although
included in that fief are a number of other manors, escheated to the
Crown from time to time and for various reasons.

In 1030 Duke Robert I granted the Bessin Fief to the Abbey of Mont St
Michel when the Duke and Alain, Count of Brittany, signed a peace

treaty at the Mount. The treaty had been brought about by Mauger, Archbishop of Rouen. Anquetil, Viscount of the Bessin, was probably deprived of his fief because he had supported the count.

Five years later, when Duke Robert died and was succeeded by his son Duke William II, the fief was restored to Anquetil's son Ranulf, as the new duke was anxious to obtain the viscount's support even if it meant forfeiting that of the abbey. However, the duke compensated the abbey by granting it the islands of Alderney and Sark. In 1057 the abbey was deprived of both islands, but was again compensated, this time by a grant of the Manor of Noirmont in Jersey.

In about 1030 Duke Robert I of Normandy and Edward the Atheling, later King Edward the Confessor, while sailing in a fleet bound from Normandy to England were obliged to put into Jersey owing to contrary winds and remained in that island for some time. As the winds persisted in the same quarter they prevented a continuation of their journey to England and they returned with the fleet to Normandy.

On 14th October 1066 Duke William II of Normandy won the Battle of Hastings and became King William I of England, and ever since, except for a few short breaks, the Channel Islands have been associated with the Crown of England. They are, therefore, with the exception of England, the oldest parts of the British Commonwealth.

On the death of William the Conqueror in 1087 Robert, his eldest son, nicknamed 'Short Hose', succeeded him as Duke Robert II of Normandy (1087–1106), and his brother, William Rufus, became King William II of England (1087–1100). William was succeeded by his younger son Henry, nicknamed 'Beauclerc', as King Henry I (1100–35). In 1106 having defeated Duke Robert II at Tinchebrai, King Henry captured the duchy, which was again united with the English Crown (1106–35). Robert was taken to England and remained a prisoner for the rest of his life. He died in Cardiff Castle and was buried in Gloucester Cathedral. Normandy accepted King Henry's authority and London became the centre of the Anglo-Norman state. In 1135, upon the accession of King Stephen to the English throne, Normandy passed to Geoffrey Plantagenet, Count of Anjou, who ruled (1135–51) in the name of his little son, Henry, King Henry's grandson. At some time in or shortly after 1142 the Channel Islands were under the count's control.

The House of Anjou or Plantagenet provided eight kings of England of whom the first three were King Henry II (1154–89), King Richard I (1189–99), and King John, nicknamed 'Lackland' (1199–1216). At the accession of Henry II, Normandy and England were united again.

It is known that all the parish churches in Jersey and Guernsey existed as early as the eleventh century although little, if anything, remains of the original in the present buildings. In addition, there were in the islands many chapels, the number of which increased as the years went by, as well as a Leper House, St Nicholas of Grandport, which possibly was situated near Gorey in Jersey.

Two bishops and a number of religious houses, principally in Normandy, became possessed of manors, land and rights in the Channel Islands following their annexation to the duchy. The bishops were those of Coutances and Avranches. The former owned a small manor in Jersey and held one-half of the tithes of St Saviour's Church in that island; also a manor in Guernsey. In passing, it might be mentioned that the Chapter of Coutances and the Archdeacon of Val de Vire held the advowson of that church to which they appointed a vicar, not a rector as in the case of the other eleven parish churches. The latter (Avranches) owned a manor in the parishes of St John and Trinity in Jersey. Today there is still a manor called Avranches and the *evêque* (bishop) referred to in the name of the Vingtaine called Ville à l'Evêque and the district of the same name, both in the parish of Trinity, is the Bishop of Avranches.

The abbeys which owned manors, land and rights in the Channel Islands were Mont St Michel (Jersey and Guernsey), St Sauveur Le Vicomte, Our Lady of the Vow near Cherbourg, Holy Trinity of Caen (Jersey and Guernsey), St Mary of Bellosanne, St Nicholas of Blanchelande (Jersey and Guernsey), St Vigor of Cérisy, Holy Trinity of Lessay, Montivilliers, St Mary of Val Richer, St Margaret of Vignatz, Cormery in the Touraine, de la Croix St Leufroy at Evreux, and St Martin at Marmoutier.

The only abbey established in the Channel Islands was the Abbey of St Helier, founded during the twelfth century by William FitzHamon. The precise date of the foundation is not known, Dupont placed the date at 1125 and the editor of the *Cartulaire* at about 1155. FitzHamon was in the service of Prince Henry, later Henry II, in 1149–50, before his accession to the Duchy of Normandy, and continued in his service for the first twelve years of his reign. In 1166 he accompanied the King on his campaign in Brittany and became Seneschal of Nantes. He died probably about 1176.

The Abbey Church and ancillary buildings were built on L'Islet, the small island in St Aubin's Bay on which Elizabeth Castle now stands, and where St Helier was reputed to have lived and been murdered some centuries earlier. The abbey was occupied by Canons Regular of the Order of St Augustine. According to a document of 1461 there were three Abbots of St Helier before the abbey was reduced to the status of a priory. Only the name of the last abbot (Benjamin) is known.

The Abbey of Our Lady of the Vow, situated on the island of Le Hommet, near Cherbourg in the Cotentin, was founded by the Empress Matilda about 1150. In about 1179, as the result of intrigue, which reflected little credit on those concerned, the former was reduced to the status of a priory. The object of this disreputable manœuvre was to bolster the slender finances of the Abbey of the Vow with the not-insubstantial possessions of the Abbey of St Helier. Abbot Benjamin was made abbot of the united abbey, no doubt as a reward for his co-operation. About 1185–89 it was laid down that the seat of the united abbey was to be at Cherbourg and the Priory at L'Islet was to have not less than five canons living under the orders of the abbot.

It appears from entries relating to Jersey in the Great Rolls of the Exchequer of Normandy that in 1180 the island was divided for fiscal purposes into three divisions or *ministeria* called Groceio, Crapout Doit, and Gorroic. The last of these names is the regular early medieval form of Gorey.

John, Count of Mortain, was made Lord of the Islands (probably only Jersey and Guernsey) some time between 1195 and 1198, and succeeded to the English throne in 1199. There is a strong but unproved tradition that he granted Jersey its constitutions and that he visited the island.

The King by charter dated 14th January 1200 granted to Piers des Préaux the islands of Jersey, Guernsey and Alderney, together with land to the value of £60 in Alton and rent to the value of £100 (Angevin) in Rouen by the service of three knights' fees until the earldom of the Isle of Wight which the King had granted him, came to him, together with the daughter of the then Earl of the Isle, or until the King had provided him with another suitable wife. The grant of the islands, land and rent was confirmed by two further charters both dated 21st June 1200, one relating to the grant of the islands and the land in England, and the other to the rent in Rouen.

In 1203 des Préaux for the salvation of the King's soul, and for the salvation of his own soul and that of his father and mother, and the souls of all his ancestors, granted and gave the island of Ecréhous to the Abbey of St Mary of Val Richer in Normandy for a church to be built there in honour of God and of the Virgin Mary.

In 1202 King Philip II of France invaded Normandy and by 1204 had driven King John from the mainland part of the Duchy. As a result of surrendering Rouen to the French in June 1204, des Préaux lost the islands, land and other benefits which the King had bestowed upon him. However, two years later the King restored to him the islands and the land in England.

Justices Itinerant visited the Channel Islands from some time prior to 1204 as is evidenced by the Norman Exchequer Roll of 1180 until the end of the reign of King Edward I and continued at irregular intervals until 1331 in the reign of King Edward III. Before 1204 the judges of the

Norman Exchequer conducted the assizes. Thereafter they were conducted by the wardens and their subordinates and under King Edward I and his successors the judges were specially named for each case. Those sent to the islands from England were generally appointed by Letters Patent. The plea rolls of the Justices Itinerant from 1299 to 1331 are extant.

It is known that in 1135 the de Carterets had a house in Jersey and it is appropriate at this point to make reference to a family which was to play so large a part in the island's history. There is no doubt that the de Carterets take pride of place among the families of Jersey. Their name is derived from the small town of Carteret which stands on the west coast of the Cotentin, almost facing Jersey. Wace mentions that two members of the family, Onfroi and Maugier de Carteret, fought at the Battle of Hastings. It has been estimated that the de Carterets have provided nine Lieutenant-Governors, fifteen Bailiffs, nine Attorneys-General, and at least forty-eight Jurats; also a Bailiff of Guernsey. A member of the family was granted Sark by Queen Elizabeth I. Two others, jointly with a third person, were granted Alderney by King Charles II. St Ouen's Manor, the original seat of the family in Jersey, is the senior and the most interesting of all the manor houses in the island. The Lord of St Ouen was by tradition the captain of the West Regiment of the Militia when that force came into being, and he took command of the troops when a governor died. When a member of the family was a jurat he claimed the privilege of sitting in the senior place on the Bench on the bailiff's left, a privilege still claimed.

Another family which has played a leading part in the history of the Channel Islands, primarily Guernsey, is that of de Sausmarez. It is said that the family is descended from the Norman family of St Hilaire de Harcourt, but this view has been contested. The name de Sausmarez, which has been spelt in many different ways, is derived from Samarès in St Clement, Jersey, where the original home of the family was situated near the Salt Marsh. The first mention of a de Sausmarez in Jersey occurs in a Bull of Pope Urban IV of 1186. Three members of the family in direct succession were called William de Salinelles. The second is recorded as having given a *vavassorie* to the Abbey of the Holy Trinity at Caen in 1221 and the third would appear to be the same person as the William de Saumareis mentioned in connection with Guernsey in a letter of 1254.

CHAPTER THREE

The Later Middle Ages—1204–1399

The loss by King John of continental Normandy
and his retention of the Channel Islands, had considerable effects on the islands and their inhabitants.

John was still King of England and was to remain so until 1216. He was
to be succeeded by five further sovereigns of the House of Anjou—
Henry III, Edward I, Edward II, Edward III and Richard II. Although
there is a strong tradition that King John visited Jersey, there is no documentary evidence to substantiate it. However, it is known that King
Henry III landed in Guernsey on 2nd May 1230 on his way to St Malo,
which is the first recorded visit of a reigning sovereign to that island.

Despite almost constant attacks by the French, the administration of
the Channel Islands gradually developed between 1204 and 1399. The
government of the islands was in the hands of either a Lord or Warden
of the Isles, the distinction between the two lying in the type of grant.
The former had a grant in fee or for life, and the latter a grant during
pleasure or for a fixed term. Occasionally joint wardens were appointed.
In addition, there were sub-wardens who discharged the duties of the
warden. In time the official who presided over the King's Court in each
of the islands of Jersey and Guernsey came to be known as the bailiff,
and by the end of the thirteenth century the office was distinct from that
of warden or sub-warden. As the centuries advanced the importance of
the lords and wardens, and, later, of the governors, declined and that of
the bailiffs increased. Between 1288 and 1331 English Justices Itinerant
visited the islands.

During the 195 years covered in this chapter a large number of people
were either lords or wardens of the Islands. Among them was Otto de
Grandison who was appointed by King Edward I and held the office first

27

as warden and later as lord of the Isles from 1275 until his death in 1328, with only one break from 1294–98 when Sir Henry de Cobham was warden (1294–97) followed by Nicholas de Cheny (1297–98). Grandison was primarily a soldier, but he was also Seneschal of Gascony, an office held by a number of other wardens of the Islands during the thirteenth century. He was succeeded by John de Roches from 1328 to 1330, who found the castles in a ruinous state and caused them to be repaired.

The family of Lemprière, which was to play a prominent part in the history of Jersey, first made its appearance in that island towards the end of the thirteenth century. It originated in the Cotentin, where it owned a small manor called de l'Emperière at Crosville near St Sauveur-sur-Douve. In 1274 Willelmus dictus Imperator, otherwise Guillaume dit l'Empereur, was a jurat, holding a manor called the Manor of Guillaume in the parish of St Helier, which in time became known as the Manor of the Lemprières, and was ultimately absorbed into the Manor of Mélèches. Members of the Lemprière family have at various times held all the principal public offices in Jersey.

The Carey family whose members were to play an equally prominent part in the history of Guernsey is first recorded in that island about 1288. The family probably originated in the district of Lisieux in Normandy.

In 1204 King John lost continental Normandy to Philip II (Augustus) of France. Although the French twice captured the Channel Islands the English recaptured them and the islanders remained loyal to King John. However, in order to ensure this loyalty the King took hostages and placed them in safe custody in various parts of England. In 1214 he sent a letter to the islanders stating that he was "very grateful for your good services and fidelity which you have manifested in our behalf for our affairs and honour. We send you your hostages that they remain with you, as we have full confidence in your fidelity", and at the same time he sent letters to the various officials, including the Prior of Winchester, the Sheriff of Northampton, the Sheriff of Nottingham, the Abbot of Gloucester, the Prior of St Albans and the Abbot of Ramsey, who were holding hostages, with orders to release them. The following year the King ordered the release from Porchester Castle of thirty-four hostages taken from Sark.

The loss by King John of continental Normandy and his retention of the Channel Islands, had considerable effects on the islands and their inhabitants. Firstly, there was the matter of defence. Before 1204 the islands had had nothing to fear from Normandy, as they were part of the duchy, but from then on Normandy was part of a foreign country with whom England, and later Great Britain, was to be frequently and for long periods at war. Therefore, it was necessary to defend the islands and consequently two castles were built, one at Gorey in Jersey and the other on an islet off the town of St Peter Port in Guernsey. The first reference to the former occurs in 1212. The building of the latter is known to have been commenced as early as 1206, although it is not mentioned by name until 1226. Secondly, the connection between the islands and the machinery of ducal government had been severed and the islands were in the future to be governed by the King in Council through a warden of the Isles, at the same time retaining in large measure their own customs and legal institutions. Thirdly, some families with property both in the islands and continental Normandy were placed in a predicament as they had to decide whether to be loyal to King John and forfeit their property on the mainland or to King Philip II of France and forfeit their insular lands. Generally they decided not on a basis of loyalty, but according to their best financial interests, Renaud de Carteret being one of the few to decide on a contrary basis. Fourthly, a peculiar state of affairs existed so far as the Church was concerned, because the islands remained in the Norman diocese of Coutances, although part of the realm and territories of the King of England—a situation which was to continue until 1569.

In 1214 Philip d'Aubigny was appointed Warden of Sark.

The King died in 1216 and was succeeded by his son, King Henry III, who in 1226 confirmed that the Channel Islands should continue to enjoy the same liberties as they had done in the reigns of King Henry II and King Richard I.

By the Treaty of Lambeth in 1217, Louis (later King Louis VIII), son of King Philip II of France, ordered the associates of Eustace the Monk to hand the Channel Islands back to King Henry III and it is believed that all the islands were back in English hands by the end of the year. The same year Eustace was captured by the English at the naval Battle of Sandwich and beheaded. Under the Treaty of Paris of 1259, which ratified a treaty drawn up at Abbeville the previous year, King Henry renounced all claims to continental Normandy, but the Channel Islands were not specifically mentioned. Despite this renunciation, English sovereigns did not entirely forget their claim to Normandy, and as late as the coronation of King George III in 1761 someone representing the Duke of Normandy walked in the Abbey procession taking precedence over the Archbishop of Canterbury. At Périgueux in 1311 some effort was made to settle points of dispute which arose out of the treaty. The French claimed that under its provisions the Channel Islands were theirs; the English refused to surrender them.

In 1279 King Edward I despatched to his bailiffs in the Channel Islands a specially cut seal of office bearing the royal arms to be used to authenticate certain documents. About 1290 a separate seal was sent to each bailiff, but the seal of office originally issued remained in use at least until 1291. The ancient seal now in the keeping of the Bailiff of Jersey is of great antiquity. It was replaced by a replica made at the Royal Mint in 1931. On the reverse side of the seal is a representation either of the arms of the current bailiff or, in the case of a bailiff without arms, his initials. The ancient seal, preserved in the record room of the Guernsey Greffe, dates from 1472; the present seal was made at the Royal Mint in 1938. During the French occupation of Jersey 1461-68, the Commonwealth and Protectorate 1649-60 and the German occupation 1940-45, the seals continued to be affixed to documents. In course of time and without royal authority the Bailiwicks of Jersey and Guernsey adopted the arms on King Edward's seal as their own. The single and very minor difference between the arms of the two bailiwicks is the sprig appearing above the Guernsey arms.

As has been said earlier, there were many French attacks on the Channel Islands during this period. A petition addressed by the islanders to King Edward in about 1294 complained that:

... The body of our Lord was there cut down with swords & spat upon. The images were cut down with swords ... The chalices were destroyed & taken away. The men & women were killed 1500 in number. The houses were burnt and the corn, whereby they had nothing to eat. Their money and all their other chattels were carried off. Of the chasubles and the vestments they made trappings for horses and when the horses had served them they hamstrung them ...

If the facts stated in the petition were true, and there is no reason to doubt them, the population of the island must have been at least decimated, as it is doubtful whether at that time it amounted to 15,000 or even approached that figure.

In Guernsey there is a spot called Bailiff's Cross. The name originated in an event of 1320. In that year various officials of Otto de Grandison, included amongst whom was Gautier de la Salle, seized Renouf Gautier and took him to Castle Cornet, where they tortured and killed him. Gerard Philippe, Renouf's nephew, a prominent islander, petitioned the King for his protection against the officials concerned as he wished to prove to the King and Council how they murdered his uncle. Justice began to work and de la Salle was tried before Peter Le Marchant, the Bailiff, convicted and hanged at the Courtil de Gibet, St Andrew's. Tradition says that de la Salle stopped on his way to the gallows to make his last confession and obtain absolution, or, less likely, his last communion, at the place now known as Bailiff's Cross, although there is no proof that he ever held that office. The others involved in the murder fled and were later pardoned.

The Channel Islanders became so exasperated with the fines exacted from them on every possible pretext by the Justices Itinerant and the disregard of their privileges and franchises that in 1331, just prior to the arrival of further justices, a number of them under the leadership of the Prior of St Clement, Jersey, and the Prior of the Vale, Guernsey, met at St Helier's Priory and took a solemn oath to defend their liberties. Five hundred of the protestors presented themselves before the justices in Guernsey and demanded recognition of their ancient rights. The justices looked upon the proceedings with disfavour and when the protestors saw this they shouted in defiance. The justices ordered the viscount to arrest the ringleaders, who were subsequently tried and acquitted. Later the protestors were summoned to appear before the justices at Longueville in Jersey. Only one, Philip de St Martin, appeared and he was fined. The justices ordered the arrest of those who failed to appear, but what happened to them is not on record.

The Hundred Years' War which arose out of King Edward III's claim to the French throne through his mother, Isabel, daughter of King Philip IV of France, started in 1337 and continued until 1453. During the greater part of that time attacks on the Channel Islands were being constantly made by the French.

The islanders claimed that they were exempted from all liability to military service. However, conditions became so bad in the islands that inevitably they became involved in their own defence and in 1335 John de Roches was ordered to array the men of the islands and to take such measures as he might deem fit for the defence of the islands. A similar order was sent in 1337 to Thomas Ferrers, Warden (1337-41 and 1343-48) commanding him to organize levies in thousands, hundreds and twenties and to arm them and to use them as necessary to repel hostile attacks, and the following year a number of Jerseymen were employed and paid as regular members of the garrison.

In 1339 Sir Nicholas Béhuchet, Admiral of France, captured Guernsey and the lesser islands; he also attacked Jersey. The following year Sir Robert Bertrand, Lord of Bricquebec, Marshal of France, with Nicholas Helie, Vice-Admiral, invaded Jersey and ravaged the island, although they did not attempt to take Gorey Castle. The inhabitants sent a detailed account of the attack to the King's Council in which they estimated Bertrand's force at 8,000 men, and stated that the invasion fleet comprised seventeen Genoese galleys and about thirty-five ships from Normandy. The account ended with an urgent appeal for help, at the same time pointing out that the island had been ravaged by the King's enemies three times in one year. In 1340 the English won the Battle of Sluys and King Edward III caused Béhuchet to be hanged from the yard-arm; they also recaptured Guernsey, Alderney and Sark, although Castle Cornet remained in the hands of the French until 1345 when it was recaptured by Thomas de Ferrers with the help of Sir Godfrey de Harcourt. In

1356–57 the French recaptured Castle Cornet and held it for some months.

When it became known in Jersey that Castle Cornet was in French hands a force of Jerseymen was raised for its relief. The French commander was captured and the castle was surrendered in return for his release. In the course of the relief operation the Jerseymen executed a prominent Guernseyman called William Le Feyvre for treason. Those responsible for the execution were brought before the Royal Court of Guernsey. At the hearing Nicholaa Le Feyvre, the dead man's widow, alleged that her husband had been executed by the Jerseymen because "of ancient enmity and their own malice". The accused were found guilty and banished. Sir Renaud (Reginald) de Carteret (died 1382), Lord of the Manor of St Ouen, and Raoul Lemprière (died about 1378), Lord of the Manor of Rozel, Bailiff of Jersey (1362–64), who had been in the relieving force and were present in court challenged the verdict of guilty which had been returned against their fellow islanders, stating that the responsibility for Le Feyvre's death lay as much with them as with those who had been condemned. Both de Carteret and Lemprière were also adjudged guilty of Le Feyvre's death and were imprisoned. Ultimately all those who had been convicted were pardoned.

In 1346 England won the Battle of Crécy and ten years later the Battle of Poitiers. These two victories led to the Treaty of Calais (otherwise known as the Treaty of Brétigny) of 1360 by which it was agreed that England should retain certain lands and islands, which included the Channel Islands, although they were not specifically named.

The war was resumed in 1369 and by 1375 the English were driven out of most of France by Bertrand du Guesclin, Constable of France. In 1372 Owen of Wales (died 1378), a soldier in the French service, was in command of a French expedition which landed in Guernsey, but he was unable to take Castle Cornet and as a result departed. This invasion of Guernsey is the subject of a ballad. In 1372–73 Sark was raided by the French who caused such devastation that the island was completely abandoned until the middle of the sixteenth century. The following year Gorey Castle was besieged by du Guesclin, but although he captured the outer defences he did not succeed in taking the castle, which was eventually relieved by the English. John de St Martin, Bailiff (1370 and 1372–74) was twice tried and acquitted on a charge of betraying Gorey Castle to the French.

In 1380 Jean de Vienne, a French admiral, attacked Jersey, and captured its castles, but was driven out two years later.

Life in the Channel Islands during the period covered by this chapter was virtually intolerable. The islanders were living in daily dread of raids by the French, raids which meant death and destruction; robbery and violence. Crops were burnt and the countryside laid waste. Even the

Dug up in St Helier in 1889, this gold torque probably reached Jersey
during the late Bronze Age

Statue Menhir at Castel Church, Guernsey—probably second or third century

Grandmother of the Cemetery at the entrance of the churchyard of St Martin's Church, Guernsey—probably sixth century

churches were not immune from the violence of the invaders. Those who were not within the walls of Gorey Castle, Le Château de Sedement and Grosnez Castle in Jersey, or Castle Cornet, La Tour Beauregard, Château d'Orgueil or Le Château des Marais, Vale Castle or Jerbourg Castle in Guernsey were at the mercy of an invading force. The castles of Sedement, Grosnez and Jerbourg were not ordinary castles, but rather places of refuge where the civilian population, with their cattle and valuables, were able to obtain some protection. In addition to the ravages of war there was pestilence which reached the Channel Islands in 1347.

The town of St Peter Port was gradually developing. The church is known to have existed as early as 1048. The building of Castle Cornet was started in 1206. In 1275 King Edward I ordered the building of a new pier between the town and the castle and laid down the method by which the necessary funds were to be raised. The pier was destroyed by the French during their attack on Guernsey 1294–95, but in 1305 the King ordered that it be rebuilt. The town had grown to be of sufficient importance by 1309 to justify the transference to it of the market from Les Landes du Marché where it is said to have been held since about 600; a fish market had been established in St Peter Port either during or before the thirteenth century. Certainly by 1331 the King had a grange or barn in the town where his rents in kind were stored. In February 1350 King Edward III ordered that the town be enclosed by a wall. Initially the order was not carried out and in August of the same year a second order was issued reiterating the first, but despite this it is doubtful whether the wall was ever built. In 1357 La Tour Beauregard was under construction. In passing it should be mentioned that in 1392 St Apolline's Chapel was founded. It was built in St Saviour's parish not far from Perelle Bay and was originally called Our Lady of Perelle.

In the thirteenth and fourteenth centuries St Peter Port was important and many ships called there each year. By present-day standards these vessels would be considered little more than cockleshells. During the eleven months from Michaelmas 1329 some 487 foreign ships called at St Peter Port. The number of such ships which called at Jersey was substantially less. Many of the ships calling at Guernsey came from Gascony, which was also part of the Angevin Empire; others came from England, Spain and elsewhere. In those days ships hugged the coast and consequently all the shipping from the south bound to England and the northern coasts of Europe passed close to Guernsey, which was a landmark for sailors. This accounted for the large number of ships wrecked off the island, particularly the west coast. The right to the proceeds of wrecks principally belonged to the Crown. The ships from Gascony carried cargoes of wine, salt and spices; those sailing to Gascony carried wool, cloth, hides, metals, grain and salted fish. So much land in Gascony was covered with vineyards that it was necessary for the Gascons to import much of their food and the Channel Islands provided one of a number of sources of supply. A number of Gascon merchants also had commercial interests in the islands.

In the Middle Ages fishing for conger and mackerel was an important industry in the Channel Islands. The first reference to the fishery in the islands occurs in the Norman Exchequer Roll of 1195 where there is mention of an *éperquerie* held by Vital de Biele under a Charter of King Richard I. An *éperquerie* was a place where the congers were dried. There is a place on the north-west coast of Sark called L'Eperquerie and two others in Guernsey, Pézeries at Pleinmont and Péqueries Bay between Grandes Rocques and Grand Havre, which recall the fishery. The King had the right of *éperquerie* by which he could require the fishermen to take the fish to certain places for sale to merchants to whom he had granted the right of pre-emption. The custom of fish was levied on all fish exported to Normandy or other places outside the kingdom.

It is interesting to note that in the thirteenth century Guernsey shipping shared with Dieppe preferential treatment in the port of Rouen.

CHAPTER FOUR

The Red Rose and the White—1399–1485

> It is not to be supposed that the inhabitants of the
> Channel Islands would with any warmth embrace the
> party of the White or the Red Roses, or feel much
> interest in the struggle. They do not appear to have
> been in any way engaged in this contest.
> Charles Le Quesne (1811–56)

Two dynasties governed England between 1399 and 1485. The house of
Lancaster provided three kings—Henry IV, Henry V and Henry VI; its
symbol was the red rose. The house of York, its symbol the white rose,
provided three kings—Edward IV, Edward V and Richard III. Civil
Wars known as the Wars of the Roses racked England during thirty
years of the period, the contending parties being the Yorkists and the
Lancastrians.

Edward, Earl of Rutland, later Duke of York, was Warden of the
Isles from 1396 until his death at Agincourt in 1415. Thereafter until late
in the fifteenth century the Channel Islands were governed by Lords
of the Isles who had a grant either in fee or for life, similar to that
which King John, when Earl of Mortain, and Peter des Préaux had
enjoyed. John, Duke of Bedford, Regent of France, third son of King
Henry IV, held the Lordship 1415–35 and Humphrey, Duke of Gloucester,
youngest son of King Henry IV 1437–47. It is known that the latter was
in residence at Gorey Castle in 1445. In 1444 King Henry VI granted the
reversion of the lordship to Henry de Beauchamp, Duke of Warwick,
with remainder to his heirs, but he predeceased the Duke of Gloucester,
who died in 1447. Lady Anne de Beauchamp, infant daughter of Henry de
Beauchamp, became Lady of the Isles on the death of the Duke of
Gloucester, and held the office until her death in 1449. During her

minority the guard of the Isles was in fact conferred on Viscount Beaumont and Ralph Butler, Viscount Sudeley, afterwards Earl of Wiltshire and Ormonde. Both were killed in battle, Beaumont at the battle of Northampton in 1460 and Sudeley at the battle of Towton Field in 1461. Anne's heirs were her four aunts of whom Anne de Beauchamp, wife of Sir Richard Neville, was sister of the whole blood to Henry Beauchamp, Duke of Warwick, and as such inherited the bulk of her niece's honours. On the death of Anne, Lady of the Isles, Neville was created Earl of Warwick, but the following year, 1450, the Patent was revoked and he and his wife, Anne de Beauchamp, were created conjointly Earl and Countess of Warwick and granted all the honours and possessions of Henry, Duke of Warwick, with remainder to her heirs. Richard, Earl of Warwick, was attained in 1459 and lost his honours and estates. However, they were restored to him in 1461 and he remained Lord of the Isles, in right of his wife, until he was killed at the battle of Barnet in 1471. Killed fighting under the duke at the same battle was Geoffrey Walsh, Lord of the Manor of St Germain, in the island of Jersey, who had been Constable of Castle Cornet in 1457 and Lieutenant-Governor of Guernsey in 1468. Some of Walsh's Jersey tenants had followed him into battle and were killed; others were hanged at Southampton. The fortunate managed to get back to Jersey. In 1487 Anne, widow of the Earl of Warwick, conveyed the Channel Islands to the King.

John Nanfan was appointed warden of the islands on two occasions, the first 1452–57 and the second from 1460–61. The French occupied Jersey from 1461 to 1468. In the latter year the island was recaptured by the English under Sir Richard Harliston, who was appointed governor about 1470. From then on no further lords or wardens of the islands were appointed and each bailiwick had its own governor. Edward de Courtney was Governor of Guernsey 1476–77, his brother William de Courtney succeeded him in 1477, and was in turn succeeded by Sir John Dichefield in 1478.

Sir Edward Brampton, otherwise Duarte Brandão (1440?–1508), Governor of Guernsey, was undoubtedly the most colourful and unusual person to hold that office. Brampton was a Portuguese Jew of humble birth who is first heard of in London in 1468 living in the Home for Converted Jews, which then existed in Chancery Lane on the site of what is now the Public Record Office. At first he was known as Edward Brandon, but later changed his surname to Brampton. He prospered greatly and became an English subject. On 24th August 1482 he was appointed Governor of Guernsey, an office which he held until he was succeeded by Thomas Rydley, who was appointed Governor in his place on 25th January 1485.

Guernsey's liberties, customs and usages in the year 1441 were set out in a document called *Le Précepte d'Assise*, which is divided into three parts—preamble, findings of the Court and notarial attestation. The first two parts are written in French and the third in Latin. An Order in Council of 1580 based on the report of the Royal Commission of 1579 takes note of both *Le Précepte d'Assise* and the *Extente* of 1331 as varying the customary law of Normandy. The same Order in Council gave instructions that a compilation should be made of local customs varying from those of Normandy and sent to the Council. The result was the *Approbation des Lois, Coutumes, et Usages de l'Isle de Guernesey* of 1582.

Of the many raids made on the Channel Islands in medieval times, none is better recorded than that of a Castillian, Pero Niño, Count of Buelna, in 1406. Together with Pierre de Pontbriand, surnamed Hector, a Breton Knight, Pero Niño planned an expedition against Jersey. On 7th October the invading force, comprising about 1,000 archers and crossbowmen, reached Jersey. They landed at night, when the tide was high, at L'Islet, in St Aubin's Bay, where stood St Helier's Priory. At dawn next day the invaders advanced across the sands towards the mainland and were opposed by the English and local defenders, probably commanded by Sir John Pykworth, Keeper. A fierce and bloody fight ensued, the standard of St George was captured and the defenders withdrew, but the invaders were in no condition to pursue them. The following day the invaders advanced across the island towards Gorey Castle, ravaging the countryside as they went. When they reached the heights of Grouville a skirmish took place near the spot now called Le Jardin de la Croix de la Bataille. An English herald came from the castle and appealed for mercy on the grounds that the islanders were christians and the Queen of Castile was English by birth. Niño asked to meet four or five of the leading inhabitants. His request was agreed to and at the meeting which followed a ransom, said to be of 10,000 gold crowns, was agreed on, part of which was to be paid immediately and part in due course, four hostages being given as security for the balance. In addition, an annual tribute was to be paid to Niño of twelve lances, twelve battle axes, twelve bows with their complement of arrows, and twelve trumpets. The next day, 9th October, the invaders sailed away with such of the ransom money as had been paid, the hostages, and a large quantity of plunder, principally horses and cows.

Early in the reign of King Henry V, in 1414, the alien priories were suppressed and their property seized by the Crown. As a result of this Jersey lost the priories of St Clement, St Mary of Lecq, St Mary of Bonne Nuit, St Michael of Noirmont and St Peter, but the priory of St Helier escaped suppression and survived until the Reformation; Guernsey lost the priories of Lihou and the Vale.

During the summer of 1461 Pierre de Brezé, Grand Seneschal of

Normandy, an Angevin who was the nephew of Regnier, King of Sicily and Duke of Anjou, and first cousin of Margaret of Anjou, consort of King Henry VI of England, sent an expedition to Jersey under the command of Jean de Carbonnel, Lord of Sourdeval and Robert de Floques, formerly Bailiff of Evreux. The expedition was successful partly due to the negligence of John Nanfan, the warden, and partly because of treachery, notably of members of the de St Martin family. The de St Martins probably originated from the village of St Martin le Gaillard in Normandy. They had the reputation of having French sympathies. Suspicion had pointed its finger at John de St Martin, the bailiff, who had been twice tried and acquitted on a charge of betraying Gorey Castle to Bertrand du Guesclin in 1373. However, there was no doubt at all that some years later in 1452 Thomas de St Martin, a jurat, went over to the French.

Whatever the cause, the expedition was successful and the whole of Jersey (not only the six eastern parishes, as was once believed), but not the other Channel Islands, was occupied by the French in the Lancastrian interest until 1468. During those years de Brezé, and after his death in 1465, Jacques, his son, were lords (as opposed to wardens) of the Isles.

In 1462 Pierre de Brezé promulgated a number of ordinances which are of importance for, among other things, they define the functions of the bailiff and jurats.

In the document containing the ordinances occurs the first known reference to Gorey Castle as Mont Orgueil Castle.

During the reigns of King Henry VII and King Henry VIII there was an officer of the College of Heralds called Mont Orgueil, who almost certainly derived his name from Mont Orgueil Castle in Jersey. As far as is known there was only one holder of the office, Randulph Jackson, who was appointed a pursuivant about 1494; he was promoted herald by Patent in 1516, still being called Mont Orgueil, and granted twenty marks a year. Jackson's christian name appeared sometimes as Randle and his surname as Holmes. He was made Chester Herald by patent in 1533 and vanished from the scene in 1545.

In 1468 Vice-Admiral Sir Richard Harliston arrived with the English fleet at Jersey and Mont Orgueil Castle was blockaded from the sea and besieged from the land with the aid of Philip de Carteret (born about 1432), Lord of St Ouen, and other Jerseymen, as well as a force of Guernseymen. The siege lasted from 17th May until the beginning of October. Charles de France, Duke of Normandy, made efforts to assist the beleaguered garrison. Numerous attacks were made on the castle and the garrison made a number of sorties. Renaud Lemprière (1418–67), Lord of Rozel, was killed while attacking the castle. Some years earlier he had been accused by the French of plotting against them, but was acquitted. Eventually, early in October, de Carbonnel surrendered on honourable terms and retired with the garrison to Normandy.

King Edward IV showed his gratitude to the men and commonalty of Jersey by granting them by Charter dated 28th January 1469 not only confirmation of the privileges contained in the Charter of King Richard II, but also further privileges. On 10th March 1469 the King granted to Peter Le Serkees, Peter Téhy, John de Soulement, Nicholas Le Petit, and John Le Moigne of Jersey and John Peryn, John Tyaut, William Duport, Jordan Rogier, Thomas de Havilland, Laurence Carey, William Mainguy, Renouf Agenor, Ralph Cousin, and Nicholas de Lisle of Guernsey, who had spent £2,833 6s 8d in recovering Jersey from the French, for a term of years certain trading privileges to enable them to recoup their losses.

Thomas de Havilland (about 1440–81), who was a jurat of the Royal Court of Guernsey in 1474, was of an old family of that island which had settled there as early as 1176. The name de Havilland is derived from the Fiefs of Haverland, near Valognes, in Normandy. As the result of being granted trading privileges, Thomas established his son James at Poole, Dorset, and thus began the family's association with that town. James was mayor in 1494 and 1498. His son, who also was called James, followed in his father's footsteps and was mayor in 1502 and 1506. His son, Christopher, who was the progenitor of the Dorset and Gloucestershire branches of the family, was mayor in 1519. Other members of the family who held that office were Richard in 1512, 1519 and 1529, John in 1514 and 1526, William in 1523, 1533, 1537 and 1544, and Christopher in 1519. The Reverend Matthew Havilland was minister at St James's Church, the old parish church, replaced by the present one in 1819, from 1566 until he was deprived in 1570.

When Harliston recaptured Mont Orgueil Castle he built the large tower at the first gateway and ever afterwards it has borne his name. His daughter, Margaret, married Philip de Carteret (died 1502?), Lord of the Manor of St Ouen, by whom she had twenty sons and a daughter. In 1484 Harliston, acting in the King's name, gave his son-in-law a licence to crenellate St Ouen's Manor.

Education in Jersey took a major step forward when Jehan Hue (died 1508), Rector of St Saviour, founded St Mannelier's School in 1477. By deed dated 7th October of that year he gave land near St Mannelier's Chapel (in Jersey St Maglorius is known as St Mannelier), St Saviour, as a site for the school. Subsequently the scheme was approved by the dean, the Vicar General of Coutances and, ultimately, by the Bishop of Coutances.

As has been stated earlier, from the time of the political separation of the Channel Islands from continental Normandy in 1204 the islands were constantly being raided by the French and others and the islanders must have lived in constant dread of these raids which jeopardized their lives, homes, livestock and crops.

This constant strife between England and France resulted in a system of safe conducts being evolved whereby the islanders were able to obtain for payment Letters of Protection from the French, generally valid for three months, which enabled them to carry on trade between the islands and between the islands and England and if the need arose to take refuge in the ports of Brittany and Normandy. Furthermore, if any islanders should be engaged in war at the instance of the King of England it would not affect the validity of Letters of Protection issued to islanders who were not involved.

Despite these Letters of Protection the situation became so bad that King Edward IV and the islanders jointly petitioned Pope Sixtus IV for help. As a result the Pope issued a Monition on 27th February 1481 ordering the pirates who had been attacking the islands to cease from doing so under pain of excommunication, anathema and other sanctions. The Pope further ordered that the Monition be made known by posting the papal letters containing it on the doors of the churches of Canterbury, London, Salisbury, Nantes, St Pol-de-Léon, Tréguier and St Peter Port. Two years later on 1st March 1483, at the instance of King Edward IV, the Pope reissued the Monition as a Bull, which ordered that the islands and the surrounding waters, so far as the eye could see, should be treated as neutral in time of war, with immunity inside the area for enemy ships and goods. The neutrality of the islands in war-time was generally observed until the privilege was abolished in 1689, and in the Charters granted to Jersey and Guernsey by Queen Elizabeth I it was specifically stated that trade would be allowed in time of war with all, including the enemy.

King Edward died in 1483. He was succeeded by his son a boy of thirteen as King Edward V, who a few months later was murdered in the Tower of London. He in turn was succeeded by Richard III, who was crowned King at Westminster on 6th July. A little over two years later Richard would be dead and the house of York would be no more.

CHAPTER FIVE

Tudor Times—1485–1603

> . . . I can now tell you by experience that it is a
> blessed life to live in those little Isles. When I
> consider the course of things in this worlde I persuade
> myself that God loveth those Isles and careth for
> them.
>
> Amias Poulett (died 1588)

On 22nd August 1485 Henry Tudor, Earl of Richmond, defeated his rival, King Richard III, at the Battle of Bosworth; the Wars of the Roses were at an end and the Tudor Rose, a combination of the red rose of Lancaster and the white rose of York, became the symbol of a new dynasty which was to preside over the destinies of England for 118 years. King Henry's consort was Elizabeth of York.

According to Jersey tradition King Henry VII, when Earl of Richmond, landed in the island in 1483 after an unsuccessful attempt to win the throne of England and was assisted by Clement Le Hardy (died about 1494). The story is related in the inscription on the monument to Rear-Admiral Sir Thomas Le Hardy, Kt, in Westminster Abbey, against the west wall on the south side of the Great West Door. It reads:

. . . Clement was made a Lieutenant Governor, and had the Office of Bailiff or Chief Magistrate) of the Island, with the Seigneurie de Meleche, confer'd upon him for life, by Henry the 7, as a Reward for the most important Service he had rendered him when Earl of Richmond, after the Disappointment he had met with in his first attempt upon England; where being separated from the rest of his fleet by a Storm, he landed privately in Jersey, intending to stay there till he could obtain leave from the French King to come into his Dominions, and was Shelter'd at the House of the said Clement, who protected him, and convey'd him safely to Normandy at the Hazard of his own life, notwithstanding a Proclamation from Richard the 3, for apprehending the said Earl, had been publish'd in the Island . . .

This tradition is unsupported by documentary evidence, although it is true that Henry Tudor made an unsuccessful attempt on England in 1483 and when he became King, Clement Le Hardy was made Bailiff of Jersey, an office which he held until 1493.

In 1486 the King confirmed the charter of King Richard II acquitting the people of the Channel Islands from tolls, etc, in England.

When King Henry VII came to the throne he did not confirm Harliston in the Governorship of Jersey, and sent Edmund Weston as a Royal Commissioner to take possession of Jersey and Mont Orgueil Castle. Harliston refused to hand over the castle where he remained under siege for six months. The besieging force consisted of twenty-five English soldiers, supported by the local militia. The wheel of fortune had gone full circle, the besieger had become the besieged. When eventually he did surrender Harliston retired to Flanders where he entered the service of the Duchess of Burgundy, sister of King Edward IV. In 1486 he supported the Earl of Lincoln in Lambert Simnel's rising and was attainted, but was pardoned later the same year. He was in trouble again in 1495 for supporting Perkin Warbeck's rebellion (1492–98).

Harliston's successor was Matthew Baker, Constable of Kenilworth Castle, an Esquire of the Body to the King, who held the office from 1486–97. He in turn was succeeded by Thomas Overay who held office until 1500 and was followed by John Lemprière (1500–02) as temporary governor, under the title of Lieutenant of Mont Orgueil and of the island, Sir Hugh Vaughan (1502–32), Sir Anthony Ughtred (1532–34), Sir Arthur Darcy (1534–36), and Thomas, Lord Vaux (1536–37), a cousin of Anne Boleyn.

Baker and Philip de Carteret became enemies. Matters were not improved when Baker demanded to see the title deeds of the lords of the manors to prove the ownership of their estates. As Les Chroniques de Jersey relate, in 1494 Baker who nursed a mortal hatred in his heart against de Carteret devised a scheme to make it look as though de Carteret was guilty of treason with a view to getting rid of him once and for all. Baker forged a letter purporting to have been written by de Carteret to some Norman gentry offering to betray Mont Orgueil Castle to them and arranged for it to be dropped in a road near Longueville by which he was accustomed to travel on his way from the Castle to St Helier. As Baker was riding along this road one of his men called Rogier Le Boutillier, a rascally knave whom de Carteret had once saved from the gallows, picked up the letter and gave it to Baker. Having got the letter Baker produced it at court before everyone and accused the Lord of St Ouen of treason. When de Carteret denied the accusation Le Boutillier challenged him to ordeal by battle and despite the former's demur on the ground of the challenger's criminal record the bailiff ruled that the combat should take place. Le Hardy, the bailiff, having been in communication with Baker about the case, sent both de Carteret and Le Boutillier to prison in Mont Orgueil Castle. The former was kept in close confinement and harshly treated while the latter was allowed to go where he wished and was well nourished so that he would be in good condition for the combat. The governor hastened to England in order to make things right with the King and Council. However, he did not reckon on the spirit of Margaret de Carteret and her devotion to her husband. Three or four days before the governor left for England she was brought to bed of a child. She saw the great danger in which her husband was; also that his estates were in peril and that she and her children might well be ruined. Taking courage and putting her whole trust in God Margaret de Carteret took a boat to Guernsey where she stayed in the house of William de Beauvoir, a jurat, who put her aboard a boat for England. When she arrived at Poole, Baker was there on the quay waiting for the boat in order to hear the latest news from Jersey. Just as the boat arrived there was a heavy storm and Baker and his party were forced to shelter in a house. So it was that Margaret de Carteret managed to land without Baker seeing her. As de Beauvoir knew that Baker would be in Poole he arranged for Margaret de Carteret to stay with a de Havilland who lived in the town. Next morning at daybreak de Havilland put her on horseback and rode with her to Salisbury without Baker being aware of what was happening. She made a good journey to the King's court where she obtained an audience with the sovereign through the good offices of Richard Fox, Bishop of Winchester, who liked de Carteret very much through long acquaintance. With his help Margaret de Carteret saw and spoke with the King who granted her husband his release until his case was tried before the Privy Council. As she descended the steps of the presence chamber Baker ascended them on his way to see the King and Margaret de Carteret made her way with all speed to Hampton (as Southampton was called then). There she found a ship ready to sail for Jersey where she arrived the day before that fixed for her husband's trial by combat. She presented to the Royal Court the order which she had obtained from the King and secured de Carteret's release. A few days later he went to England bearing testimonials of his loyalty to the crown, and was acquitted by the Privy Council. If the trial by combat had taken place there is no doubt that de Carteret would have been beaten because covered traps had been dug where the contest was to have been fought so as to ensure that he would have fallen and been defeated.

This remarkable story is unfortunately unsupported by outside evidence. Fox was not Bishop of Winchester in 1494. He was Bishop of Bath and Wells (1492-94), of Durham (1494-1501) and of Winchester (1501-28). However, on 3rd November 1494 a Writ of Privy Seal was issued which dealt with complaints made by the people of Jersey concerning Baker, who is referred to by name. It stated that no Governor of the island was in future to name, present, institute or create any bailiff or dean or exercise jurisdiction; also that actions against the jurats were to be brought before the Privy Council. It forbade the governor to imprison anyone without the authority of the royal court except for treason. It authorized the inhabitants to go and come from the island without further permission from the king or the governor. It confirmed the islanders' ancient privileges. Finally, it stated that all troubles and hindrances placed by the governor contrary to the ancient laws and customs were quashed, rejected and annulled. On 17th June 1495 an Order in Council was made of a far more comprehensive nature. Among many other things it referred to the redress of injuries caused by the governor. It contained a direction to the governor and his deputy neither to allow the islanders to visit Mont Orgueil Castle on St George's Day as they had been accustomed to do nor to allow any persons to come to the castle except in such a manner and in such numbers as they might be easily controlled and put out as occasion should demand. It also provided that each matter which came before the jurats should be registered and signed by those of them before whom it came and was adjudged and remain for a record so that each of the parties might have recourse as occasion should demand. All the records of the royal court were destroyed in 1502 in a fire which burnt down the house of Thomas Lemprière, Bailiff (1495–1513 and 1515?), close by the Royal Court House, possibly in Morier Lane (now the southern end of Halkett Place running into Hill Street).

Sir Hugh Vaughan was appointed Governor of Jersey in 1502 and held the office for thirty years. He was a Welshman, originally a tailor, who because of his good looks, bravery and high spirits had attracted the attention of the Earl of Richmond. When the earl became King he appointed Vaughan a gentleman usher and in 1503 made him a knight.

Vaughan was one of the worst governors Jersey ever had. He carried off young women by force so that they dared not venture out alone for fear of him. If he wanted a man's land he demanded to see his title deeds and when they were produced tore them up. He caused people to be beaten so that they nearly died. In 1513 the governor's behaviour had become so bad that the bailiff went to England to complain of it to the King.

In order to protect his position, the governor allied himself with the de Carteret family. He promised Helier the bailiffship and took his brothers, Richard and John, into his service. He then sent Helier to Wolsey with a gift of Norman cloth and a letter stating that he had appointed de Carteret bailiff.

As a result of the bailiff's complaint royal commissioners in the persons of George Treneton and Reginald Meinours were sent to Jersey in 1515 to inquire by means of sworn jurors into the governor's conduct. The terms of their commission were widely drawn and contained no "suggestion that it was due primarily to complaints against him". The commissioners' report whitewashed the governor and he came out of the affair remarkably well considering his outrageous conduct. In 1529 the islanders made representations to the Privy Council complaining that the royal commissioners had shown partiality towards the governor. Further royal commissioners, Richard Foster, Yeoman of the Chamber, Robert Kirke, John Dumaresq, Lord of the Manor of Bagot, and John Lemprière, Lord of the Manor of Rozel, were sent to Jersey in 1531 and conducted their inquiry by means of sworn jurors. The inquiry was very different from that of 1515 in that every charge was directed against the governor. At the conclusion of the inquiry the jurors in reply to a direct question stated that the commissioners had conducted themselves properly and impartially. It was clear that the English authorities were anxious to avoid the criticism of partiality which had been made against the previous commissioners. The commissioners' report showed the governor in his true colours. It is said that he retired against his will in 1532.

In 1524 the dean and John Lemprière, Lord of the Manor of Rozel, were appointed joint-bailiffs, during the dispute between Vaughan and de Carteret. In criminal cases Lemprière was to act alone as it would have been improper for the dean to do so. In 1528 Vaughan appointed Jasper Pen bailiff, a position which he held for some months.

In 1496 King Henry VII by Letters Patent gave to two Jerseymen, John Neel (died 1497), Dean of the Chapel to Arthur, Prince of Wales, and Vincent Téhy (flourished 1469–98), a merchant of Southampton who had been mayor of that town in 1484, authority to found and endow two schools in Jersey. The following year Thomas de St Martin, Lord of the Manor of Trinity and First Usher of the Prince of Wales, Sire Jehan Hue, Rector of St Saviour's, and William Wolf, as Attorneys of Neel and Téhy presented the Letters Patent before the governor, bailiff, rectors, constables, centeniers and vingteniers, and regulations were promulgated for the conduct of the two schools. The first school, dedicated to St Mary Magdalen, was to occupy the house built by the States near St Mannelier's chapel in accordance with Hue's original foundation, and was to serve the six eastern parishes. The second, St Anastase's, was to be attached to a chapel dedicated to that saint and situated at St Peter's and was to serve the six western parishes. The teaching at both schools was to be free for ever. Daily offices were to be performed for the king and the founders, and masses were to be said in the churches for the founders.

As has already been noticed, until the Papal Bull of Neutrality, the

Channel Islands had for many years been constantly invaded and devastated, principally by the French. Even when those hazards had been removed, life for most islanders consisted principally of work, unpaid service to their particular island, parish and feudal lord, and religious observance. Pleasures were few and what there were were simple and homespun. It was a Catholic world; religion was an integral part of everyday existence. The only buildings of any significance other than fortifications, such as Mont Orgueil Castle, Castle Cornet, La Tour Beauregard and St Aubin's Tower, and a few domestic buildings, such as St Ouen's Manor, were the parish churches. There it was that the ordinary people, whose homes were humble and whose goods were few, could see beauty and colour in the buildings themselves, in the stained glass windows, the statues, wall paintings and other adornments. There the people found in the mass, in prayer and devotion, some measure of consolation for their hard and arid existence; there they learnt that for the faithful and contrite there would be life eternal and for unrepentant sinners hellfire.

Some of the faithful, those with the courage and the money, made arduous and dangerous pilgrimages to the holy places of Christendom, such as the shrine of St James of Compostella, Rome, or Jerusalem itself. When they returned home they related their experiences to their families and friends, who regarded them with a combination of awe and respect for their courage and piety. In 1428 sixty pilgrims sailed from Jersey to the shrine of St James of Compostella. The scallop shell was worn as a badge by all those who made a pilgrimage to there. It is known that George Lemprière, a Jerseyman, who was Constable of St Saviour in 1464, made this particular pilgrimage. John Bonamy, with other Guernseymen, amongst whom was probably John de Lisle, made a pilgrimage to Rome in 1500. The pilgrims started from Guernsey on 10th March. They travelled across France, their route taking them through Caen in Normandy down to Marseilles in the south where they took a boat for Genoa. After arriving there they again travelled overland passing through Lucca, Florence, Siena and Viterbo until at last they reached Rome on 20th April. Bonamy caused a mass to be sung in the crypt of the Church of St Sebastian for nineteen people, including his father, Peter Bonamy, his mother, Marguerite Bonamy (née Patris), Nicholas Fashion, Bailiff of Guernsey (1481–88), and Thomas de la Court, Lord of the Manor of Trinity in Jersey and a jurat of the Royal Court of Guernsey. Richard Mabon, Dean of Jersey (born 1484—died 1543) made the pilgrimage to Jerusalem about 1515, when the days of pilgrimages from the Channel Islands were coming to an end. His picture painted by Hans Holbein the Younger in 1533 which hangs in the Rijksmuseum at Enschede in the Netherlands is the oldest known portrait of a Jerseyman. Mabon is shown wearing a black biretta and a dark blue cape, with a red and white cross on the breast, the habit of the Crutched Friars, the Order of the Holy Cross. Holbein also painted Lord and Lady Vaux.

Change was in the air. Learning and science were struggling forward; new lands were being discovered. The old ways were being questioned; the doctrines and teaching of Holy Church herself were being challenged. In 1517 Martin Luther, a German priest, nailed his theses on the sale of indulgences and other matters to the door of Wittenberg Castle Church. The Reformation had started, but did not reach the Channel Islands until the reign of Edward VI; so that as late as 1524 the beautiful Hamptonne Chapel was added to St Lawrence's Church, Jersey, and still later, in 1537, a nave aisle was added to St Brelade's Church in the same island.

The principal instrument of change so far as England, Ireland and the Channel Islands were concerned was to be King Henry VIII who ascended the throne on the death of his father in 1509 and was to reign until 1547. He is remembered by most people for having had six wives rather than for having made the break with Rome, an event of outstanding importance which was to have a profound effect on the country and its people for centuries to come. However, at the outset of his reign the King was a good Catholic and had the title *Fidei Defensor* conferred upon him by the Pope in 1521.

In November 1509 the King promoted Thomas Wolsey to the Council Board, with the office of almoner to the royal household. Wolsey's progress up the ladder of success was swift. He was successively promoted Bishop of Lincoln, Archbishop of York and, in September 1515, was made a cardinal; finally, in December of the same year he was made Lord Chancellor. His glittering career was brought to an untimely end by his failure to obtain an annulment of the King's marriage to Catherine of Aragon.

Even if the Pope had been prepared to allow the dissolution of the marriage, he dared not agree to it because he was in the power of the Emperor Charles V whose imperial soldiers had sacked Rome in 1527 and who was determined that King Henry should not divorce Catherine of Aragon who was his aunt.

A Jerseyman who held important positions in England during the reign of King Henry VIII was Thomas de Soulemont (died 1541), who was Dean of Jersey (1534-41) and French Secretary to the King from some time before October 1534. In 1537 he became clerk to Thomas Cromwell and in 1540, Clerk of the Parliaments. He appears from all accounts to have been a pleasant person.

The Reformation was accepted in the Channel Islands with only minor resistance; Jersey acquiesced in the change more readily than Guernsey. On 17th March 1549 the Privy Council sent a letter to the inhabitants of Jersey thanking them for embracing His Majesty's laws in the order of

Divine Service. No one in the islands died for their faith during the reigns of King Henry VIII and King Edward VI, but a few people were punished for possessing rosary beads and attending mass in private. The Reformation was given special impetus in Jersey by the appointment of Sir Hugh Poulett, a staunch protestant, as governor, in 1549. Commissioners in the persons of Hugh Poulett, Helier de Carteret, Adam Martin and Charles Mabon were appointed on 25th April 1550 to sell and dispose of all manors, lands, tenements, parsonages, tithes, rents and revenues belonging to the chantries, free chapels, fraternities, obits, founded masses and other rights, titles and hereditaments pursuant to the Act of Parliament confiscating the same; also to sell all the church bells, bell metal, ornaments, stocks, stores, superfluous buildings and other goods and chattels which had also been confiscated by the same Act. The proceeds from the sales in Jersey were to be spent on the castle. The despoliation of the parish churches and chapels and the destruction of the wayside and other crosses was carried out with great thoroughness. In Jersey only one bell was left to each church but in Guernsey all the bells survived. Everything in the parish churches which appertained to the old form of worship was destroyed and the buildings were converted into unadorned whitewashed calvinist temples, in which form they were largely to remain until the restorations of the nineteenth century. Although the parish churches have survived, the chapels of which there were very many in the islands, have mostly disappeared, notable exceptions being the Fishermen's Chapel at St Brelade, Jersey, and St Apolline's Chapel at St Saviour's, Guernsey. In Jersey many of the altar slabs were incorporated in alterations being carried out at Mont Orgueil Castle.

The Crown also became possessed of the perquages or sanctuary paths in Jersey. Until the Reformation the parish churches in that island not only possessed the *Franchise de l'Eglise* or right of sanctuary in accordance with Norman Law, but, in addition, from each church there was a perquage or sanctuary path leading to the sea, although not always by the shortest route. These special paths were used by criminals who had sought refuge in the churches and wished to leave the island.

As already stated Sir Hugh Poulett was appointed Governor of Jersey in 1549. This marked the start of a connection between the island and the Poulett family whose seat was the Manor at Hinton St George, near Crewkerne, Somerset, which was to last well beyond the end of the century. Sir Hugh (died about 1578) held the governorship until about 1574. He brought with him to Jersey his brother, John Poulett (died about 1580), who was Rector of St Martin (1553–about 1565) and Dean (1543–about 1576). He was originally a staunch Catholic, but ultimately became reconciled to Protestantism and married Marguerite Mallet (*née* Lemprière), a widow, by whom he had two children, Hugh, who died

(*above*) St Martin's Church, Guernsey, one of the island's ancient parish churches—from an engraving after W. Berry published in 1815

(*below*) St Brelade's Church, Jersey, first mentioned between 1053 and 1066—from a photograph taken in about 1880

(*above*) Castle Cornet, Guernsey, first mentioned in 1206—from an engraving after W. Berry published in 1815

(*below*) Gorey Castle, Jersey, first mentioned in 1212—from a lithograph after P. J. Ouless published in 1847

without heirs in 1606, and Marguerite, who married Arthur Fortescue of Lyme Regis. Sir Amias Poulett (about 1532-88), a son of Sir Hugh, succeeded his father as Governor of Jersey and he held the office until 1590. He was Ambassador to France in 1576 and Principal Keeper of Mary, Queen of Scots. In the latter capacity it was intimated to him that Queen Elizabeth I was displeased that he had not found some way to shorten his prisoner's life. Sir Amias was prepared if need be to incur the royal displeasure, and swiftly gave the reply "My goods and my life are at Her Majestie's disposition, but God forbid I should make so foul a shipwreck of my conscience, or leave so great a blot on my poor posterity". George Poulett (1534-1621), Amias' brother, was Lieutenant-Governor of Jersey, and bailiff of the island (1583-86, 1587-91 and 1596-1614). His daughter Rachel (1564-1651) married Philip de Carteret and his son Abraham (died 1605), who married Esther de Carteret, daughter of John de Carteret, Lord of the Manor of Vinchelez de Haut, was attorney-general (1603-05). Sir Anthony Poulett (1562-1600), a son of Sir Amias, was governor from 1590-1600. He married Catherine, only daughter of Sir Henry Norris, or Norreys, first Baron Norreys of Rycote, who shared the duty of guarding Princess Elizabeth while imprisoned at Woodstock during the reign of her half-sister Queen Mary I. The oldest memorial remaining in St Helier's Church is that placed there by Sir Anthony to his brother-in-law Maximilian Norris who died aged 24 years in 1591 while serving in the army of King Henry IV of France and Navarre. Before he became of age, Sir Anthony was Captain of the Guard to Queen Elizabeth I. Sir Anthony's son John (1586-1649), who like his father was born in Jersey, was elevated to the peerage. His eldest son, Sir John Poulett, was one of the first to bring the news of the execution of King Charles I to Jersey. Sir Amias, Sir Anthony and Lady Catherine all have splendid monuments in the parish church of Hinton St George. Sir Amias died in London and was buried at St Martin-in-the-Fields where a magnificent monument was erected to his memory. However, when that church was rebuilt in 1728 the parishioners would not allow the monument to be re-erected and the first Earl Poulett had the body and the monument removed to Hinton St George. Portraits of Sir Amias and Sir Anthony hang in the museum, St Helier. The inscription above Sir Anthony's effigy reads "*Hic jacet Antonius Poulett, miles et dux insulae Jersey, qui obiit 22 die Julii Anno Dni.* 1600." The arms of the Poulett family appear on the middle ward gateway at Mont Orgueil Castle; those of Sir Anthony impaling those of his wife, with their initials beneath, appear on the same gateway, and without initials at the side of Queen Elizabeth's gate, built some time between 1594 and 1600, at Elizabeth Castle. The family motto is "*Gardez la Foi*" (Keep Faith). Thomas Fuller referring to it in his *Worthies of England* in connection with Sir Amias wrote "Which

4

harping on that one string of his fidelity, though perchance harsh music to the ears of others, was harmonious to Queen Elizabeth".

Sir Peter Mewtis was Governor of Guernsey (1546–53). On 25th September 1553 he was replaced by Leonard Chamberlain who was knighted a week later. Sir Leonard appointed his eldest son, Francis, his lieutenant, and subsequently, in 1555, Francis became joint governor with his father. Sir Leonard died in 1561, and Francis succeeded him as governor, which office he held until his death in 1570. He was succeeded by Sir Thomas Leighton who was governor until 1610. Leighton was connected with Queen Elizabeth I through his wife, Cecilia Knollys, whose grandmother was a sister of Anne Boleyn.

On 5th February 1587 Leighton wrote to the Earl of Leicester, his wife's brother-in-law, about various matters concerning Guernsey, at the same time urging the execution of Mary, Queen of Scots:

. . . suffer dewe punishments to be done uppon that wiked won, throgh whos meanes her Maties death is dayly still soghte, and will be so longe as the other hath lyffe. Wherefore my good lorde deale vehemently with her Matie, take no refusalle tille that ennymye to you and her highness be executed. And let not her Matie feare the threats of anny, for God is with her, but think suche will seke to crowne that monster lyvinge that deade will not spende won grote for her revenge . . .

The letter was delivered by Peter Carey (about 1550–1629) who was a Guernsey merchant "honneste and trusty, who is to declare farther to yor L^{d} off the Spanishe preparacione accordinge to the generalle reports of all that".

On 12th August 1594 the new Royal Rampart at Castle Cornet was dedicated by Malhommeau, the Rector of St Peter Port, in the presence of Sir Thomas Leighton, the governor, and Louis de Vic, the bailiff, and other local dignitaries.

Until the Reformation the Church had provided education and cared for the sick and the infirm; the fraternities attached to the parish churches no doubt also provided their members with help in time of sickness and distress. In Jersey there existed at the end of the fifteenth century and no doubt until the Reformation two institutions known respectively as the Hospital of Jerusalem and the Hospital of the High Footstep. The former was probably situated at La Hougue Bie, where the Jerusalem Chapel still exists; the latter was situated at Havre des Pas adjacent to La Chapelle de Notre Dame des Pas on the eastern side of the Town Hill. There was also a leper hospital called St Nicolas of Grandport at Gorey. In Guernsey there was the Hôpital de Boscq.

King Edward VI died in 1553 and was succeeded by his half-sister Mary, a staunch Roman Catholic. The new Queen set about reversing the effects of the Reformation throughout her realm and with such vigour and cruelty that she earned for herself the macabre nickname of 'Bloody Mary'. It was during her brief reign that three Guernsey women were put to death in the most gruesome way. Both the principal participants in this terrible tragedy were Jerseymen, Helier Gosselin (died 1579), Bailiff of Guernsey (1549–62), and James Amy (about 1500–about 1586), Dean of Guernsey (1547–63). Gosselin was of a Protestant family, and it had been his duty under King Edward VI to enforce the changes brought about by the Reformation; Amy was a Catholic who had acquiesced in the Reformation. In 1556, three women, Catherine Cauchés and her daughters Perotine Massey and Guillemine Guibert were accused of having stolen some pewter pots, and found not guilty. Although the jury acquitted them on 1st July, they declared that the accused "had not been obedient to the commands of Holy Church" and the bailiff handed them over to the Ecclesiastical Court, which condemned them as heretics without even hearing them. The bailiff would not accept this verdict and insisted that the women be examined. On the 13th July the dean questioned each of them in the north-east aisle of the Town Church concerning the Catholic faith. Their answers were unacceptable and the Ecclesiastical Court handed the women over to the Royal Court, which sentenced them to be burnt. The execution took place in St Peter Port. The whole of the tragic circumstances are fully recounted in the *Book of Martyrs* by John Foxe (1517–87). His account of the burning reads thus:

> The time being come when the innocent mother with her two daughters should suffer, in the place where they should consummate their martyrdom were three stakes set up. At the middle post was the mother, the eldest daughter on the right hand, the youngest on the other. They were first strangled, but the rope broke before they were dead, and the poor women fell in the fire. Perrotine, who was great with child, did fall on her side, where happened a rueful sight, not only to the eyes of all that there stood, but also to the ears of all true-hearted Christians that shall read this history. For as the belly of the woman brast asunder by the vehemency of the flame, the infant, a fair man child, fell into the fire, and being taken out of the fire by one, W. House was laid on the grass. Then was the child had to the provost, and from him to the bailiff, who gave censure that it should be carried back again and cast into the fire. And so the infant baptized in his own blood, to fill up the number of God's innocent saints was both born and died a martyr, leaving behind the world, which it never saw.

It has been suggested, probably correctly, that the bailiff and the dean felt themselves insecure owing to their past history and in order to assure the English authorities of their orthodoxy treated the three women in the barbarous manner already described.

When Queen Elizabeth came to the throne, Matthew Cauchés, Catherine Cauchés' brother, petitioned Her Majesty asking for those who had been responsible for the death of his sister and nieces to be punished. This resulted in both the bailiff and dean being deprived of office. The bailiff and jurats who had formed the court which had condemned the unfortunate women were sent to England to stand trial. However, they submitted "themselves to the Queen's Most Excellent Majesty, acknowledging their erroneous judgment", In January 1565 the Queen granted a pardon to the whole court, but Amy never resumed the office of dean.

Another grim episode, this time in Jersey, took place in 1555. A priest called Richard Averty was convicted on the 27th June for infanticide and sentenced to death. The facts of the case were that Averty, Proctor of the Ecclesiastical Court, had strangled a baby born to Marie Bellée, a domestic servant, who had been employed by him for a long time. Averty, the father of the child, baptized it, or so he said, strangled it, and buried it under the hearth in his house. The dean tried his best to save Averty and disputed the right of the royal court to deal with the matter. However, his efforts were in vain, and Averty was drawn to the gallows on a hurdle and his surplice was dragged off him before he was hanged. Averty's body was left hanging until it rotted. Two proverbs arose from this case. The first resulted from the fact that when the royal court refused to surrender him to the ecclesiastical authorities, Averty complained to the dean that he had promised to save his life. The dean replied that he would bring them to repentance. Averty retorted that that would be too late. Hence "A Richard Averty repentance" means one which comes too late. The second proverb arose from the fact that as Averty was being drawn through the stream which crossed the road at the western end of La Grande Rue he folded his surplice on either side so that it would not get wet. Ever after it is said of a sick man who winds his sheets about him that "He is doing what Richard Averty did and will not live long".

Queen Mary died in 1558 and was succeeded by her half-sister Elizabeth who reversed the pro-Catholic policies of the previous reign.

Helier de Carteret died in London in February 1561 while staying at the house of Sir Hugh Poulett, the Governor of Jersey, and was buried in St John's, Clerkenwell. The Governor wrote to the States informing them of the bailiff's death:

To my very loving friends the Jurats and others the inhabitants of the Isle of Jersey be this delivered with my very hearty commendations. These shall be to advertise you that my good friend and yours, Sr. Helier de Carteret, Bailiff of the Isle, is deceased here the 19th of this present month in travelling more about your affairs than any of his own, in the midst whereof God hath called him to his mercy, etc. Your assured friend, Hugh Paulet.

It was the purpose of the English government to enforce in the Channel Islands uniformity with the Church of England. However, there was one difficulty which for some years proved an insuperable obstacle to uniformity, it was that of language. The islanders were French-speaking and there were virtually no French-speaking Church of England clergy available in the islands except for the few Catholic clergy who had conformed. Therefore, not unnaturally, the islanders availed themselves of the services of French Protestant ministers, some of whom were men of considerable ability. This resulted in the establishment in the islands of a complete Presbyterian system of government in accordance with the practice of the French Reformed Churches. Guillaume Morise, Sieur de la Ripaudière, of Anjou organized St Helier's Parish Church in accordance with that system with elders, deacons and a consistory. Nicholas Baudouin of Rouen did likewise for St Peter's Port Parish Church. Their examples were followed throughout the islands and had the support of the governors and the civil authorities of both bailiwicks who in turn had the support of the English government. In 1564 the first General Synod was held in Guernsey.

In brief, the Presbyterian system was organized in this way. Every congregation was considered equal. At parish level there was a consistory consisting of the minister, who presided, elders and deacons, which met every Sunday. At island level was a colloquy consisting either of the governor or his lieutenant, who presided, and the minister and one elder from each parish, which met at least quarterly. The acts or minutes of the Jersey Colloquy commence in September 1577 and end on 14th November 1614; those of the Guernsey Colloquy run from 2nd August 1585 to 24th September 1619. Originally there was a meeting of the synod comprising the two colloquies once a year, but latterly it met once every two years. The discipline established in 1576 was revised in 1597. Under the first discipline the islands were each to send one minister to the French General Synod, this according to the good advice of the governors. The secular and church authorities worked hand in glove and enforced an irksome and oppressive control over the lives of the people.

In 1565 an Order in Council was issued permitting the parish churches of St Helier and St Peter Port to follow the Presbyterian system provided that the other churches were in uniformity with the Church of England. The proviso was ignored as were a number of injunctions from the Bishop of Winchester requiring all but the two exempted churches to use the Church of England Prayer Book and to have six sermons a year setting forth the Crown's supremacy in ecclesiastical matters.

In 1400 the Channel Islands had been transferred by a Bull of the Pope at Rome from the Clementine Bishop of Coutances to a Bishop of Nantes, who was unable to occupy his see because it was still in the possession of a Clementine bishop. In 1496 Pope Alexander VI had transferred the

Channel Islands from the Diocese of Coutances to that of Salisbury, but this transfer never took effect. In 1499, by a further Bull, Pope Alexander cancelled this transfer and instead transferred the islands to the Diocese of Winchester, again without effect, although the Bull was followed by a letter from King Henry VII to the Bishop of Winchester signifying that the transfer had taken place. Bishop Langton of Winchester exercised jurisdiction in Jersey on 1st January 1500, but from then until 1569 the Bishop of Coutances continued to exercise ecclesiastical authority in that island and he instituted Edward Hamon to the Rectory of St John as late as May 1557. The Bishop of Coutances might have continued his authority even longer had it not been that he insisted on pressing too strongly for his dues. In passing, it is amusing to note that in 1500 Richard Le Haguais took the precaution of being appointed to the Rectory of St Brelade both by the Bishop of Coutances and the Bishop of Winchester. The position of the Channel Islands as part of the Diocese of Winchester was once and for all declared in an Order in Council of March 1569, confirming a letter of Queen Elizabeth I of the previous June.

Sark was invaded and captured for King Henry II of France in 1549 and four years later was recaptured for Queen Mary I of England by her allies the Flemings. Sir Hugh Poulett, the Governor of Jersey, caused the three forts erected by the French to be destroyed, but no garrison was installed and Sark became a haunt of pirates who preyed on shipping as it passed through the islands. In 1563 Helier de Carteret, Lord of the Manor of St Ouen in Jersey, obtained permission to colonize Sark and in 1565 Queen Elizabeth I granted him the Lordship of the island by Letters Patent on the understanding that he would colonize it with forty men. Sark was principally colonized from Jersey, although in 1567 de Carteret to his friend Nicholas Gosselin, a Guernseyman, son of Helier Gosselin, Bailiff of Guernsey, the Tenement of Beauregard, for his help in securing the grant of Sark. Among the island's early settlers were a number of Englishmen, some of whom were serving the garrison at Mont Orgueil Castle—Edward Brayer, Jasper Dare, Edward Gregory and William Smith.

Slowly, painfully slowly, higher education was being brought to the islanders. The fifteenth century had seen the foundation in Jersey of the schools of St Mannelier and St Anastase; the sixteenth century saw the foundation of Elizabeth College in Guernsey, and the efforts of Laurens Baudains (about 1546–1611) to found a college in Jersey. In 1596 Baudains presented Dannemarche Mill and eighteen quarters of wheat rent to the States and the next year obtained Letters Patent from Queen Elizabeth I permitting others to add to the endowment up to 200 quarters. The first master, Edmund Snape, chaplain to the garrison at Mont Orgueil Castle, was appointed by the States in 1598, but he left the island a few months later. The following year the States added twenty quarters to the endowment from the revenues of St Mannelier and St Anastase. In 1600 the States authorized the two senior boys to conduct the college, then in St Helier, as sub-regents.

By Letters Patent dated 25th May 1563 royal commissioners were appointed to examine the state of the harbour and the island of Guernsey generally, and in particular to endow a royal school. The letter of the commissioners dated 27th September 1563 contains the statutes of the new school, Elizabeth College. The royal endowments were made in two grants. The first comprising of tenements and lands of a convent of Franciscan friars, together with eighty quarters of wheat rent, was made in 1563; the second, comprising further buildings and lands, which had formerly belonged to the friars, was made in 1568.

The first headmaster of the newly-founded college was Adrian Saravia (1531-1613) who held the post from 1563-68. He was a native of Artois and had originally been a Franciscan friar. He became a Calvinist and was appointed pastor in Antwerp. Owing to religious troubles in the Netherlands he moved with his family to Guernsey in 1560. Four years later he is mentioned as assistant to Nicholas Baudouin, whom Calvin sent to Guernsey. Saravia later went to England and was one of the translators of the Authorized Version of the Bible.

In the sixteenth century Alderney was a haunt of pirates. In 1565 or early in the following year seventeen pirates were caught in the island and brought to Guernsey accused of piracy, homicide and felony. Included among them were Robert Ahyer (Ahier), T. Lawrence, alias Lorens (Laurens) and Edward Regnold (Renault) whose surnames suggest that they may have been Jerseymen. The accused were examined by Francis Chamberlain, the governor, and John After, the dean, who reported their findings to Queen Elizabeth who ordered:

> . . . considering that these men have remained there now a great while in Prison that you shall cause two or three of them, such as you shall think most culpable and fittest for example sake; to be executed out of hand, and for ye Rest we will that you shall upon baill or otherwise as by your discretion shall be thought best deliver them and set them at liberty to repair heither and sue out their pardon w'ch upon your Recommendation we shall be contented to graunt unto them . . .

Richard Hygkens was the one selected to pay for his villainies in full and it was ordered that he should be:

> . . . pynioned by ye officer of justice and by him lead . . . to St. Martin's Point nere ye full sea mark and there by ye same officer shall be hanged and strangled till thou be dead . . .

Chamberlain's successor, Sir Thomas Leighton, during his term of office imposed a heavy fine on the people of Alderney for failing to go to the assistance of shipping attacked by pirates in the vicinity of the island. There is little doubt that the islanders were in league with pirates and allowed pirate ships to anchor in the island's bays and to use the island as a base from whence to carry out depredations on shipping in the English Channel.

In 1585 were written *Les Chroniques de Jersey* (to which reference has already been made) by an author whose identity has never been discovered, although it is clear from what he wrote that he was either a member or a friend of the de Carteret family. The chronicles constitute a history of the de Carterets from early times to the date when they were written, and careful checking of the text has shown that despite the author's obvious partiality for the de Carterets his facts for the most part are accurate. A number of handwritten copies of the chronicles were in circulation in Jersey and it was not until 1832 that a printed edition was published in Guernsey by G. S. Syvret. Unfortunately he did not print from the best manuscript available and a further edition published in 1858 in Jersey by Philip Falle is to be preferred.

The Channel Islands have had a long connection with Southampton, dating at least from the time of the Norman Conquest. Early in the sixteenth century most trade between the islands and England passed through that port, although previously a considerable amount of trade went through Poole. It was through Southampton that a great deal of the islands' knitted goods were sent to the English market and in 1587 the islands' merchants were asking for permission to sell their goods in the market of Hampton (Southampton). In 1604, when plague ravaged the port, a collection was made at the instance of the Royal Court of Jersey to help the poor of the town cruelly affected by the outbreak. The Channel Islands also contributed to the support of the French Reformed Church in Southampton and in 1750 some fifty of the islands' merchants undertook to pay a penny on each tod of wool imported to defray the expenses of the minister. Between 1409 and 1846 no less than twenty Jerseymen or persons with Jersey connections held the office of Mayor of Southampton, twenty-eight the office of Sheriff, some of whom later became mayor, and five were ministers of the French Episcopal Church in the town. It was probably a Jerseyman, Richard Estur, who presented the municipal seal in 1587. Two of those of Jersey descent who held the office of mayor were father and son, both called John Major, the surname being an anglicized form of the name Mauger. They were the grandson and great-grandson respectively of John Mauger, a Jerseyman, who settled in Southampton towards the end of the fifteenth century.

Southampton was not the only port with which the Channel Islands were trading in Elizabethan times. Coal, then referred to as sea coals, were imported principally in Jersey- and Guernsey-owned ships from South Wales through the ports of Carmarthen, Llanelli, Neath and particularly Swansea. The Jersey trade was one-sided, vessels from that island with very few exceptions arriving in the South Wales ports in ballast. The Guernsey trade was more reciprocal.

By the end of the century the islands' participation in the Newfoundland fisheries had become well established. The fisheries provided a new and welcome means of livelihood; one which was to last for nearly three centuries.

Knitting was a well-established industry in the Channel Islands by the sixteenth century, and had certainly existed in the fifteenth century. The knitted goods produced by the islanders had reached such a high standard that they were to be found in England in the wardrobes of the wealthy. On 1st January 1556 the Governor of Guernsey presented various woollen articles to Queen Mary I. It is known that in 1578 Guernsey woollens were in the Scottish royal wardrobe and in 1586 in the English royal wardrobe. At her execution in 1587 Mary Queen of Scots wore a pair of Guernsey knitted stockings.

Sir Anthony Poulett, the Governor of Jersey, died on 22nd July 1600. Within a few days Sir Walter Raleigh (1554–1618), Captain of the Queen's Guard, Warden of the Stanneries of Cornwall and Devon, Grand Steward of the Duchy of Cornwall and of Exeter, and Lieutenant of Her Majesty in the County of Cornwall, was angling for the governorship. On 26th August he secured the appointment together with a grant of the Manor of St Germain. The Crown reserved to itself £300 out of the governor's revenues. On 20th September Raleigh arrived in Jersey, and on the same day took his oath before the States. Raleigh appointed George Poulett, the bailiff, uncle of his predecessor, his lieutenant-governor. The first of Raleigh's two visits to Jersey lasted to 16th October. Two days before he left the island the States made an Act stating that the governor had appointed Charles Hamelin to be Master of the Hunt for the whole island. In September 1602 Hamelin was succeeded by Peter de la Rocque and Helier Le Tubelin as joint masters.

Raleigh's second visit lasted from 3rd July to about 10th August 1602. On 20th July he wrote to Sir Robert Cecil:

> I beseech you to bestow a line on me, that live in desolation, And if you find no cause to staye me here, I would willingly returne . . . I arrived here the 3rd, so I have walked here these 17 dayes in the wilderness.

Queen Elizabeth I died on 30th March 1603. Her death marked the end of the Tudor dynasty and of the Elizabethan age, a golden era in the history of England.

CHAPTER SIX

Early Stuart Times—1603–41

... And certainly, it could not be but an eyesore to
the French, to have these Isles within their sight, and
not within their power; to see them at the least in
possession of their ancient enemy the English ...

Peter Heylyn (1600–62)

Queen Elizabeth was succeeded on the throne of England by King
James VI of Scotland, as King James I. The King's consort was Queen
Anne of Denmark. Shortly after the commencement of the new reign the
King deprived Raleigh of the Governorship of Jersey, because he believed
that he had conspired against him with the object of placing Arabella
Stuart on the throne in his place. Raleigh survived until 1618 when he was
executed in the Tower of London. He was succeeded by Sir John Peyton,
Lieutenant of the Tower, who remained governor until his death in 1630.
Peyton was succeeded in that office by Sir Thomas Jermyn in 1631.

Leighton continued as Governor of Guernsey until his death in 1610
and was succeeded by George, Lord Carew, later created Earl of Totnes,
who resigned in 1621. The same year Henry Danvers, later created Earl of
Danby, was appointed governor and Sir Peter Osborne, Danvers' brother-
in-law, lieutenant-governor in succession to Amias de Carteret, who was
also bailiff; in addition Osborne obtained a grant of the reversion of the
governorship. Osborne was the father of Dorothy Osborne who married
Sir William Temple. Lady Temple's letters to her husband are well known
and were first published in 1888. Little did Osborne think when he assumed
the office of lieutenant-governor that over twenty years later he would
have to endure so many hardships and dangers in maintaining Castle
Cornet for his sovereign.

George Poulett was still Bailiff of Jersey and remained so until his resignation in 1614 when he was succeeded by John Herault (1569–1626) who had secured the reversion of the office in 1611 and paid him a sum of money to induce him to retire. Herault was removed from office in 1620 and reinstated in 1624, and for part of the time during which Herault was suspended Sir William Parkhurst was appointed to execute the office of bailiff. Following Herault's death Sir Philip de Carteret (1584–1643), eldest son of Sir Philip de Carteret and Rachel de Carteret (*née* Poulett), was appointed bailiff in 1627 and lieutenant-governor in 1634.The latter office entitled him to live at Mont Orgueil Castle, which he did with his wife Anne de Carteret (*née* Dowse), daughter of Sir Francis Dowse of Nether Wallop, Hampshire, and their eleven children, leaving his mother in solitary state at St Ouen's Manor. The de Carterets lived in some splendour at the castle and entertained a number of distinguished visitors.

Amias de Carteret (about 1559–1631) had been appointed Bailiff of Guernsey in 1601 and was to hold the office until his death in 1631. He was the second son of Helier de Carteret, Lord of the Manor of St Ouen and Colonizer of Sark, and Marguerite, daughter of Helier de Carteret, Bailiff of Jersey. He married Catherine Lemprière, daughter of William Lempriere, Lord of Trinity Manor. He became a jurat and an influential man in his native island before becoming Bailiff of Guernsey. Both he and his wife were buried in St Peter Port Church. John de Quetteville succeeded de Carteret as bailiff.

The town of St Helier in the early years of the seventeenth century was still small in extent and contained few buildings of any interest. The parish church was a Calvinist temple devoid of all ornamentation; the neighbouring chapel of the Madelaine had been secularized, as had been La Chapelle de Notre Dame des Pas, close to the west end of Havre des Pas. The court house was as it had been from time immemorial. The Market Place was unpaved and the market cross had fallen victim to the Reformation. The houses, either one- or two-storeyed, were thatched. Beyond the town at the west end of La Grande Rue (now Broad Street) were sand-dunes; beyond the east end was Le Manoir de la Motte, otherwise called La Maison de Téhy. The Abbey Church now shared the islet in St Aubin's Bay with Elizabeth Castle.

Outside St Helier, buildings remained much as they had been in the previous century. The parish churches had suffered in the same way as that of St Helier; the manorial and other chapels had fallen into disuse, and the vast majority of them would disappear with the passing of the years. In St Aubin's Bay were St Aubin's Tower (1542) and Elizabeth Castle (commenced about 1551), so named by Raleigh. The latter was referred to as the 'New Castle' and Mont Orgueil Castle as the 'Old Castle'.

St Peter Port consisted of Cornet Street, Fountain Street, La Grande

Rue (now called High Street), La Rue des Forges (now called Smith Street) and The Pollet, with other very narrow thoroughfares within Les Barrières de la Ville. The junction of La Grande Rue, La Rue des Forges and The Pollet was known as Le Grand Carrefour. The parish church had been converted into a Calvinist temple like St Helier's Church in Jersey. Elizabeth College occupied the buildings of the Friary of the Cordeliers or Franciscan friars. It was known as La Grande Ecole as distinct from the parish school which was known as La Petite Ecole. On Easter Day 1513 Thomas Le Marquant and Jannette Le Marquant (née Thelry), his wife, appeared in St Peter Port Church before the bailiff and three jurats and made a formal declaration of their gift of a house and garden on the north side of St Julien's Chapel for use as a parish school, also two quarters of annual wheat rent for the schoolmaster, who every evening before they went home was to repeat to the scholars, who in turn were to repeat, an Anthem of Our Lady, with a *De Profundis* and an *Ave Maria*, for the souls of the donors, the souls of all their friends and benefactors, also for all souls for whom God would have men pray. The King's Barn or La Plaiderie still occupied the site where it had been since as long ago as 1248. La Croix de Glatigny or Town Cross, which had stood to the east of La Plaiderie, had been destroyed at the Reformation. La Tour Beauregard had been demolished, precisely at what date is not known. The houses were finer than any to be found in St Helier and some of them had pious inscriptions carved on their frontages. The town was very picturesque and remained so until considerable rebuilding was carried out at the end of the eighteenth and the early nineteenth centuries. William Camden (1551–1623) described the town as:

> . . . an haven within an hollow Bay
> bending inward like an halfemoone,
> able to receive tall ships; upon which standeth Saint Peters,
> a little towne built with a long and narrow street.

While Peter Heylyn wrote of "the large capaciousnesse of the Harbour" as "the principall honour and glory" of the island. The south pier was completed in 1590 and a harbour supervisor was appointed by the States in 1611.

In Alderney Fort Essex was built between 1546 and 1554.

Almost from the outset of the new reign disputes, both civil and ecclesiastical, arose in Jersey. There was also discontent in Guernsey, which in 1604 resulted in a petition being sent from that island to the Privy Council and deputies being heard on the complaints before the council. The council's decision was embodied in an order of 9th June 1605.

The States of Guernsey would appear to have originated from the same

Order in Council and their deliberations are recorded from 1605. However, the order refers to "the ancient use and authority of assembling the States for ordering the principal affairs of the island" which would indicate that the States had been in existence many years earlier.

Guernsey was dissatisfied with the terms of the Order in Council of 9th June 1605 and tried to organize common action with Jersey to bring about reforms in the islands. In June 1606 representatives of the States of both islands met in St Peter Port and drew up proposals for submission to the King, which included the establishment of a States General and a Court of Appeal for the islands, it being the intention that no further appeals would be sent to the Privy Council. Nothing resulted from the joint proposals.

However, on 25th July 1607 commissioners in the persons of Sir Robert Gardiner and Dr James Hussey, one of the Masters of the Court of Chancery, with John Herault as local expert, were sent to Jersey and Guernsey to inquire into the affairs of both islands under identical commissions. They were to report on the state of the laws and customs of the islands, to make a list of the rents and revenues of the Crown, to settle differences between the governors on the one hand and the bailiffs, jurats and the islanders on the other and to determine certain cases of little importance where an appeal had been made to the Privy Council. The report of the commissioners with some slight amendments was approved by Order in Council of 30th June 1608.

By Letters Patent of 9th August 1615 Herault was appointed Bailiff of Jersey, the emoluments of that office were augmented and it was ordered that the right of nomination of the bailiff, dean, attorney-general and solicitor-general was reserved to the Crown. This order reserving the nomination of the Crown appointments constituted a signal victory for the bailiff who had for long disputed the pretended right of the governor to nominate the bailiff. The part of the Letters Patent relating to the Crown appointments ran thus:

. . . We, by the advice and mature deliberation of our Counsell, have commanded and ordered, and by these Presents our Heirs, and Successors do command and order that henceforth no Bailiffe, Deane, Vicomte, Procuror, Advocate to Us shall be made and appointed, but immediately by Letters Patent under our Seal, in the Name and by the Authority of Us, our Heirs, and Successors, Kings of this Realm of England, and Dukes of Normandy, and not otherwise. As we do likewise command and enjoyne, and by these Presents do straightly command and enjoyne the said Sir John Peyton, and all others Captains or Governors of the said Island present and to come never hereafter to attempt or intermeddle in any way in the Nomination, Institution and Appointment of the said Offices of Bailiffe, Deane, Vicomte, our Attorney, or Advocate, or any other

Public Officers of Justice within the said Isle, or in any way to infringe or violate, either the Privileges granted to the Inhabitants thereof by the most excellent Prince of famous Memory King Henry the Seventh, or the Statutes and Ordinances made by the same King for the good and peaceable Government of the same Island, upon paine to incur our indignation, and further Punishment at our Pleasure . . .

On 25th March 1617 further commissioners, Sir Edward Conway and Sir William Bird, were appointed to examine the defects and abuses in the military and civil government of Jersey. As a result of the commissioners' report the Privy Council made certain ordinances on 15th June 1618 which it ordered should be observed and put into execution for the safekeeping of the King's castles, the administration of justice and the general peace and harmony of the island. The ordinances settled once and for all the precedence of bailiff and governor:

It is ordered first that the Bailiff shall, in the cohue and seat of justice and likewise in the assembly of the States, take the seat of precedence as formerly, and that in all places and assemblies the Governor take place and have precedence which is due unto him as Governor, without further question.

This was a further victory for Herault brought about by his courage, skill and tenacity. Among other things the ordinances directed that a dean should be appointed and granted to the island the right to levy a tax upon wine sold in taverns, for the defence of the island, and to levy a petty custom upon imports, for a harbour.

The sympathies of the Governor of Jersey were with Anglicanism and although at first he took no special steps to introduce it into Jersey he was merely biding his time for an opportunity to strike at Presbyterianism. In 1603 the King confirmed the ecclesiastical arrangements existing in the islands. However, by 1607 the English authorities had formed the definite intention of bringing Jersey into conformity with the Church of England. Eventually the governor found the opportunity he had been looking for and so far as Presbyterianism was concerned the game was up. The governor had been given his chance when a living fell vacant and he appointed a young Jerseyman, Eli Messervy, who had studied at Oxford and had taken Anglican orders to fill it. The colloquy were powerless to do anything as the governor was clearly within his rights in making the appointment. On 2nd November 1613 letters were sent from the Privy Council to Jersey and Guernsey announcing the King's intention to introduce Anglicanism into the islands. Jersey was given the opportunity to state its case before the council, but it was all in vain, which is not surprising in view of the fact that the committee to which the matter was referred consisted of only three members of whom the Archbishop of Canterbury was one. The committee considered that the office of dean should be revived, the holder to be an islander, and that a body of canons be drawn up. Messervy was admitted to his benefice. It was now only a matter of time before Jersey would be brought into conformity. It will be recalled that the ordinances of 1618 specifically ordered that a dean should be appointed.

The first Anglican Dean of Jersey, David Bandinel (died 1645), Rector of St Brelade, was appointed by Letters Patent of 28th January 1620 and sworn in at a meeting of the States on 15th April. Bandinel was probably Italian by birth, but was naturalized in 1602, the papers being signed by Raleigh. He married Elizabeth Stallenge, daughter of William Stallenge, Clerk of Naval Receipts at Plymouth.

The next step in the establishment of the Anglican Church in Jersey was the drawing up of the Canons Ecclesiastical. The canons, fifty-eight in number, were promulgated in 1623 and are entered in the first book of the Ecclesiastical Court. Down the years they have been modified to some small extent, but the majority of them remain unaltered and in force. It had been intended that Guernsey should also have Canons Ecclestiastical, but the proposal excited the strongest opposition in that island and was dropped.

The English authorities had little success in its endeavour to bring Guernsey into uniformity with the Church of England. The island was fortunate that the governor was an absentee and not interested in its ecclesiastical affairs and that the lieutenant-governor, who was also the bailiff, was Presbyterian in his sympathies, that the States and the colloquy were united when the local system of church government was threatened, and that John de la Marche, the young minister who was sent to argue its case proved himself to be an able advocate. The King with whom de la Marche had two personal interviews, eventually decided to leave matters as they were. In the face of such united opposition the English authorities had felt it unwise to forfeit the goodwill and loyalty of the islanders and thus possibly endanger the safety of the island.

In order to ensure an adequate supply of Church of England clergy for the Channel Islands King Charles I, at the instance of Archbishop Laud, by Letters Patent dated June 1636 founded three fellowships, one each at Exeter, Jesus and Pembroke Colleges, Oxford, for students from Jersey and Guernsey, to be held by natives of each island alternately, it being "his Majesties intention that within convenient tyme the sayd Fellowes or Scholars shall return to the sayd severall Ilands upon fitt Promocions to them offerred there". The properties which were used to endow the fellowships had belonged to Sir Miles Hobart, Alderman of London, and had fallen to the Crown by escheat, through lack of heirs. They comprised seven messuages and two gardens in Lad Lane in the parish of St Lawrence Jewry held in free burgage of the City of London and a moiety of a cottage at Medmenham, Buckinghamshire, with 123 acres of land, 52 of meadows, 53 of pasture, and 205 of woods. The King named the first fellows; afterwards the dean and jurats of either island were to nominate. Daniel Brevint (1617–95), the son of Daniel Brevint and grandson of Cosme Brevint, and John Poingdestre (1609–91) were the first named. In 1636 Brevint, who had been educated at the Protestant University of Saumur and taken the degree of Master of Arts when he was only seventeen, was nominated Jersey Fellow of Jesus College. In 1649 he preached before King Charles II in St Helier's Church. In 1660 he was appointed Prebendary of Durham, in 1663 Oxford University conferred on him the degree of Doctor of Divinity, and in 1682 he was appointed Dean of Lincoln. Poingdestre took his degree of Master of Arts at Cambridge in 1633. He then went to Exeter College, Oxford, as Gentleman Commoner in 1635, and the following year was nominated a Jersey Fellow of the College. In 1669 he was appointed Lieutenant-Bailiff of Jersey, but he retired from the position in 1676, although he remained a jurat. He was learned in the laws and customs of his native island, about which he wrote three books.

Despite the great attention given to religion, witchcraft claimed a small and sinister following. Witchcraft had been practised in Europe for centuries. There is no doubt that it was organized as a widespread secret society throughout Western Europe including the Channel Islands. Between the years 1550 and 1649 seventy-seven witchcraft trials are recorded in Guernsey and sixty-six in Jersey between 1562 and 1736. Sixty-one of the Guernsey trials took place between 1603 and 1630 when Amias de Carteret was Bailiff (1601–31); twenty-six of the Jersey trials took place between 1605 and 1626. Although the administration of justice at that period was rough and ready, there is little doubt that many of the persons brought to trial had indulged in witchcraft. The practice of the evil arts ran in families, the Alexandres, Grandins and Tourgis in Jersey; the Becquets and de Callais in Guernsey. The surnames Alexandre, Becquet and Tourgis appear on the lists of accused in both islands. In Jersey the death sentence imposed on a condemned witch provided for death by hanging and for the body to be burnt; in Guernsey the sentence almost always provided for torture followed by death by burning. In the former island the place of execution was St Helier except for condemned persons who resided either on the Manor of St Ouen or the Manor of Samarès, in which case the sentence was carried out on the manorial gallows. In the latter island the place of execution was on Tower Hill, close to La Tour de Beauregard, which was used as a prison. In Jersey the memory of Marie Tourgis executed in 1618 is preserved in a local saying

(*above*) St Apolline's Chapel, Guernsey—founded in 1392

(*below*) Elizabeth Castle, Jersey, first mentioned in 1550—from an early eighteenth-century engraving

Fort Essex, Alderney, probably built 1546–54—from a nineteenth-century lithograph

directed at a naughty young child by a disgruntled grown-up—"If you're such a bad girl, I'll send for Marie Tourgis."

King James had died in 1625 and been succeeded by his son, Charles, Prince of Wales, as King Charles I. The new King's consort was Queen Henrietta Maria. Almost from its outset the reign was far from happy and relations between the King and his people, particularly the puritans, steadily deteriorated. The sad story is too well known to need recapitulation.

During this period Mont Orgueil Castle was on occasion used as a state prison. One prisoner sent there by the English authorities was William Prynne (1600–69). He was a graduate of Oxford University and a barrister-at-law of Lincoln's Inn; he was also a puritan pamphleteer. His writings had twice got him into serious trouble with the authorities. He had been pilloried, his ears had been cropped, and the letters SL, standing for 'seditious libeller', had been branded on each of his cheeks. His books had been burnt by the hangman and he had been expelled from his University and Inn of Court; he was also fined. He was twice imprisoned in the Tower of London and then sent to prison in Caernarvon Castle, from which he was transferred to Mont Orgueil Castle "in a bruised ship-wracked vessell, full of leakes, and after foureteene weekes voyage in the Winter season, through dangerous stormes and seas, which spoyled most of his stuffe and bedding, and threatening often ship-wrack to him." Prynne was to remain in Mont Orgueil Castle from 1638 to 1640. While there he was well treated by Sir Philip de Carteret, the lieutenant-governor, and during his incarceration wrote *Mount Orgueil, or Divine and Profitable Meditations, raised from the contemplation of these three leaves of Nature's volume. 1, Rockes, 2, Seas, 3, Gardens, digested into three distinct poems, to which is prefixed a poetical description of Mont Orgueil Castle in the Island of Jersey*, published in London in 1641. The work as a whole is dedicated "To the Right Worshipfull his ever Honoured worthy Friend, Sir Philip Carteret", but each section has a separate dedication. The first, entitled "Rockes" is dedicated "To the Right Worshipfull his most highly honoured, speciall Kind Friend, the truly vertuous, and religious Lady, Anne Carteret", de Carteret's wife; the second, "Seas" "To the Worship-full his highly Honoured Friend Mrs Elizabeth Carteret", de Carteret's daughter; and the third, "Gardens", "To the Worshipfull his ever Honoured Kinde Friends, Mrs Douse, and Mrs Margaret Carteret", who were also de Carteret's daughters. Later de Carteret's kindness was repaid by Prynne not merely in poetry, but in a very practical manner.

In 1641 England was on the brink of civil war. Parliament and people had lost patience with the King. The Channel Islands were not directly concerned in the dispute. Since the death of Queen Elizabeth I there had been almost constant arguments and disputes between the islanders on the one hand and the English authorities on the other on constitutional and ecclesiastical matters, but at no time had events taken a serious turn. Soon, however, the situation was to change and the Channel Islands were to find themselves caught up and embroiled in a bloody revolution—the Great Rebellion.

CHAPTER SEVEN

The Great Rebellion and the Commonwealth—1642–60

It is a difficult province to write the history of the civil wars of a great and powerful nation, where the King was engaged with one part of his subjects against the other and both sides were sufficiently inflamed.

Edward Hyde, Earl of Clarendon (1609–74)

If war may be divided into categories, civil war is undoubtedly the worst. Families are divided, father against son, and brother against brother. The bitterness engendered by such divisions runs deep. The English Civil War was no exception. Death and destruction, brutality and suffering, were commonplace throughout the length and breadth of the land. Yet out of those years of fighting and death there has arisen a romantic legend peopled with gallant Cavaliers and grim-faced Roundheads. The legend has some basis of truth for there are few wars and bloody encounters that do not throw up the heroes and the brave, the noble and the self-sacrificing. The Civil War had its full complement of these, among whom were to be numbered not a few, either of the islands or serving in the islands. Men like Sir Philip and Sir George de Carteret, Sir Amias Andros, Sir Edward Hyde and Sir Peter Osborne, who risked all in support of the royalist cause. And certainly there was no shortage of grim-faced Roundheads.

It is well at the outset of this account of the Civil War in the Channel Islands to note the holders of the principal offices in both Jersey and Guernsey at the start of hostilities. In Jersey Sir Thomas Jermyn was governor, Sir Philip de Carteret was both lieutenant-governor and bailiff;

David Bandinel was dean. In Guernsey the Earl of Danby was governor; Sir Peter Osborne, Bt, was lieutenant-governor; John de Quetteville was bailiff. There was no dean in that island where the Presbyterian form of church government held sway.

Many of the characters who trod Jersey's stage during those troublous years of the Civil War find a place in the *Diary* kept in the years 1643–51 by John Chevalier (about 1589–1675), a Jerseyman and ardent royalist. He was a Vingtenier of St Helier from 1638–51, an Officer for the *Extente* of 1665, and Deacon of St Helier's Parish Church. From the vantage point of Chevalier's house, which, according to tradition, stood on the site of the present Chamber of Commerce building in the Royal Square (then the Market Place) of St Helier, he observed and carefully recorded the day-to-day events of the period, missing little of any consequence for he was of an inquisitive turn of mind. The original *Diary* is preserved in the Museum at St Helier and has been published by the Société Jersiaise in the original old French in which it was written.

From the start of the Civil War Jersey supported the King, and Guernsey, including Alderney and Sark, supported Parliament. The reasons which had caused Englishmen and Scotsmen to take up arms against their sovereign were not the same as those which caused the overwhelming majority of Guernseymen to support Parliament. The Star Chamber, the High Commission Court and Ship Money held little meaning for them. There is little doubt that their principal if not sole reason for supporting Parliament was religious. The King with High Church views, his belief in the Divine Right of Kings and his French Catholic wife had little appeal for the Calvinistic Guernseymen who clung tenaciously to their Presbyterian form of church government. It was only to be expected that they would side with Parliament which numbered among its ranks many low churchmen and non-conformists. Had it not been for Sir Philip de Carteret and Captain George Carteret it might well have been that the majority of Jerseymen would also have supported Parliament for similar reasons, for they too had strong Calvinistic leanings and had only been brought into conformity with the Church of England as recently as 1620. On the other hand some Jerseymen who might otherwise have supported the King supported Parliament neither for religious reasons nor because they were opposed to the King, but because they were enemies or rivals of Sir Philip de Carteret and hoped either for revenge or to wrest from him some of the power which he wielded.

Envy and jealousy lead to hatred and hatred is a potent force. Nine men in Jersey—Francis de Carteret, Lord of the Manor of La Hague, Henry Dumaresq, Lord of the Manor of Samarès, Michael Lemprière, Lord of the Manor of Diélament, Benjamin Bisson and Abraham Herault, all of whom were jurats and David Bandinel, the dean, his son James,

Rector of St Mary, and Peter d'Assigny, Rector of St Helier—had a deep hatred for Sir Philip de Carteret, a hatred which pursued him all his life.

Michael Lemprière (1606–71) was the younger son of Hugh Lemprière, lieutenant-bailiff, by his second wife, Jeanne Lemprière (née Herault). He was educated at the Protestant University of Saumur where he acquired his Calvinistic beliefs. He married Sarah, daughter of Francis de Carteret. David Bandinel had a grudge against Sir Philip de Carteret in connection with the tithes of the Parish of St Saviour. Sir Philip in his capacity of farmer of the royal revenues had endeavoured to deprive the dean of the tithes, but the King by letter of 17th September 1642 ordered that the tithes be restored to the dean until the dispute regarding them had been resolved, which ultimately it was in favour of the dean. James Bandinel (1602–45), was the dean's son. Peter d'Assigny (flourished 1635–60) was French by birth. He married three times. It is surprising that he should have been numbered among Sir Philip de Carteret's enemies as he had received nothing but kindness from him. Sir Philip had lent him money and obtained the Rectorship of St Helier for him, and he and Lady de Carteret were godparents to his son Philip. Furthermore, on the last occasion that Sir Philip had attended church he had called on Mrs d'Assigny who was "in child-bed".

In 1642 de Carteret's enemies drew up a petition containing twenty-one articles of complaint against him to be sent to Parliament. Through Prynne's good offices the petition did not reach the Commons, although it was seen by a few of the members. However, it did reach the Lords and a day was appointed for hearing it. The complaints against de Carteret could not be fully investigated because Bandinel and Dumaresq were unable to produce their witnesses who were in Jersey, and in any case were unable to show that they were acting either in the name of the States or the inhabitants of the island. In consequence de Carteret was allowed to return to Jersey.

In the articles of complaint contained in the petition are to be found the reasons for the hatred against de Carteret. It should be explained before considering the complaints that de Carteret held three crown appointments, those of lieutenant-governor, bailiff and receiver general, and was farmer of the Crown revenues. The first four complaints related to the offices of governor and lieutenant-governor. The complaints alleged that the holder of the office of governor should be a native of England or Wales, an experienced soldier and resident in the island. They opposed the idea that the governor should live away from Jersey as this meant that his revenues went out of and in consequence impoverished the island. In particular they complained that de Carteret appointed a nephew of his, only twenty-three years of age, to discharge the duties of lieutenant-governor. Articles 5, 7 and 8 of the complaints were that de Carteret filled the various public offices with his own relatives and supporters thus concentrating too much power in his own hand. Article 6 complained that the holding by de Carteret of the offices of lieutenant-governor and bailiff and farmer of the Crown revenues was incompatible. Article 9 alleged that in open court de Carteret had threatened those jurats who opposed him. Article 10 alleged that de Carteret had imposed customs duties on imports into the island contrary to Law. Article 11 alleged that he sold at a high rate licences for the import from England of those goods for which warrants and patents were granted—wool, leather and coal—thus causing the price of those commodities to be inflated. Article 12 alleged that he kept no chaplain at either castle. Article 13 alleged that without any preliminary judicial proceedings he had commanded persons to appear before the lords within forty days and when they made their appearance he did not proceed against them. Article 14 alleged that he had committed some to prison and released others from prison without lawful authority. Article 15 alleged that he rendered no account of monies received from the English Exchequer or the Lord Treasurer for soldiers billeted in the island in 1628 and 1629; that he only paid some people when it pleased him and others nothing and that he obtained discharges from the constables in respect of payments which had not been made. Article 16 accused him of releasing convicted coiners imprisoned in the castles in return for substantial payments. Article 17 that he had entertained foreigners in the castles contrary to custom. Article 18 that he had secured alterations in the laws without the consent of the States. Article 19 that he had raised the price of wheat rents due to the King contrary to custom. Article 20 alleged that unsuitable persons had become jurats without election and against whom there were great exceptions and requested that such persons be removed. Article 21 requested that the Royal Court should visit the castles annually in accordance with custom.

The articles of complaint against de Carteret were many and weighty. Unfortunately they were never considered by the House of Lords, or by any other body, so it is impossible to know if all of the allegations were wholly or partly true. The allegations of nepotism made against de Carteret in Articles 5, 7 and 8 were true in so far that one of his cousins was attorney general, his brother was solicitor general, one of his nephews and three of his cousins were jurats, and of the twelve captains of the militia seven were de Carterets, two more were nephews, and another a brother-in-law. Even if de Carteret's relatives had obtained those offices fairly, which might conceivably have been the case, the concentration of so much influence and power in the hands of one family was undesirable and inevitably led to envy and jealousy. It was indisputable that de Carteret held offices which should not have been held by the same person at one time, and that he acted in a somewhat arrogant and autocratic manner.

Article 16 might have referred to the case of Maximilian Messervy (1616–1645) who was convicted of coining and imprisoned in Mont Orgueil Castle, from which he was released after eight months having obtained the King's pardon.

Towards the end of 1642 the support for Parliament in Guernsey had come to the notice of King Charles I. On 9th December he wrote a letter to the Earl of Danby, to his deputy, and to the bailiff and jurats of the island stating that the "ill spirit, that has thus brought woe upon this Kingdom, begins to be hearkened unto in our island of Guernsey", and assuring the authorities that he would continue, as in the past, "to preserve the true Protestant profession of the Christian religion", and to maintain "their liberties, persons, and properties of estate, as settled by the lawes and customes of that Island", and finally charging them to apprehend, imprison and severely punish those who would challenge lawful authority. The King's intervention was of no avail; the writing was on the wall for the royalist cause in Guernsey. The reference to "the true Protestant profession of the Christian religion" shows that the King realized that the islanders entertained fears for their protestant religion and bears out the contention that the Guernseymen's support for Parliament arose from an intense opposition to everything that smacked of high churchmanship and popery.

In 1643 the Committee of the Lords and Commons for the safety of the Kingdom appointed Robert, Earl of Warwick, Governor of all the Channel Islands, with Robert Russell as lieutenant-governor. The committee appointed five commissioners in Jersey whom they directed, among other things, to apprehend de Carteret and bring him to Parliament to answer charges which had been brought against him. The committee also appointed thirteen commissioners, of whom six would form a quorum, to govern Guernsey, Alderney and Sark; Peter de Beauvoir was appointed president. Among the specific instructions given to the commissioners was one to "seize upon the person of Sir Peter Osborne", and another to take into their possession the castle, and "fight with, kill and slaye" all who would make any resistance to the execution of the commission. John de Quetteville, the bailiff, was suspended from office and sent to England to answer charges which had been presented against him. The committee appointed Michael Lemprière Bailiff of Jersey.

In Jersey de Carteret summoned a meeting of the States for 23rd March at which he presented his commission from the King, and Lemprière presented his from Parliament. The States allowed the former to be read, but not the latter. An unsuccessful attempt was made by Lemprière to leave the chamber, but he was forcibly detained. The Parliamentary commissioners summoned detachments of the militia to Lemprière's aid, and de Carteret realizing that his escort of thirty or forty soldiers would not be equal to the militiamen raised the sitting of the States and retired to Elizabeth Castle.

The States sent a letter to Parliament supporting de Carteret and offering security for his appearance to answer the charges against him. They undertook to preserve peace in the island so that the people might enjoy their ancient liberties and privileges.

Lady Anne de Carteret and her son Philip (1620–62) were at Mont Orgueil, then usually referred to as 'the Old Castle'. Philip was colonel of the castle under his mother. Sir Philip was desirous of visiting them and in the company of twelve fully armed friends managed to evade his enemies and reach the castle where he stayed for one night before returning to Elizabeth Castle, never to set foot again on the mainland of Jersey.

The King sent a proclamation to de Carteret granting a pardon to all the inhabitants of Jersey, excepting only the dean and the Parliamentary commissioners. Endorsed on the proclamation was a direction that it should be read at the first opportunity. Accordingly de Carteret ordered the viscount to read it and provided him with an escort of soldiers under the command of Captain Lane. When the viscount started reading the proclamation in the market place the people began to run in from all sides and the soldiers thinking that the crowd was hostile withdrew as did the viscount. It would seem from Chevalier's account of the incident that the crowd was not hostile and nothing untoward would have happened if the viscount and his escort had held their ground. As it was de Carteret was outraged that the proclamation had not been read and by way of punishment and in order to bring refractory elements into submission bombarded the town of St Helier having forewarned the inhabitants of his intention to do so. The parish church was hit twice during the bombardment. It should be added that earlier on the same day (2nd June) on which these events had occurred de Carteret had sent a message to the commissioners proposing a meeting at a point half-way between the land and Elizabeth Castle.

During the bombardment an ineffective assault was made on the town by between forty and fifty soldiers from the castle who were under the command of Captains Lane and Gwinet. In the course of the attack some of the assailants were wounded, including Captain Gwinet who suffered grave injury to one of his arms.

The bombardment and the armed assault marked the beginning of open war between the Royalists and the Parliamentarians. No longer was the garrison of Elizabeth Castle able to obtain supplies from the island and in future had to rely on Captain George Carteret to furnish its needs.

The commissioners were in a constant state of preparedness and had men posted throughout the island. A number of Royalists were seized and sent as prisoners to the Parliamentary ships which had been sent from

Guernsey to lend support to the commissioners. Subsequently the prisoners were returned to land.

During this time the maintenance of law and order had become lax and a number of the inhabitants gave themselves over to drunken and riotous behaviour.

Unsuccessful efforts were made by de Carteret to reach some understanding with the commissioners and the Parliamentarian party. His oft-repeated entreaties contained in a number of long letters sent to various persons, including a number of his friends, went unanswered. Those who would have written to him were frightened to do so.

He then arranged for an edict from King Louis XIV of France forbidding the export of goods to the Channel Islands without the licence of one or other of the governors, and Captain George Carteret caused it to be published at Barneville. Although from the outset the edict was a dead letter, and withdrawn on representations from the French customs officers, the news of it caused great indignation in the islands.

The commissioners endeavoured to obtain the surrender of Mont Orgeuil Castle, but without avail.

On 29th July de Carteret's son Gideon died. Soon after de Carteret himself fell ill. By 16th August he was near to death and got the castle porter to write a letter to the commissioners containing his last requests:

Gentlemen,

I having received the king's gracious pardon, embraced it with a great deal of joy, hoping that before God shall call me away, I should see some beginning of the quiet of those disorders of this country, which seeing is not likely to prove, it is God's pleasure to call me to His mercy, that I may not witness the further increase of the miseries of this country. I desire in your Christian charity that you will permit Monsieur la Cloche, or any other that you will send, to administer unto me such Christian comforts as are necessary and usual in these extremities; and that you will permit my poor wife to come unto me, to do me the last duty, that of closing my eyes. The Lord forgive you, as I forgive you all. I pray you, suffer this bearer to go to the old castle to fetch my wife, and send some other to Monsieur la Cloche with all speed. This is the last request I shall ever make unto you. The Lord be merciful to you all. From the Castle Elizabeth, this 16th day of August 1643.

Your loving friend,
Ph. Carteret

The commissioners' hatred for de Carteret was unremitting as is shown by the second paragraph of their reply to his letter, which reads:

As for your desire to have some of the three ministers you desire, we cannot comply, as they are suspected by the people to have confederated with you in oppressing the country. We have sent to Mr Thomas Payne, if he please, to go to you, or any other you desire, whom we will permit. But while we were writing this letter, there met together a troop of horsemen and some foot companies that publicly require you to deliver into their hands the Cornish captain you entertain in the castle, promising to give caution or hostage that no harm shall be done to him. On that condition, your wife, a minister, or your mother and sisters, mightily desirous to see you, may have access to the castle. Mr Payne, the minister, refused even now to go and see you. You will do well, sir, in case God shall see fit to call you, to remit the custody of the castle into the hands of the estate, to keep it for his Majesty's service. And so we remain your friends *usque ad aras*,

Henry Dumaresq
Abraham Herault
Benjamin Bisson
Michael Lemprière

The consciences of the commissioners ultimately stirred and a few hours before his death Lady de Carteret was allowed to see her husband who by then was almost unconscious and only able to raise his right hand as though to make a sign. So on 23rd August 1643 after five months' confinement in Elizabeth Castle and thirteen days of illness died Sir Philip de Carteret, Lord of the Manors of St Ouen, Rozel and Sark, Lieutenant-Governor and Bailiff of Jersey, a faithful servant of the King.

Lady de Carteret and Philip de Carteret continued to hold Mont Orgueil and Elizabeth Castle for the King. The town was frequently bombarded from the latter.

The hatred which Bandinel and d'Assigny had for de Carteret is well illustrated by the story told by Chevalier as to how six hours before his death they prevented a basket of fruit being sent to him. "The fruit will be better for us than for Sir Philip," said d'Assigny.

On 26th August Lieutenant Leonard Lydcott the Parliamentary lieutenant-governor arrived in Jersey. He was a young man, newly married, and was accompanied by his wife, his father, his brother, his mother-in-law, his sister-in-law, three captains, three lieutenants, five or six men, and his servants and those of his wife. But there were no troops because the Parliamentary authorities had been assured that they would not be necessary as Jersey was strong for Parliament.

Three days later a meeting of the States was held at which Lemprière's Patent as parliamentary bailiff was read, as well as Lydcott's commission, and each of them took the oath of office. In passing, it should be mentioned that the oaths were in the traditional wording acknowledging Charles Stuart as King.

The Parliamentary Lieutenant-Governor of Guernsey by letter dated 16th September 1643 in the name of the King and Parliament called upon the Royalist lieutenant-governor to surrender Castle Cornet under threat of violence. Sir Peter by letter of 18th September refused to give up the castle. A further exchange of letters which took place during the following February was of no effect.

James Guille, Peter de Beauvoir, Michael de Sausmarez, John Bonamy, Thomas Carey and John Carey wrote to the Governor of Guernsey in October 1643 telling him how three of the commissioners were captured by a ruse. Captain Bowden, who had been a known supporter of the Parliamentarians arrived in Guernsey from Dartmouth on the 21st of the month. He anchored his ship to the south of Castle Cornet and sent a boat to shore with letters for the Parliamentary lieutenant-governor and commissioners asking them to come aboard his ship to discuss important matters on the pretence that he was ill. Three of the commissioners, Peter de Beauvoir, James de Havilland and Peter Carey, responded to the invitation and were taken prisoner. They were subsequently transferred to Castle Cornet and after being there for some time determined to escape, which they ultimately did.

There now entered upon the scene, particularly so far as Jersey was concerned, Captain George Carteret (about 1609-80) who was the eldest son of Elias de Carteret and Elizabeth de Carteret (née Dumaresq). He dropped the 'de' before his surname and is referred to in Pepys' *Diary* and other contemporary writings as Cartwright. He entered the Royal Navy and in 1629 received his first commission as lieutenant of the *Garland*. Four years later he received his first command, that of the *Eighth Lion's Whelp*. His progress was steady and in 1637 he was made vice-admiral of the expedition against the North African pirate stronghold at Sallee. Carteret won a great reputation on that occasion. Nearly all the ships in port were sunk and the King of Morocco was compelled to release his European captives. The following year Carteret returned to Sallee in command of the *Convertine* with the Moorish ambassador aboard. During the voyage he kept a diary, *A Journall Keepte by me George Carteret in His Matie's Shippe the Convertine being bound for the Coast of Barbary*, which has been published. Carteret continued to make progress and in 1639 he was appointed Comptroller of the Navy. The next year in the chapel at Mont Orgueil Castle he married his cousin Elizabeth de Carteret, daughter of Sir Philip de Carteret, to whom William Prynne had dedicated the second part of his *Divine and Profitable Meditations*.

In 1642 Parliament appointed Carteret Vice-Admiral of the Fleet, an office which he refused at the King's command. After the Civil War had started Carteret was established at St Malo as King's Faciendary selling captured Parliamentary ships and with the proceeds buying supplies for the Royalists. In 1638 the King had promised Carteret that he would succeed his father-in-law as bailiff, and in 1643 he granted him the

Manors of Mélèsches, Grainville and Noirmont "on account of the good and faithful service bravely and successfully performed and accomplished ... against the Turks". In August 1643 Sir Philip died and in October the call came to Captain Carteret, an outstanding naval officer, a Royalist champion, a good friend and a formidable foe. So far as Jersey was concerned he was the man of the hour.

Carteret arrived at Mont Orgueil Castle from St Malo on Sunday 19th November 1643. On the Monday the parishioners of St Martin and Grouville rallied to him and took the oath of allegiance to the King. The next day the parishioners of St Brelade seized St Aubin's Fort for the King, and on the 22nd Carteret moved on the town of St Helier accompanied by horse and foot, made up of men from St Martin and Grouville, English, Scots, Irish and a few French, and with flags flying and drums beating. No resistance was offered; Parliamentarian support had melted away and the principal Parliamentarians fled the island.

After two days Carteret sent the men of St Martin and Grouville back to their homes, retaining only a small force in St Helier to guard the town as well as the Parliamentary guns, powder and munitions which had been captured.

Carteret issued an order summoning the members of the States and the principal inhabitants to attend at Trinity Church at between 9 and 10 am on 23rd November. In fact, the States did not assemble until the 24th when Carteret presented his Letters Patent as lieutenant-governor and bailiff and took both oaths of office.

Following his swearing in Carteret required the soldiers in the castles to take an oath of allegiance to the King; also the men of the island, parish by parish. In addition he issued a statement to be read in each of the parish churches on Sunday 3rd December, assuring the people that the King would maintain the true protestant religion.

Very wisely d'Assigny fled the Island, and although Royalist troops were billetted in his house and drank his cider, his life was safe. Unwisely Bisson and the two Bandinels remained and were imprisoned, as were others who had supported Parliament. The Royal Court of Jersey was not and is not competent to deal with cases of high treason. Carteret, therefore, asked the King for commissioners to try such cases as had resulted from the island having for some years fallen under the sway of Parliament. The King agreed to the request and sent three commissioners, John Poley, John Nicholas Vaughan and Henry Janson, to try the accused.

Death saved the dean from trial and almost certain execution. He and his son had been imprisoned in Elizabeth Castle and were later removed to Mont Orgueil Castle where they enjoyed considerable liberty and were allowed to have visits from their wives and friends, who were permitted to bring them provisions and comforts. However, when the Bandinels heard that Archbishop Laud had been executed in London they knew that their cloth would not save them and accordingly decided to escape. One night they managed to break out of their rooms and by means of a rope and towels tied together they managed to descend down the outside of the walls of the castle. The rector was the first to go down the rope. He found it too short and fell on the rocks, bruising himself extensively. The dean followed, but the rope broke and he was dashed on the rocks, receiving multiple injuries.

The rector, thinking his father was dead, covered him with his doublet and fled in panic. The dean was discovered next morning still alive and died the following day.

The rector was recaptured and sent back to Mont Orgueil Castle. He was so ill that two doctors stated that he was unfit to stand his trial, which was postponed. He lingered on for almost a year as a cripple and invalid.

Captain Carteret and his cousin Philip organized an attack on Sark in May 1644. On the night of 26th–27th May about a hundred men left Jersey in four shallops. Two were under the command of Captain Lane with orders to land at L'Eperquerie; the other two under the command of Captain Chamberlain were to land at Dixcart Bay. Lane's party was challenged by sentries and as a consequence did not effect a landing, but returned to Jersey. Chamberlain's party, about thirty-two in number, effected a landing, overpowered the guard and captured the Captain's house where the Captain was surprised in bed and surrendered. They would undoubtedly have secured the island for the King, at least temporarily, had it not been for the failure of Lane's party to effect a landing. As it was, when daylight came, the women of the island (the men had for the most part been made prisoners) realized how few invaders there were and set light to their beacon as a sign to Guernsey that they needed help. Armed men arrived from Guernsey and Chamberlain and his party were taken prisoners and with their shallops were taken to Guernsey. Chamberlain was imprisoned with his feet in irons. There was great rejoicing in Guernsey where the church bells were rung and the guns fired as signs of victory. Lane fled from Jersey in disgrace and went to England where he was imprisoned by the Parliamentarians until he was released on rejoining their party.

John Lilburne (about 1614–57), the political agitator, wrote a pamphlet entitled *Copy of a Letter to a Friend*, published in 1645, directed against William Prynne for the support he had lent to Sir Philip de Carteret. Prynne wrote in reply *The Lyar Confounded*, published the same year, to which Michael Lemprière, Henry Dumaresq and Abraham Herault replied in *Pseudo-Mastix; The Lyar's Whipp*, published in 1646.

On 17th April 1646 the *Proud Black Eagle* commanded by Captain

Baldwin Wake, in company with two other ships, one the *Dogger Bank* and the other probably the *Phoenix*, arrived at Jersey from the Scilly Isles and dropped anchor off Elizabeth Castle. On the *Proud Black Eagle* was Charles, Prince of Wales (1630–85), who was to remain in Jersey for two months during which time he was to live at Elizabeth Castle. With him came an entourage of lords, knights and gentlemen and their ladies, as well as clergy, servants, artisans and sundry others totalling some 300 persons, among whom were Sir Edward Hyde, later to be created Earl of Clarendon, the Lord Chancellor, Lord Berkshire, Lord Brentford, Lord Capel, Lord Hopton, Lord Wentworth, Sir Richard Fanshawe, the Prince's Secretary, Sir Richard Grenville and Sir Henry Mainwaring. The following day Lord Wentworth was sent to inform the Queen of the Prince's arrival in Jersey. Lord Digby arrived on the 27th April and Lord Culpepper two days later.

Elizabeth Castle was filled to capacity with the Prince and his suite and those who were unable to find accommodation there were housed in the town of St Helier. Among the latter were Sir Richard Fanshawe and Lady Fanshawe who were "quartered at a widow's house in the market-place, Madame de Pommes, a stocking merchant", where Lady Fanshawe was delivered of her second child, a daughter christened Ann, on the 7th June.

The task of feeding this influx of Royalists was considerable. Each day two parishes were required to provide meat for the Prince and deliver it to the castle. Meat for the other refugees was to be brought to the Market Place in St Helier and sold at controlled prices. The fishermen were ordered to bring in substantial supplies of fish under threat of corporal punishment. Food was also imported from Normandy. The islanders were precluded from satisfying their own requirements of food until the refugees had been satisfied.

The Prince was accorded a warm welcome by the inhabitants. Many hastened to kneel before him and kiss his hand. On Sunday the 19th *feux-de-joie* were fired and bonfires lit at dusk.

The following Sunday the prince attended service at St Helier's Parish Church. He went in procession from Elizabeth Castle to the church. A large crowd including many women and girls turned out to see the prince and accompanied him and his escort, comprising between eighty and a hundred cavaliers and between 200 and 300 musketeers, from the castle to the church. There was a considerable crowd around the church and the cemetery. Musketeers lined the approaches to the church and prevented unauthorized persons from entering. Inside the building a table and chair had been provided for the prince in front of the minister's chair. On the table was a cover and a cushion; beneath the table was another cushion to be used as a kneeler. The floor round about was covered with carpets and strewn with sweet smelling flowers. There were other chairs for the most important members of the prince's train; the remainder of the congregation had to stand. The service was conducted in English by a royal chaplain. Dr Poley stood at the prince's side throughout the proceedings holding the prayer book for him, turning the pages, finding the psalms and pointing out the passages referred to by the chaplain. The prince received Holy Communion in the same church on 17th May.

Three days later a review was held on the beach in St Aubin's Bay at which was present the prince, accompanied by the lords and gentlemen who formed his suite. On his arrival the royal visitor was greeted with cries of "Long live the Prince" from the large crowd of men, women and children who had gathered to see him. When the prince approached Philip de Carteret's regiment de Carteret dismounted and fell on his knees before him. The prince also dismounted and asked de Carteret his name and when he replied he took his sword and touched him on his head and shoulders and said "Arise, Sir Philip" to the delight of the crowd.

At this time the Royalist lieutenant-governor of Guernsey was replaced. As a face-saving device Osborne was permitted to appoint his successor, Sir Baldwin Wake. The latter arrived at Castle Cornet from Jersey to take up his duties on 15th May. Osborne arrived in Jersey on the 29th. Relations between him and Carteret were very strained and during his stay in the Island he resided with Lord Hopton in St Helier. Osborne left Jersey on 9th August for St Malo, where one of his sons was living, and where he himself lived until the autumn of 1649, when he returned to England.

The bad relations which existed between Carteret and Osborne arose from the fact that the former, although prepared to send supplies to Castle Cornet, only did so for payment. Carteret was not a man to give anything away; Osborne, on the other hand, had to do the paying and as a result had become impoverished, apart from the fact that his house and estate in England had been confiscated. Furthermore, Osborne complained of the quality of the supplies received from Carteret; also it was alleged that the latter had misappropriated monies raised in Jersey for supplies for Castle Cornet. In fairness to Carteret, it must be pointed out that he had considerable problems to contend with in Jersey and had great trouble in raising money and obtaining supplies for the defence of the island. In addition, many among the population were far from being Royalists and even those who were had grown hostile to him because of the strictness of his government and the way in which he compelled them to pay taxes.

In October 1646 John Osborne wrote to his father Sir Peter from Rouen: "It is secretly whispered heer, but it is publiquely talked of in Paris, that both the islands are to be delivered to the French, and my Lord Jermyn is to be made Duke and Pair of France. This intelligence I have from a very good friend of yours and mine . . ." There were many other reports to the same effect: "A worthy Lady who was lately at St Germain's [had said] that She was told by some of the Ladies about the Queen, that this Island (Jersey) was to be delivered up to the French of a good Sum of Money." "A Very discreet and knowing Gentleman, now residing at Paris [reported] that he received the Same information by Several Gentlemen conversant in the Secrets of the Court, and that Lord Jermyn was to have 200,000 Pistoles for the Delivery." There was yet another report "from a Person of Known reputation, that he heard from very good hands, that Lord Jermyn was to be made a Duke of France and to receive 200,000 Pistoles, for which he was to deliver up the two Islands of Jersey and Guernsey". "A very honest Gentleman" and "a Gentleman, who is a Known Creature of the Lord Jermyn" reported likewise. The Royalists in Jersey were deeply concerned at what they heard and four of them, Capel, Hopton, Hyde and Carteret entered into Articles of Association on 19th October 1646. The first article provided that Capel should go to France and then on to Holland to ascertain whether the reports were true and, if they were, to return to Jersey to consult as to what was to be done. The second that Carteret would inform the Earl of Northumberland that if the worst came to the worst he would give up Jersey to Parliament. The third that if Capel found that on inquiry that the reports were true he would ask the Dutch for aid. The fourth that steps would be taken to defend Castle Cornet. The fifth that the associates even if separated would act together.

On 26th October Capel left for Paris where Cardinel Mazarin denied the rumours, despite the fact that it was obvious that they had some basis of truth.

In June Jermyn, the Royalist Governor, visited Jersey bringing with him his secretary, Abraham Cowley, the poet. They were to visit the island again in 1651. Cowley wrote a poem entitled *An answer to a copy of verses sent me to Jersey* which includes the following lines:

> But it produced such base, rough, crabbed hedge
> Rhymes, as ev'en set the hearers ears on edge.
> Written by ——————————— Esquire, the
> Year of our Lord six hundred thirty three.
> Brave Jersey Muse! and he's for this high stile
> Call'd to this day the Homer of the isle.
> Alas, to men here no words less hard be
> To rhime with, than Mount-Orgueil is to me.
> Mount-Orgueil, which in scorn o'th' Muses law
> With no yoke-fellow word will daign to draw.
> Stubborn Mount-Orgueil! 'tis a work to make it
> Come into Rhyme, more hard than 'twere to take it.

(*above*) The town of St Aubin, Jersey, which emerged into history in the seventeenth century. A view in about 1870

(*below*) Seventeenth-century La Moye farmhouse, Jersey—as it was around 1900

Front entrance of La
Pompe, La Contrée de
Mouilpieds, St Martin,
Guernsey, with typical
Guernsey Arch dated 1600.
The door was carved by
John Burgess (1818–1904)

The anonymous 'Esquire' was Prynne.

The reason for Jermyn's visit to Jersey with other envoys from the Queen was to persuade the prince to leave the island and to go to France. The prince's Council objected most strongly to the suggested course of action, but their protestations were in vain and the prince left Jersey for Paris on 25th June.

The prince was truly grateful for the hospitality which he had received in Jersey and commanded Fanshawe, his secretary, to send the following letter of appreciation to the States:

> Trusty and welbeloved, We cannot before our departure hence but expresse ye great Sence and acknowledgm^t we have of ye Extraordinary proofes We have found dureing o^r Residence here of ye good affeccons of ye Inhabitants of this Island to the Crowne and to our person, assureing you hereby that We shall embrace and seeke all opportunities to testifie ye same by ye most reall wayes, and so much we desire yo^u in our name to make knowne to ye Island^{rs}, which we shall make good upon all occasions, And so We bid yo^u very heartily Farwell. Given at our Court at Jersey the 22th of June 1646.

In February 1647 Hyde was invited by the Carterets to live at Elizabeth Castle where he had a three-storey house built at the south-west angle of the Priory Church in the lower ward. This is where he wrote part of his *History of the Great Rebellion*. He also had a walled-in garden on the castle green of which he wrote to Lord Cottington in the following spring "I am busy about nothinge butt settinge lettice, onions, carretts, wish that you would send me some seedes that you may be sure of sallets when you come". The Chancellor's House, as Hyde's residence was called, was destroyed in 1651 at the same time as the Priory Church.

There was a great deal of discontent in Guernsey in 1647 and in November of that year Parliament appointed four commissioners, Edmond Ludlow, John Weaver, John Birch and John Harrington, all Members of the House of Commons, or any two or more of them to hear and examine the complaints and grievances of the inhabitants.

The commissioners having failed to execute their commission, Charles de la Marche, "Minister and Deputy for the well affected in the Island of Guernezie", petitioned the committee for the Safety of the Kingdom in 1648 stating that the island was "in more apparent danger of revolt than at any time since" the Civil War and making allegations against Russell, the deputy-governor, and his associates and requesting that until the commissioners carried out their inquiry the government and militia of Guernsey should be entrusted to those named in the ordinance of both Houses of Parliament of March 1642.

As the commissioners had still done nothing, Henry de la Marche,

6

who had formerly been one of the committee appointed for the safety of the island, later the same year, addressed a petition to the commissioners which started by complaining that:

The Governor, Bayly, and Jurates doe persecute the people. They puffes at them. All their thoughts are that your worships will never enquire, and that noe man shall beholde their actions; either Church or Commonwealth; —they shall never be brought to account.

In October 1649 Colonel Alban Coxe was appointed by Thomas, Lord Fairfax, Lord General of all the land forces under the pay of Parliament in England, Wales and in the islands of Guernsey and Jersey, governor of the former island in Russell's absence.

John de Quetteville, former Bailiff of Guernsey, died in 1648 or 1649. He had been suspended from office by the Guernsey Commissioners in 1643.

The King was executed on 30th January 1649. The Prince of Wales was proclaimed King in Edinburgh on 5th February and in Jersey on 17th February. The proclamation was read by Lawrence Hamptonne (1600–65), the viscount, first on Saturday in the Market Place in St Helier, then next day at Elizabeth Castle after morning service, and finally on the following Wednesday at Mont Orgueil Castle, after which it was nailed on the door of the Royal Court House. The original document, written in French, is preserved in the museum at St Helier. In English it reads:

Whereas the rebels have by a horrible outrage laid violent hands on the person of King Charles the First of glorious memory, by whose death the Sovereign Crowns of the Kingdoms of England, Scotland, France and Ireland belong to and wholly and legally devolve upon His Highness the very high and mighty Prince Charles.

We the Lieutenant-Governor and Bailiff and Jurats of this Island of Jersey, assisted by the King's Officers and by the principal inhabitants of the said Island, with one heart and voice publish and proclaim that His Highness, the very high and mighty Prince Charles, has now by the death of our late Sovereign of glorious memory, lawfully become by right of legitimate succession and direct descent, our only and Sovereign Lord, Charles the Second, by the Grace of God, King of England, Scotland, France and Ireland, Defender of the Faith, etc., to whom we acknowledge our duty of implicit obedience and fidelity, honour and service. And we pray God by whom Kings reign, to stablish and confirm King Charles the Second in all his just rights, and on his Throne, and to grant him a long and happy reign over us.

Dated the 17th day of February 1648 [1649]

LONG LIVE KING CHARLES THE SECOND

(here follow the signatures)

On 17th September 1649 Charles II returned to Jersey. Since he had left the island in 1646 he had become a King, albeit without a kingdom, and the father of a son James (Jemmy) Scott, known as Fitzroy and as Crofts, later to be created Duke of Monmouth and Buccleuch, who was born at Rotterdam on 9th April 1649. Jemmy's mother was Lucy Walter (1630?–58), a beautiful young woman whom Charles met and fell in love with during his exile and became the first of his many mistresses. With the King came his brother James, Duke of York (1633–1701).

Chevalier described the King, who was then nineteen years old, as being of good stature, with dark brown hair, a grave face and a pale complexion, and the duke, who was then nearly sixteen years old, as being tall for his age and slender. The King was affable to all, and the duke was of a lively disposition. They both wore mourning for their father, as did all those who accompanied them. The King's mourning clothes were violet, the only relief being a silver star on the left side of his cloak, a blue scarf and a blue garter around his left knee; everyone else, including the servants, wore black. The duke, like his brother, had a silver star on his cloak and wore a blue scarf.

The King and the duke were accompanied by over 300 persons, from lords, knights and gentlemen on the one hand to bootmakers, laundresses and tailors on the other. The King also brought with him three coaches and 120 horses, including eighteen coach horses.

On 11th December the King touched eleven persons, both male and female, for scrofula in the Priory Church at Elizabeth Castle. Scrofula, sometimes known as 'the King's Evil', was a complaint which the sovereign was believed to have the power to heal. The King and the duke sat together on one side of the choir with the sufferers facing them on the other. The King's doctor then led each of the sufferers to the King. As each knelt before him the King placed his hand on their head and breast saying as he did so "May God heal thee". At the same time an English minister read a few words in English. Each sufferer was then brought before the King a second time and knelt down while the King placed a ribbon with a gold piece on it round their neck. The gold pieces, either angels or half-angels, were supplied by the sufferers themselves. The King touched again, this time two children, on 22nd January 1650, and yet again seven or eight persons on 10th February, and three more on the following day.

When the King left Jersey for Breda he bought the governorship of the island from Jermyn for £3,000 and conferred it on the Duke of York who held the appointment from 13th February 1650 until 21st August of the same year when he left Jersey. The King made his brother Governor in order to keep him away from Breda and to compensate him for being left behind.

In 1650, while staying in Jersey the King gave an uninhabited island called Smith's Island off the coast of Virginia in North America to Carteret in perpetuity with the right to build a church and castle and to govern in such a manner as he thought fit. Carteret was also granted permission to recruit 300 persons to settle on the island which was to be called New Jersey. On 3rd May Carteret despatched a fully equipped ship, *The Gunder*, with twenty-five or thirty men aboard in charge of Philip de Soulemont, an advocate, to settle New Jersey. Some of the settlers were equipped by Carteret's brother Philip. Unfortunately the vessel and all its passengers and crew were captured by a Parliamentary vessel off Guernsey and taken to Falmouth.

The Parliamentarians made an unsuccessful assault on Castle Cornet in March 1651 in the belief that there were only forty-two defenders of whom eighteen were sick. A letter dated 16th May sent from Guernsey described what happened:

> . . . at the first onset (which was performed with as great courage and resolution, as hath been observed since these wars) thirteen of the enemy were disabled, being wounded or slain, which being added to the eighteen which were said to be sick, there remained but eleven, but we found it otherwise, and that there was above three score able men in it, many of them Reformadoes, &c., which is sufficient to keep the castle against three thousand. Our ladders beaten down and broken with stones, timber, case-shot from the flankers, &c., many of our men wounded, and thirty-two slain, two Captains wounded, one Lieutenant and one Ensign slain in the place.

On 3rd September 1651 the Battle of Worcester was fought which resulted in a crushing defeat for the Royalists. It was to Cromwell 'the crowning mercy', and to King Charles II it was the start of a great escape adventure.

While the King was in Dorset on his way to the coast and exile, Bridport and other nearby coastal towns were full of redcoats mustering before embarkation on the fleet shortly to set out to reduce Jersey and Castle Cornet to obedience to the Commonwealth.

This fleet comprising some eighty vessels, under the command of Admiral and General at Sea Robert Blake, after a false start, finally set sail from Weymouth on the 19th October. Blake's flagship was the *Happy Entrance*, the largest of the men-at-war. The land forces totalling about 2,000 men comprised Heane's regiment, six companies of Sir Hardress Waller's foot and two troops of horse commanded by Captains Margerum and West. Two further companies were added at Guernsey. Heane was accompanied by Michael Lemprière, the Parliamentary Bailiff of Jersey, Lemprière's nephew Colonel Stocall (1620–about 1665), and Captain Daniel Norman (died about 1668).

The fleet anchored off Sark on the evening of its departure from England. It set sail again the following day and by noon anchored off St Ouen's Bay. The bells of the twelve parish churches were rung to summon the militia to arms. Carteret, the Royalist Lieutenant-Governor, went to St Ouen's Bay with regular forces, as well as part of the militia. Nothing further happened that day, but the following morning a double shallop was sent from the flagship with a letter from Heane asking the islanders to surrender. Carteret fired on the boat, which was compelled to retire, a move which was most unpopular among his men and the islanders in general, who were in no mood for heroics if they might be avoided.

The naval ships then started to bombard the shore but with little effect. The defenders reply was of even less effect. The rough weather, which had persisted from the outset of the expedition continued unabated, and Blake decided to sail his fleet to St Brelade's Bay on the south coast. Carteret had no alternative but to send reinforcements to support the militia defending the bay, and when Blake's ships arrived they were fired upon by troops on the beach and from two batteries.

In an endeavour to divide Carteret's forces as much as possible, Blake despatched some of his fleet to St Aubin's Bay and to St Clement's Bay and sent back other ships to St Ouen's Bay. The defendants did not know from hour to hour when and where a landing might be attempted. Carteret's position was becoming more and more difficult as time went by, not only because of Blake's manœuvres, but also because of the poor morale among the militiamen and the inhabitants, who had had more than their fill of the Great Rebellion and not least of the strict government and constant taxation imposed upon them by Carteret. The Royalist defence was on the point of collapse.

St Aubin's Tower was surrendered on 23rd October and Mont Orgueil on the 25th, although it was not evacuated until three days later. The whole of Jersey was in the hands of the Parliamentarians, with the sole exception of Elizabeth Castle, and it was inevitable that sooner or later it too would be surrendered. However, the garrison might have held out for some considerable length of time if it had not been for a mortar piece which the Parliamentarians had brought over from England for use in the siege. The story of the reduction of the Castle in 1651 is told in *A perfect Narrative of the particular service performed by Thomas Wright, Firemaster, with a Mortar-piece of fifteen inches and a half diameter, against the Castle of Elizabeth in the Isle of Jersey* published in 1652 in which are given particulars of each shot fired and the damage caused. It was the third shot fired on Monday 15th November, which caused the greatest damage. Wright recounts what happened:

Yet I proceeded to make a third shot upon the same line, and having altered my degrees of elevation, and my proportion of powder to a much larger length, then the last, I did my self fire to the Granado and Gun as before and had wonderfull great successe and operation in the execution; For this shot struke quite through the Roof of the Church, and fell into a Warehouse underneath the Church, where the Enemy had their Magazine of powder and other things, which by the Granados breaking there, it was all set on fire, their Church thrown down, and many dwelling houses, Warehouses and buildings there, of about 200 foot square were totally ruinated by this blowe; and as I was after informed by many Gent' that came out of the Castle, there were in the said houses and Sellers about 30 Tun of Syder, 12 Tuns of Sack, great store of Corn and Bisket, with a vast number of Fish and other provisions of victuall, and for the War. Also a large Cestern which was made for the receiving of rain-water, very serviceable for the Castle, and joyned to the said buildings, was utterly made unusefull.

Although the bombardment continued the fatal blow had been struck with the third shot. The morale of the garrison was lowered considerably and some began to desert. Lady Carteret and others left for France on the day following the blowing up of the magazine. Messengers in the persons of John Poingdestre and Durel were sent to the King informing him of the desperate situation of the garrison, and asking for reinforcements. The King was unable to comply with the request and sent the messengers back with the answer that Carteret should surrender to the Parliamentary forces, and make the best terms he could. Carteret was still reluctant to surrender but on Heane's third summons he did so, having agreed terms which proved to be generous, in particular to himself. The Articles of Rendition were signed on 12th December, Elizabeth Castle to be surrendered on the 15th. The actual evacuation took place a day late owing to the inclemency of the weather.

Castle Cornet, the last Royalist stronghold, surrendered on 15th December and was evacuated on the 19th. The Articles of Rendition provided for an honourable surrender on generous terms. On the due day the garrison marched out of the Castle with drums beating, colours flying, bullet in mouth and match lighted at both ends and laid down their arms. Nearly nine years had passed since the start of the siege and before it was ended the Commonwealth had been established over two years.

Heane was appointed Parliamentary governor of Jersey in 1651. He was replaced by Colonel Robert Gibbon some time before 1655, the year in which the latter died. Gibbon was succeeded by two deputy governors. The first, Austin Buckler, was appointed about 1657; the second, Richard Yardley, was appointed some time before 1658 and remained in office until 1659. Colonel John Mason was appointed governor in 1660 by virtue of a Parliamentary commission of 28th June of the previous year, which named him at once governor, colonel of a regiment of Jersey trained bands (militia) and commander-in-chief.

Michael Lemprière resumed the office of bailiff. New Letters Patent regularizing his appointment were granted in 1655 to replace those of 1643 issued in the name of King Charles I. Lemprière discharged his duties conscientiously and efficiently, and showed a genuine regard for the constitution and privileges of the island, as is evidenced by a letter dated 2nd February 1652 sent by him to the Speaker of the House of Commons. There is no doubt that the Jersey Parliamentarians were as desirous of preserving the island's constitution and privileges as were the Royalists. James Stocall, Colonel of the East Regiment of Militia, backed up his uncle's letter by writing a pamphlet entitled *Freedome or, The Description of the Excellent Civill Government of the Island of JERSEY*, dedicated to Lieutenant-General Fleetwood, and published in London in 1652. Stocall contended that "there is no need of change in the Forme of the Civill Government", but conceded that it might be desirable that "a Representor, or two in Parliament, to the end of a stronger Union to this Nation, and of a speedier expedition of Necessaries, from that Superior Power unto our people, were for the future allowed to Jersey and Guernezé, and that without diminution of their Freedom, Liberties, and Priviledges whatsoever, not repugnant to the safe and well-being of the Commonwealth".

One of Lemprière's duties as bailiff, which no other holder of that office before or since has had, was the performance of weddings. A typical entry of a marriage under the Commonwealth appears in the register of St Lawrence's Church as follows: "Dr Denis Le Guerdain was married to Mademoiselle Marie Heraut in the 'New Style' on 3rd November, 1656". So far as weddings were concerned the rectors were purely registrars.

Only one jurat, Abraham Herault (died 1655), remained on the bench and a petition signed by the constables, centeniers and others, and dated 8th June 1652 was sent to the Council asking for jurats to be appointed so that justice could be administered as formerly. However, elections were not held to fill the vacancies but instead on the last day of February 1655 the Lord Protector issued, contrary to custom and on the basis of a once and for all expedient, an Order under his privy seal nominating a complete new bench of twelve jurats: Abraham Herault, Aaron Guerdain, Philip de Carteret, M.D., Lord of the Manor of La Hague, Nicholas Lemprière, Denis Guerdain, Philip Messervy, Philip Le Febvre, James Lemprière, Thomas Le Marinel, Simon Le Sebirel, John de Rue and Simon Esnouf. Aaron Guerdain, M.D. (died 1676), who was Master of the Mint, then situated in the Tower of London, declined to serve. Denis Guerdain (died 1668), physician, was Aaron's brother. As three of those nominated refused to take the necessary oath an election for jurats was held in 1657.

A charge of nepotism could have been levelled against the bailiff every bit as much as it had been against Sir Philip de Carteret for among those appointed jurats were his brother, Nicholas Lemprière (1611–67), a physician, a nephew, two cousins and a brother-in-law. In addition, a connection by marriage was viscount, and Aaron Stocall, a nephew, was solicitor-general (1655–60).

By Commission of 14th March 1655 the governor, the bailiff, Edward Horsman, John Brun and William Harding were appointed commissioners to compound with the Royalists. All persons whose income from land did not exceed £7 per annum, or whose personal property was under £100 were neither fined nor did they have to pay any compensation. The composition for others did not exceed two years' income from their real estate, or one-tenth of their personal estate. The fine had to be paid within six months, and in default of payment the commissioners were enpowered to take possession of the property for a term of seven years.

It is not the purpose of this account of the Great Rebellion as it affected the Channel Islands to consider the merits of the respective causes of King and Parliament. However, it may be observed, as in so many other instances, that those who claimed to oppose tyranny were themselves tyrants when they came to power.

In Jersey the Parliamentary governors, deputy governors and military authorities were more tyrannical than any of their Royalist predecessors. In addition to the billeting of troops on civilians, which was strongly resented by the population, the military committed every type of outrage. Three pamphlets, all dated 1659, detail a number of the complaints. The first entitled *Articles of Impeachment Exhibited against Col. Robert Gibbons and Cap. Richard Yeardley, Late Governors of the Isle of Jersey* was by someone either with or using the initials "A.B."; the second and third respectively entitled *Blood-Thirsty Cyrus Unsatisfied with Blood, or The Boundless Cruelty of an Anabaptist's Tyranny, Manifested in a Letter of Colonel John Mason's Governour of Jersey of November 3d. last* and *Satan in Samuel's Mantle, or the Cruelty of Germany acted in Jersey* were by Thomas Ashton (about 1631–70) a Master of Arts of Brasenose College, Oxford, described as " 'a malepert preacher in and near Oxon', chaplain to the forces in Jersey in 1656, beneficed in Herts".

When Osborne returned to England his house, Chicksands Priory, which stood between the villages of Campton and Haynes in Bedfordshire, as well as part of his estates, were restored to him, probably through the good offices of his father-in-law, Sir John Danvers. There it was that on 11th March 1654 Osborne died, some two years after his wife. He was buried in Campton Church, where the parish register describes him as "a friend to the poor, a lover of learning, a maintainer of divine exercises". E. A. Parry, writing as editor of *Letters from Dorothy Osborne to Sir William Temple* adds this appreciation: "Wiser men and greater men there were many in those stirring times, but none more valiant, honourable, and true-hearted than Sir Peter Osborne".

The Navy Commissioners in 1654 ordered a new frigate to be built at Maldon. It was named *Jersey* to commemorate the recapture of the island of Jersey by Parliamentary forces. Although at the Restoration many of the navy's ships which had been named during the Commonwealth were renamed, the King retained the name of *Jersey* to commemorate his visits to Jersey during the Civil War. Benjamin Carteret was Lieutenant of the frigate in 1665 and James Carteret (died 1682), Sir George's youngest son, became its commander in 1667.

Cromwell, the Lord Protector, died on 3rd September 1658 and was succeeded by his son Richard Cromwell who earnt for himself the nickname of 'Tumbledown Dick'. The new first lady, Dorothy Cromwell (1628–76), was the daughter of Richard Major, a descendant of John Mauger, son of John Mauger of Handois in Jersey, who had settled in Southampton towards the end of the fifteenth century.

To his most Serene Highness, Richard, Lord Protector of the Commonwealth of England, Scotland, and Ireland, and the Dominions thereunto appertaining. The humble Request of the Bayliff, Jurates, and Common Councill, and other well-affected Inhabitants of the Island of Guernzey.

Sheweth, That having had a deep feeling in the general Consternation, which all well-affected persons have received by the death of his late most renowned Highness, They have also great share in the great Exultation, which doth possess the Hearts of all such who make profession of Piety, and who do see your Highness Act for God and his People in his Government; and as your most humble Suppliants have nothing more precious than their fidelity towards your Highness, being that which doth embolden them to prostrate themselves in all Humility before your Highness, Humbly supplicating, That you will please to confirm that Priviledges, Franchises, and Immunities, which they do enjoy by their Ancient Charters; and seeing the inhabitants of the said Isle are become very Numerous, and of above 6000 persons who get their living by knitting of Stockings, and other Manufactures of Wooll, and that One Thousand Todds of it is the least quantity which is necessary for them to keep them at work; which quantity being equally distributed amongst the said persons, will not amount to more than four pounds and an half for each for one whole year: We do with all Humility supplicate your Highness, That it may please your Grace to grant to the Poor Inhabitants of the said Isle the same favour and grace, (having already been granted to the Inhabitants of Jersey, by your Highness most renowned Father of happy memory) and according to the cordial affection which they bear to your Highness, and their duty to addresse themselves with favour to the Throne of Grace.

They pray God, that he may be pleased to continue his blessing upon your Highness Person, Prosperity, and Government, &c.

The above address which was presented to the Lord Protector by Peter and William de Beauvoir was the subject of an anonymous pamphlet attacking them entitled *An Epitomie of Tyranny in the Island of Guernzey Sent in a Letter to a Person of Quality in London Concerning the late Irregular Transactions there in relation to a certain Deputation and Addresse made to Richard late (sic) Protector.*

Richard Cromwell was not half the man his father had been and it was only a matter of time before there was a widespread movement for the restoration of the monarchy. George Monck, later Duke of Albemarle, entered into direct communication with the King for his return. The result was the Declaration of Breda of April 1660 in which the King promised to leave all difficult problems to future Parliaments. The following month King Charles' exile was over; Richard Cromwell's had just begun.

It was during these troublous times that the lily which was to become known as the Guernsey Lily, *Nerine sarniensis*, was introduced into that island. A great deal has been written about this attractive flower. James Douglas published an account of it entitled *Lilium Sarniense* as early as 1725 followed by a second edition, *A Description of the Guernsey Lily*, in 1737; a broadsheet entitled *The Golden Red Lily* was published in 1729. It would appear that a small quantity of bulbs was given to a member of the de Sausmarez family by a traveller from abroad whose ship was stranded on the Guernsey shore and who was hospitably entertained in the island during his short sojourn there.

CHAPTER EIGHT

The Restoration, the Later Stuarts and the Foundation of New Jersey—1660–1714

> . . . In a word, the joy was so unexpressible and so
> universal, that his majesty said smilingly to some
> about him, that he doubted it had been his own fault
> that he had been absent so long, for he saw nobody
> that did not protest he had ever wished for his
> return . . .
>
> Edward Hyde, Earl of Clarendon (1609–74)

The year 1660 saw King Charles II home from his travels to enjoy his own again. On 2nd June he was proclaimed King in Jersey for the second time and on 31st May in Guernsey for the first time. In St Helier the traditional place for reading proclamations was the Market Place; in St Peter Port there were six such places—La Plaiderie, Le Grand Carrefour, at the foot of Berthelot Street, La Rue du Pilori, now Quay Street, at the church and on the pier. On 3rd September James, Duke of York, married Anne Hyde (1637–71), daughter of the Earl of Clarendon, by whom he had eight children, six of whom were to die in infancy and two of whom, Mary and Anne, were to become queens regnant of England, Scotland and Ireland. Henry Jermyn, Earl of St Albans, resumed the office of Governor of Jersey and Sir Hugh Pollard, Bt, was appointed Governor of Guernsey. The latter to be replaced in 1662 by Christopher, Lord Hatton, with reversion to his son, also named Christopher, who succeeded him on his death in 1670 and was created a viscount in 1682. General Charles Churchill, a son of Sir Winston Churchill and brother of John Churchill, first Duke of Marlborough, was appointed Governor of Guernsey in 1706. He had played a conspicuous part in the Battle of Blenheim in 1704. Sir

George Carteret was Bailiff of Jersey, but resigned in 1661 in favour of his cousin and brother-in-law, Sir Philip de Carteret (1620–62). Amias Andros was Bailiff of Guernsey until his death in 1674, when he was succeeded by his son Edmund.

Jersey had supported the Royalists until defeated by the forces of the Commonwealth; Guernsey, on the other hand, from the outset had supported the Parliamentarians. Therefore, at the Restoration Jersey felt it could expect well of King Charles II, whereas Guernsey considered it expedient to take steps to placate him. Accordingly the States of that island hastened to send deputies with a petition to his Majesty asking for his gracious pardon for their misdeeds. In reply the Privy Council made the following order:

At the court of Whitehall, the 18th of August, 1660; present, the King's most excellent majesty in council.

Upon reading the petition of Amias Andros, of Saumarez, bailiff of the island of Guernsey, and Nathaniel Darell, both of them his majesty's servants, and deputies of the island of Guernsey, on behalf of the inhabitants of the said island, humbly acknowledging their great guilt and unfeigned grief of heart, for having, since the disorders these many years past, submitted to the usurping powers (which at last tyrannized over his majesty's subjects), and quitted their duties of obedience to their native sovereign, for which great crimes, imploring his majesty's gracious pardon; it is ordered by this board (his majesty being present) that Mr Attorney-General do forthwith draw up, in due manner, a full and effectual pardon for all the inhabitants of the said island of Guernsey; the said pardon to proceed in the accustomed manner to pass the great seal of England, so to remain as a monument of his majesty's most royal clemency to all in the said pardon. That Sir Henry Devic, knight and baronet, Mr Amias Andros, of Saumarez, bailiff of the said island, Edmond Andros, son of the said Amias, Charles Andros, brother of the said Amias, and Nathaniel Darell, have, to their great honour, during the late rebellion, continued inviolably faithful to his majesty, and consequently have no need to be included in this general pardon.

Sir Henry de Vic, Bt (1597–1672), was the son of John de Vic, the King's Attorney, by Elizabeth Pageot, his father's second wife. He was French Secretary to King Charles I in 1635, was knighted in 1641, while British Resident in Brussels and was in exile with King Charles II, who created him a baronet in 1649. He was later Comptroller of the Household to James, Duke of York and Chancellor of the Order of the Garter (1660–71), a position once held by Sir Amias Poulett. He married Margaret de Carteret, third daughter of Sir Philip de Carteret to whom, with her sister Elizabeth, William Prynne had dedicated the third part of his *Divine and Profitable Meditations*. Their only daughter Anne Charlotte married John, Lord Frescheville and was a lady-in-waiting to Queen Anne. Henry de Vic died in 1672 and was buried in Westminster Abbey.

Amias and Edmund Andros were members of a distinguished Guernsey family. The surname Andros is a corruption of the English surname Andrews. The founder of the family in Guernsey was John Andrews known in that island as Andros who went there as lieutenant to Sir Peter Mewtis, the governor. In 1542 he married Judith de Sausmarez who inherited Sausmarez Manor from her brother George, the lord of the manor, who died in 1557. The Andros were connected to the Chamberlains, Leonard Chamberlain having married Dorothy Andros, daughter of Richard Andros of Woodstock, and when John Andros died at Calais in 1554 Sir Leonard was appointed guardian of his young son. John Andros' great-great grandson Amias Andros (1610–74) was Marshal of the Ceremonies at the Court of King Charles I. On 6th June 1637 he did homage in person for his manor of Sausmarez. In 1650 he had been appointed Bailiff of Guernsey, but as the island was under Parliamentary control he was unable to take office. Amias' son Edmund (1637–1714) had a distinguished career. In 1660 he was appointed Gentleman in Ordinary to the Queen of Bohemia. The same year he was sent to America and became Governor-General of New York. He was appointed Bailiff of Guernsey in 1674, knighted in 1681, and made a Gentleman in Ordinary to the King in 1683. On 1st August 1686 he was appointed Governor, Captain-General and Vice-Admiral of Massachusetts, New Hampshire, Maine, New Plymouth and certain dependent territories, and soon afterwards of Rhode Island and Connecticut; to these were added the governorships of Virginia and Maryland in 1692.

Captain Nathaniel Darell was Lieutenant-Governor of Guernsey. He married Anne de Beauvoir, widow of Thomas Le Marchant and sister of Peter de Beauvoir, who with Peter Carey and James de Havilland had been imprisoned in Castle Cornet.

The royal clemency brought heartfelt relief to the people of Guernsey, which found expression in the following letter sent to the King by the bailiff and jurats:

Your majesty's most gracious letters, brought unto us by Colonel Jonathan Atkyns, your majesty's commissioner in this, your poor island of Guernsey, have so revived the drooping and dejected spirits of the magistrates and people in it, and have had such an influence upon the hearts and hands of all of them, that we could wish your majesty were informed of the fruits of your own labours, and with what joy, what alacrity we received them,—what blessings, what acclamations of joy and gratitude there were expressed in all places after the reading of them, for your majesty's long life and prosperous reign, with blessings upon all your majesty's undertakings, certainly great. As condemned persons, unexpectedly hearing that joyful acclamation of pardon and liberty, cast off all remembrance of past miseries; so this jurisdiction, your majesty's most humble and faithful subjects and servants, with the rest of the inhabitants, hearing and seeing beyond expectation those gracious promises of encouragement under your majesty's own hand, and seconded from your own mouth by that worthy gentleman whom your majesty has been pleased to entrust with the government of this island, as also the assurance we had before of it by that worthy gentleman, Captain Sheldon, your majesty's deputy-governor, all this has wrought such a change in us all, when we reflect on our past conduct, that we can never sufficiently admire and acknowledge your majesty's incomparable goodness and mercy towards us, for which we bless God and your majesty, devoting ourselves, our services, the remainder of our poor estates, and all that is near and dear to us for the advancement of your majesty's service in general, or for the defence of this poor island, part of the remains of your ancient duchy of Normandy which (with God's blessing, and under the conduct of those gallant gentlemen your majesty has been pleased lately to send to command over us) we will defend and secure against all attempts whatsoever; so prostrating ourselves at your majesty's feet with all humility, we subscribe ourselves, &c., &c.

The Lord Protector's "well-affected inhabitants of the island of Guernsey" had now become his "majesty's most humble and faithful subjects and servants". The Great Rebellion was indeed dead in the Channel Islands.

In the event Jersey's loyalty to King and Guernsey's to Parliament made little difference in the general treatment they received at the Restoration and, as his predecessors had done, King Charles II granted a charter to each Bailiwick confirming their privileges; Jersey's was granted in 1662 and Guernsey's in 1668.

King Charles II granted to Jersey by Letters Patent dated 14th April 1669 the right to levy duty on wines and spirits consumed in the island the proceeds from which were to be devoted to the building of a college, a house of correction and a harbour. The first two objects were not proceeded with, and even the building of a harbour at St Aubin, for which there was a long felt and pressing need, was delayed, and the work was not completed until the end of the century. When St Aubin's harbour was finished the proceeds of the wine and spirit duty were then applied towards building a harbour at St Helier, which sadly lacked such a facility.

In ecclesiastical matters the English Government continued with the policy of bringing the Channel Islands effectively within the fold of the Church of England. An Anglican Dean was appointed to Guernsey, the Prayer Book was translated into French for the use of the Channel Islanders, and further scholarships were founded for natives of the islands to ensure a supply of Anglican clergy. John de Sausmarez (died 1697) was appointed Dean of Guernsey in 1663 and for his work in that capacity was rewarded with a canonry of Windsor in 1671 and created a Doctor of Divinity. In 1684 de Sausmarez was nominated to the rectory of Great Haseley but was not admitted owing to the opposition of the dean who claimed the living. John Le Vavasseur dit Durel (1625–83) was ordained deacon and priest in the chapel of Sir R. Brown in Paris in 1651. After the Restoration he was entrusted with the translation of the Prayer Book into French. He completed the work by 1663, but it was not published until 1667. This translation with only minor modifications was used in the islands' churches for over 200 years. In 1661 Durel was the Minister of the French Episcopal Chapel in the Savoy, London. Two years later he was appointed Prebendary of Salisbury and the next year a canon of Windsor. In 1668 he was appointed Prebendary of Durham; in July 1677 he was appointed Dean of the Chapel Royal Windsor and later the same year made Registrar of the Order of the Garter. Both de Sausmarez and Durel are buried in St George's Chapel at Windsor; the monument to the former survives in the North Choir Aisle, while that to the latter has been destroyed. George Morley (1597–1684), Bishop of Winchester, by indenture of foundation dated 4th May 1678 founded five scholarships "for the encouragement of virtue, education, and the advancement and propagation of true religion" in Jersey and Guernsey. The scholars were to be of Pembroke College, Oxford, and were to be called "Bishop Morley's Scholars". An attempt to provide Guernsey with Canons Ecclesiastical similar to those of Jersey proved unsuccessful.

On 5th March 1649 King Charles II had sent a letter to Sir George Carteret. It was written by a secretary, but on it he wrote in his own hand:

Carteret, I will add this to you under my owne hand that I can never forgett the good services you have done to my father and to me; and if God bless me, you shall find I doe remember them to the advantage of you and yours and for this you have the word of Your very loving friend Charles R.

The King kept his word and loyalty was rewarded in full measure.

In 1663 King Charles II gave to Jersey a silver-gilt mace on which is an inscription in Latin, which in English reads:

Not all does he deem worthy of such a reward. Charles II, King of Great Britain, France and Ireland, as a proof of his royal affection towards the isle of JERSEY (in which he has been twice received in safety when he was excluded from the remainder of his domains), has willed that this Royal Mace should be consecrated to posterity and has ordered that hereafter it shall be carried before the Bailiffs, in perpetual remembrance of their fidelity, not only to his august father Charles I, but to His Majesty during the fury of the Civil Wars, when the Island was maintained by the illustrious Philip and George de Carteret, Knights, Bailiffs and Governors of the said Island.

The mace is a splendid example of its type being 4 feet 9½ inches long and weighing 237 ounces Troy. It has neither maker's mark nor hallmark and is made up of eleven separate pieces. The head is decorated entirely with repoussé work. It is divided by armless winged cherubs, ending in acanthus foliage, into four compartments, containing respectively a rose, thistle, harp and fleur-de-lys, all surmounted by an imperial crown and dividing the royal cypher C.R. The head is closed by a plate bearing the royal arms, and is surmounted by an imperial crown with fillet supporting a cresting of Maltese crosses and fleurs-de-lys elevated on rays, from within which there spring four arches bearing the orb and cross. The shaft is chased with roses and thistles and has two round bulging knops decorated with acanthus foliage. The neckband is enriched with four scroll brackets with figurehead terminals. The mace was regilded in 1918.

Since its presentation the mace has always been carried before the bailiff at sittings of the Royal Court and the States and on ceremonial occasions and this was so even during the German occupation.

Understandably, the principal object of the King's gratitude was Sir George Carteret. At the Restoration he was appointed Vice-Chamberlain of the Royal Household, a position promised to him in 1647, which he held until 1670. The office entitled him to apartments in Whitehall Palace and a residence, Cranbourne, a royal lodge in Windsor Park. He was made a Privy Councillor and Treasurer of the Navy. He had been Comptroller of the Navy twenty-one years before in the reign of King Charles I. Carteret was given manors in Cornwall and Devon in repayment of a loan to King Charles I. In 1661 he resigned the office of Bailiff of Jersey. He rode in the King's procession through London from the Tower to Whitehall on the day before the coronation. A fact noted by Samuel Pepys in his *Diary* where he wrote: "There followed the Vice-Chamberlain, Sir George Carteret, a company of men all like Turks; but I know not yet what they are for." In the same year he was elected Member of Parliament for Portsmouth, a seat which he held until 1669. The following year he was appointed one of the commissioners for administering Tangier, which was part of the dowry of Catherine, daughter of the King of Portugal, when she married King Charles II. The same year the King granted Carteret the right to hold a feudal court on his Manor of Handois in Jersey. In 1663 he was one of the eight Lords Proprietors to whom the King re-granted all the land between Virginia and Florida, a district called Carolina. The coats of arms of the Lords

Proprietors were depicted on the reverse of their seal; as they were on Richard Blome's map of Carolina made about 1672. A Philip de Carteret has left an account, dated December 1674, of how he had employed himself and his servants since 1666 in establishing a plantation for the Earl of Craven, Lord Berkeley, Sir George Carteret and Sir Peter Colleton at Albemarle in Carolina; also of the storms and hurricanes which occurred after his arrival in the province. The settlement at Albemarle had been established in April 1670 and was largely abandoned in 1680 for a new site where Charleston now stands. In 1664 Carteret was elected Master of Trinity House, an office which he held until May 1665. The Duke of York made a substantial grant of land in North America to Carteret and Lord John Berkeley in 1664, which land was to be known as New Jersey and now comprises the state of that name. When Carteret found himself under attack for alleged misappropriation of navy funds he was appointed Vice-Treasurer of Ireland, a post which he held from 1667–73. In 1670 the King made a grant to six Lords Proprietors, one of whom was Carteret, of "all those islands commonly called the Bahama Islands with power to appoint Governors, make laws, wage wars, and transport colonists from England". The next year Carteret was appointed one of the Commissioners of Trade and Plantations. The oath of office was administered to him and the other commissioners on 26th May 1671, a fact recorded in the *Diary* of John Evelyn, who was himself one of the commissioners. In 1672 Carteret was one of the foundation members of the Company of Royal Adventurers Trading to Africa which acquired the East India Company's forts on the Gambia and Gold Coast. The next year Carteret was appointed one of the commissioners to discharge the duties of the office of Lord High Admiral after the Duke of York had been compelled to surrender that office on the passing of the Test Act. He remained a commissioner until 1679. Carteret was appointed in 1673 one of the commissioners "for the rebuilding, new erecting, finishing and adorning" of St Paul's Cathedral after the fire of London.

When Carteret was Treasurer of the Navy Samuel Pepys was Clerk of the Acts and Carteret is often mentioned in the *Diary*. Over the years Carteret supported Pepys in the Navy Board and the latter reciprocated by giving considerable assistance in arranging the marriage of Carteret's son Philip to Lady Jemima Montagu, daughter of the Earl of Sandwich. Pepys was not impressed by Philip Carteret's conduct in the matter and wrote in the *Diary* "But, Lord! What silly discourse we had by the way as to love-matters, he being the most awkward man ever met with in my life as to that business". The marriage duly took place and Pepys was in the wedding party and in the *Diary* he describes the events of the day concluding ". . . and so after prayers, soberly to bed; only I got into the bridegroom's chamber while he undressed himself, and there was very

7

merry, till he was called to the bride's chamber, and into bed they went. I kissed the bride in bed, and so the curtains drawne with the greatest gravity that could be, and so goodnight".

Philip Carteret was knighted in 1667 and later became a Fellow of the Royal Society. He was a naval officer and for some years lived in retirement, but on the outbreak of the Third Dutch War in 1672 he was recalled to active service on the *Royal James*, the flag-ship of his father-in-law, the Earl of Sandwich. Both Carteret and the Earl died at the Battle of Solebay. The engagement is the subject of a painting by Peter Monamy (about 1670–1749), the Jersey marine artist, which is said to be his finest work.

In passing it is of interest to note that Samuel Pepys' uncle Thomas Pepys lived in Jersey. Thomas Pepys' first wife died before 1629. He married his second wife, Mary Syvret, at St Helier's Parish Church on 23rd June of that year. There were issue of the marriage Thomas, Charles and Mary, all of whom were christened at St Helier's Parish Church. His uncle and the three cousins are all mentioned by Samuel Pepys in his *Diary*. Thomas, junior, was by trade a turner and had a shop or booth in Smithfield, London. Charles married Joan Smith, a widow, at St Martin's Church, Ludgate, London, on 21st February 1662. He became master joiner at Chatham dockyard. Mary married Samuel de Santhune at the French Protestant Church, Threadneedle Street, London, on 12th November 1662. She died in December 1667 and was buried on the 26th of the month.

Sir George Carteret died on 13th January 1680 at Hawnes, his home in Bedfordshire, which had been purchased in 1667 for his son Philip and his wife, and which stood only a short distance from Chicksands Priory, the home of Sir Peter Osborne. At the time of his death the King was about to create him a baron. Despite his personal ambitions, principally, if not wholly, directed towards the acquisition of wealth, Carteret had been indefatigable in his efforts on behalf of his native island and, above all, of the Royalist cause. As the Pouletts had adhered to their family motto so he had kept to his—*loyal devoir*. The King, for his part, never forgot the promise made over thirty years before to Carteret, his friend and ever faithful servant. He honoured it not only during Carteret's life but even after his death for, by royal warrant, he gave to his widow Lady Elizabeth Carteret the same precedence that she would have had if her husband had lived to become a peer, and, furthermore, by Letters Patent dated 19th October 1681 created his grandson, Sir George Carteret, Bt, Baron Carteret of Hawnes.

Other members of the de Carteret family were rewarded for their loyalty to the King. Sir Edward de Carteret (1620–83) was appointed a Gentleman Usher in Ordinary and Daily Waiter. In 1665 he was appointed

Bailiff of Jersey, the first of six non-resident de Carteret bailiffs. By 1675 he was Keeper of the Little Park, Windsor, and in 1676 he became Gentleman Usher of the Black Rod. Sir Edward died in Jersey at St Ouen's Manor, and was buried at Trinity Church where he is commemorated by the finest monument in the island.

On 29th August 1660 King Charles II by Letters Patent confirmed the grant of the island of Alderney and the adjacent islets which he had promised on 12th May 1660 to Edward de Carteret, the same person as mentioned in the preceding paragraph, James de Carteret and Clement Le Couteur jointly, and for the survivor of them for an annual rent of thirteen shillings in consideration of good and acceptable services which they had rendered to him. On 6th September of the same year the grantees assigned their grant to Sir George Carteret.

Alderney was retained by Carteret during his life. Following his death it was sold by his trustees in 1683 to Sir Edmund Andros and Lady Mary Andros (née Craven), his wife, who surrendered their rights to the King who in turn issued a new Patent dated 28th April 1683 granting the island to Sir Edmund and his heirs for a term of ninety-nine years for the original rental of thirteen shillings per annum. The following month Sir Edmund appointed Thomas Le Mesurier, a Guernseyman, his lieutenant-governor. This was the start of the Le Mesuriers' connection with Alderney. At Sir Edmund's death the island passed to his nephew George Andros and at his death it passed to his sister Anne, wife of John Le Mesurier (1682–1722), son of Sir Edmund's lieutenant-governor and the first of the Le Mesurier Governors of Alderney.

Sir Edward de Carteret (about 1630–98), who in 1649 had been appointed cup-bearer to the Duke of York, resumed his duties at the Restoration. In 1663 the King granted him all the sanctuary paths and waste lands in Jersey in consideration of his services and those of his father Sir Philip de Carteret to the Royalist cause; he was knighted about 1668 and in 1674 he was granted the great tithes of St Helier's Parish Church. The Duke of York gave de Carteret the wedding suit which he had worn when his marriage to Marie Beatrice d'Este of Modena was ratified at Dover before the Bishop of Oxford, on 21st November 1673, together with the saddle and bridle of his horse.

The wedding suit is in fine fawn-coloured cloth, embroidered with silver and gold raised work. The coat is lined with reddish orange grosgrain silk, which is turned back at the cuffs and lavishly trimmed with a very handsome pillow lace of gold and silver thread, matching in colour the metal used for the embroidery on the suit. The Garter star in silver foil and blue and scarlet silk, embroidered with silver thread, is in its correct position on the left breast of the coat. The hemispherical buttons, of which there are many on the pocket flaps and down the middle of the front of the coat, are of gold. There are a surprising number of pockets in the suit, which are made of fine wash leather lined with silk; two are very large. In the breeches there are six pockets, three on each side.

On 14th February 1650 King Charles II while at Coutances in Normandy made a grant of the office of Sheriff of Guernsey to Edward de Carteret and to John de Carteret, his eldest son, successively, and to the survivor of them. On 8th September 1660 Edward de Carteret, who was living in Guernsey, produced his warrant of appointment to the Royal Court and was sworn in as sheriff on 4th May 1661 in the place of Abraham Carey on whom had fallen the duty of reading the Proclamation of Accession.

Despite the Act of Oblivion and Indemnity others received retribution. Dr Gilbert Millington, Sir Hardress Waller, Henry Smith, Colonel James Temple and Colonel Thomas Waite (Wayte), who were among those who condemned King Charles I to death and signed his death warrant, were imprisoned in Mont Orgueil Castle. Millington died in September or October 1666 and was buried in common ground. Waller possibly died the same year. Smith possibly died in 1668. Temple was transferred to Elizabeth Castle in 1674; the date of his death is not known. Waite died in 1688 and was buried in St Saviour's Church on 18th October of that year. His wife Jane or Jeanne Waite (née Raynes) died the following year and was buried in the same church on 19th November. Robert Overton who had been imprisoned in Jersey in the time of the Commonwealth was again sent to prison in the island in 1664. It is not known when he died, although it is known that he was still alive in 1668. John Lambert (1619–83) who was in prison in the Tower of London was transferred to Castle Cornet in 1661. The following year he stood trial for high treason in England. He was found guilty and sentenced to death, the sentence being commuted to life imprisonment. He was sent back to prison in Castle Cornet, remaining there until 1670 when he was removed to Drake's Island, also known as St Nicholas Island in Plymouth Sound where he was visited by Samuel Pepys in August 1683. Lambert's daughter, Mary, married Charles Hatton, the second son of the Governor of Guernsey, much to the horror of his father, who hastened to state that he had "turned his son out of doors and hath never since given him a penny". Lambert's feelings about the marriage are not on record.

As was mentioned earlier, Sir George Carteret and John, Lord Berkeley, Baron of Stratton, became proprietors of New Jersey in 1664. It will be recalled that a grant by the King of Smith's Island, renamed New Jersey, to Carteret in 1650 proved a failure.

Henry, Earl of Sterling and Viscount Canada, conveyed Long Island to the Duke of York about 1662 and King Charles II issued a Patent on 12th March 1664, to his brother for all the islands between Cape Cod, the

Narrows and Hudson River, including Martha's Vineyard and Nantucket; also all the lands between the Connecticut River and the east side of Delaware Bay. The landward boundary ran from the head of the Connecticut to the head of the Hudson and from there to the source of the Mohawk and finally to the east side of Delaware Bay. Within all this territory the Duke had absolute power to govern.

It was in respect of part of his American territory that the Duke on 23rd and 24th June 1664, executed deeds of lease and release to Carteret of Saltrum, Devon, and Lord Berkeley for them their heirs and assigns, of all that part of his land

> . . . lying and being to the westward of Long Island and Manhatas Island and bounded on the east part by the main sea, and part by Hudson's river, and hath upon the west, Delaware bay or river, and extending southward to the main ocean as far as Cape May, at the mouth of Delaware bay; and to the northward, as far as the northernmost branch of the said bay or river of Delaware, which is forty-one degrees and forty minutes of latitude, and crosseth over thence in a straight line to Hudson's river, in forty-one degrees of latitude; which said tract of land is hereafter to be called by the name or names of New Caesarea, or New Jersey . . .

The Lords Proprietors were given full ownership of the land and assumed that they possessed the power of government. On their seal as Lords Proprietors were depicted the arms, in duplicate of Carteret and Lord Berkeley with their respective monograms, also in duplicate. Captain Philip de Carteret (1639–82), eldest son of Helier de Carteret, Attorney-General for Jersey and Rachael de Carteret (*née* La Cloche), one of Carteret's cousins was governor from 1664 to 1676 and of East New Jersey from 1677 to 1682. He arrived in August 1665 on the ship *Philip* with some thirty gentlemen and servants, Channel Islanders, Englishmen and Frenchmen. The capital was established at Elizabethtown, now called Elizabeth, which was named after Lady Carteret. The first Assembly, convened on 26th May 1668, marked the beginning of representative government in New Jersey. Trouble broke out and in May 1672 an illegally constituted assembly which met at Elizabethtown purported to depose Philip de Carteret and to appoint James Carteret, Sir George's scalliwag of a son, "president of the Country". Philip de Carteret returned to England to obtain instructions from the Lords Proprietors and did not resume his position as governor until November 1674. The previous year Berkeley sold his half share of New Jersey to John Fenwick, acting on behalf of his fellow Quaker, Edward Byllynge. The territory was then divided into East and West Jersey by the Quintipartite Deed of 1st July 1676 the boundary between the two divisions being a line running from Little Egg Harbour to the north-west corner of the province.

After the death of Sir George Carteret in 1680 Sir Edmund Andros, the Governor of New York, who resented the alienation of New Jersey, issued a proclamation on 13th March ordering Philip de Carteret, the Governor of East New Jersey, and his officials to cease exercising jurisdiction. As de Carteret refused to comply with the terms of the proclamation Andros went with his council to Elizabethtown on 7th April and claimed that he had been commissioned to receive the whole country from the Dutch. In reply de Carteret produced his commission appointing him governor. Andros departed on the 1st May and issued a warrant for de Carteret's arrest and caused him to be abducted from his home in the most brutal fashion and imprisoned in New York where he suffered much from the injuries which he had received. In May de Carteret was presented at a New York Court of Assizes on a charge of having improperly attempted to exercise powers of government with force and was acquitted after Andros had several times attempted to prevent the jury from returning a verdict of not guilty. On the understanding that he would not "assume any jurisdiction there, civil or military" until the dispute had been settled in London, de Carteret was allowed to return home to New Jersey. Lady Elizabeth Carteret sent a letter to de Carteret in March 1681 stating that the Duke of York disowned the acts of Andros, and the Duke wrote a letter to Andros confirming that this was so.

Andros was summoned to London to answer charges against him. There was trouble in East New Jersey and de Carteret dissolved the Assembly. Then it was learnt that the trustees of Sir George Carteret's will had sold East New Jersey to a group of Quakers and de Carteret resigned the governorship. In December 1682 de Carteret died at Elizabethtown and on the 14th of the month his widow wrote to his mother informing her of the death of her son, a

> . . . dear and loving husband who ever since their barbarious and unhuman action of Sir Edmond Andross and his merciless souldiers hath been subject to frequent and many body infirmities arising from crushes and most cruel bruises from them received which is believed hath shortened and made his life many times and at his latter end uncomfortable to him . . .

Unpleasant things could happen nearer home as proved to be the case on the night of 29th December 1672 when the magazine at Castle Cornet exploded after being struck by lightning and the keep where it was situated was destroyed, as well as the medieval buildings in the courtyard to the north. There survive several contemporary accounts of the tragedy in which seven people were killed. Part of one of these accounts reads thus:

In this Nursery was killed one Mrs Willis a Dry Nurse, who was found there dead, having My Lord's 2ᵈ Daughter in her Arms fast, holding a small Silver Cup in her Hands wherewith she did play which was all rimpled and bruised and yet the Young Lady did not receive the least Hurt. This Nurse had likewise one of her Hands fast upon the Cradle where was My Lord's Youngest Daughter and the Cradle full of Rubish, but the Child received no Prejudice, and with much ado could that which she held in her Arms be pulled out, for she was cold dead.

The tragedy bore out the prediction made to the second Lord Hatton by the 'wise woman of Rockingham' which ran thus:

> Kit Hatton! Kit Hatton! I rede ye beware
> Of the flash from the cloud, and the flight through the air!
> When the Star of thy destiny looms in the sky,
> To others unclouded, but red to thine eye,
> Though men see no signs in the threatening air
> Kit Hatton! Kit Hatton! I rede ye beware!

Among the dead were the Dowager Lady Hatton and her daughter-in-law. Their viscera were buried in St Peter Port Church and their embalmed bodies were buried in the tomb of the first Lord Hatton in Westminster Abbey. The baby, Anne, eventually became the Countess of Winchelsea and Nottingham and the mother of seven sons and ten daughters.

Following the explosion at Castle Cornet and the destruction of the keep, no steps were taken to reinstate the building as its strength as a fortress had not been impaired, and only tidying up operations were carried out. Eventually, however, Colonel George Legge, Lieutenant-General of Ordnance, drew up *The Present State of Guernsey with a short Accompt of Jersey And the Forts Belonging to the said Islands*, an exhaustive report on all the garrisons and fortifications of Jersey and Guernsey, with splendid illustrations and maps by Thomas Philips, which was completed in 1680.

The appointment of Sir Edmund Andros as Bailiff of Guernsey in 1674 upset Lord Hatton, the governor, who claimed the right to dispose of that office. The matter was referred to the Privy Council who ordered that in future the King and not the governor would appoint the bailiff, dean, procureur and comptroller. Another stir was caused when Andros was appointed lieutenant-governor in February 1704. Shortly after the appointment was made it was realized that the holding of the offices of lieutenant-governor and bailiff by one person was incompatible. Accordingly in March an order was issued whereby Andros was excused carrying out the duties of bailiff. On the death of Lord Hatton in 1706 Andros' appointment as lieutenant-governor ceased and he resumed his duties as bailiff.

The year 1685 saw the death of King Charles II, the accession to the throne of his ill-starred brother, James, Duke of York, as King James II; the Duke of Monmouth's Rebellion and execution, and the revocation by King Louis XIV of the Edict of Nantes, an action which resulted in a number of French Protestants seeking refuge in the Channel Islands, some of whom were to settle there permanently.

King James II was a Roman Catholic and had every intention of re-establishing Roman Catholicism throughout his realm, including the Channel Islands. In furtherance of his objective he dismissed Charles Hatton from his position as Lieutenant-Governor of Guernsey and replaced him by Charles Maccarty, a Roman Catholic, and installed garrisons in both Jersey and Guernsey composed predominantly of soldiers of the same faith; he also caused Roman Catholic priests to be sent to the islands.

In 1687 the King granted a charter to Jersey as his predecessors had done.

During the King's short reign the first two substantial accounts of the island of Jersey ever written were presented to the Sovereign. The first, *Caesarea or a Discourse of the Island of Jersey*, was written by John Poingdestre in 1682 and the second, *A Survey of Ye Island of Jersey*, by Philip Dumaresq (1637–90), a friend and correspondent of John Evelyn, in 1685.

Samuel Pepys, the efficient Secretary of the Navy, corresponded with Philip de Carteret (1650–93), Bailiff of Jersey, with a view to obtaining information on French naval activities. In addition to supplying Pepys with as much information as he could obtain, de Carteret sent him presents of carp and red-legged partridges, and in a letter to Pepys of 3rd November 1686 wrote that those were "the only things this poor island can afford which are not in greater plenty in England". From the first paragraph of another letter from de Carteret to Pepys of 11th April 1687 it appears that the writer had been effusively thanked for a present of carp and patridges, and he promised to send more and in particular so many partridges that Pepys might reserve some for himself and present some to the King, if he thought them worthy of his majesty's acceptance, although he dared not ask that such a gift be made in his name. In the same letter de Carteret told Pepys that he had heard that Sébastien Le Prestre de Vauban (1633–1707), the famous French military engineer, had been along the coast of Normandy and Brittany as far as the Chausey Islands, and had settled on Granville for recommending to King Louis XIV as a suitable place for establishing a naval base.

(*above*) The Market Place, St Peter Port, some time between 1803
and 1816—from an engraving after M. Finucane

(*below*) The Market Place, St Peter Port, from a lithograph published by
Moss in 1838

The Death of Major Peirson—6th January 1781—from an
engraving by James Heath after J. S. Copley's picture now
in the Tate Galley, London

High Street, St Peter Port, from a lithograph after G. S. Shepherd,
published by Moss

The carp came from St Ouen's Pond, otherwise called La Mare au Seigneur. Their descendants still live in this attractive reed-fringed pond, the largest natural expanse of fresh water in the Channel Islands.

As for the partridges they had already attracted royal notice. On 16th August 1673 the Governor informed the States of Jersey that the King and the Duke of York expressly enjoined and recommended the preservation of the island's game and, in particular, the red-legged partridge. In 1675 the King showed continued interest in the matter by appointing Sir Philip de Carteret, Bt, and Sir Edward de Carteret, Kt, "Keepers of our Game Within and about Our Said Isle of Jersey During your Lives and the Life of the Longer Liver of you." The game to be protected comprised hares, rabbits, partridges and other wild fowl. All of which would seem to indicate that the King would probably have accepted a gift of some of de Carteret's partridges if Pepys had made the offer. King James II continued to show interest in Jersey's game for on 24th March 1688 he caused a letter to be sent to the Keepers of the Game stating that it was the royal will and pleasure that no one should shoot, kill or in any way destroy game from the beginning of February until the end of October. Perhaps the King recalled the pleasure he had derived from hunting partridges and hares when he was staying in Jersey during the Civil War. Chevalier recorded how the Duke, as he then was, liked shooting partridges on the wing, and rarely missed.

When in 1688 the news of the landing of William of Orange at Torbay arrived in the Channel Islands the inhabitants breathed a sigh of relief at the thought of being free of France and Popery. In Jersey the lieutenant-governor was persuaded to allow a number of the islanders equal to the number of the garrison to do duty in the castle. Ultimately the garrison was replaced by the Earl of Bath's regiment without opposition. In Guernsey the lieutenant-governor was confined and the Catholic officers and soldiers among the garrison were disarmed.

When the news that King James had been deposed reached the British colonies in America, the colonists decided to revolt against Sir Edmund Andros. One day in April 1689 while presiding in the council chamber he was set upon, bound and lodged in the fort, where he was detained for nine months, during which time he made one ineffectual attempt to escape. On 10th December 1689 Andros left Boston with a few friends to attend the Court of Enquiry which King William III had set up in England to investigate the complaints against him. Andros and his party arrived in England the following April. The Court of Enquiry exonerated Andros and he was to win the confidence of the new King and Queen and of Queen Anne, all of whom he was to serve faithfully in a number of capacities.

Andros died at his home in Denmark Hill, London, on 27th February

1714 and was buried at St Anne's, Soho. One memoir written on the life of this great Guernseyman concludes:

We see then no reason to doubt that Sir Edmund Andros was an upright and honourable man, faithful to his employer, conscientous in his religious belief, an able soldier possessed of great administrative abilities, a man worthy to be ranked among the leaders of his time.

His treatment of Philip de Carteret showed a less pleasing side of his character.

In his will Andros directed his nephew, John Andros, to build within five years of his death a "good suitable house" on or at the manor of Sausmarez and this under threat of having to pay £500 to another nephew, George Andros, should the direction not be fulfilled. John complied with his uncle's wishes with the result that there stands as part of Sausmarez Manor House a beautiful Queen Anne mansion built between 1714–18, which delights the eye of all who see it.

A Guernseyman, John Tupper, rendered signal service to the British interest before the Battle of La Hogue. It would appear that Tupper, who commanded the privateer *Monmouth Galley*, was crossing in his vessel from Guernsey to England when he spied the French fleet through the fog and, proceeding with all haste to Spithead, informed the Admiral there of the Frenchmen's presence. The English and Dutch fleets under the command of Admiral Russell met the French fleet under Tourville in the Channel off Cape La Hogue and on 19th–20th May 1692 the French were decisively beaten and the Jacobite cause suffered an irreparable set back. For the part he played in advising the British of the whereabouts of the French fleet, King William and Queen Mary presented Tupper with a gold medal and chain, which together with his portrait are on permanent loan to the Lukis and Island Museum in St Peter Port. In addition to the medal and chain Tupper was granted an augmentation to his coat of arms which took the form of a canton ermine on which were depicted in gold the chain with the medal hanging from it bearing the profiles of the King and Queen.

The intensive military preparations made in Guernsey to resist invasion from France resulted in serious complaints being presented to the King on behalf of the inhabitants of the island on 8th August 1689. This complaint was referred to Lord Hatton who gave directions on 24th August to correct the abuses complained of. It has been suggested that it was a second set of complaints from the inhabitants of Guernsey which resulted in the Order in Council of 1691.

The British and allied success at sea, which had removed the threat of invasion from Britain and the Channel Islands, was not matched by similar good fortune on land, and the campaign in Flanders was brought to a conclusion by the Treaty of Ryswick. A Jerseyman, Edward d'Auvergne (1665–1737), who went to Flanders in 1691 as chaplain to the Earl of Bath's Regiment and later to the Third Regiment of Foot Guards (Scots Guards) wrote a *History of the Campaign in Flanders* in seven volumes. That of 1693 was edited by another Jerseyman, Philip Falle (1656–1742), one of the King's Chaplains, who prefaced it with a dedication to the Duke of Ormonde. In 1699 d'Auvergne was appointed Domestic Chaplain to King William III.

Falle himself wrote *An Account of the Island of Jersey*, with a map of the island by Thomas Lemprière, published in 1694 and dedicated it to the King, which was the reason for him being granted the chaplaincy. Falle's book was based on the work of John Poingdestre written twelve years earlier. It was the standard work on Jersey for over 200 years. One writer described all other histories as being nothing more than "Falle and water".

After just over 200 years the Privilege of Neutrality was abolished by Order in Council of 8th August 1689 in the following terms:

> Whereas on the 30th of May last his Ma^{ty} in Councill was pleased to order that their Ma^{tys} Proclamation bearing the date the 18th of the said Month for Prohibiting the Importation of any Commoditys of the Growth and manufacture of France should be forthwith sent to the Bayliffs & Jurats of the Islands of Jerzey and Guernzey, who were thereby required to Cause the said Proclamation then sent unto them, to be there published and strictly observed and put into Execution; His Ma^{ty} in Councill, upon the humble Petition of the Inhabitants of the Island of Guernzey, Is this day pleased to Declare That (being at this time strictly obliged in His Treaties with His Allies and Confederats to Prohibit in all His Dominions all manner of Trade and Commerce whatsoever with France) Hee does not think it fit and Expedient to Dispense with the Execution of His said Order, in this present and Extraordinary Juncture of time; Yet, that it is not His Ma^{tys} Intention in any manner whatsoever to Revoke or Infringe any Priviledges that may have been granted by His Royall Predecessors to the Inhabitants of the said Island of Guernzey.

The Proclamation of 18th May 1689 referred to in the Order prohibited the importation of French goods into the islands.

One result of the Order in Council was to cause Channel Islanders to become smugglers on a large scale. This pursuit compensated to some extent for the loss of neutrality in the war and was profitably carried on into the early years of the nineteenth century.

Privateering was another occupation indulged in by Channel Islanders. Unlike smuggling it was legal, although, on occasion, it smacked of high adventure. During the Civil War the Jersey privateers had been the scourge of the English Channel, capturing or destroying a considerable number of Parliamentary ships. When war broke out between Britain and France in 1689 the islanders started privateering. At first they proceeded on a small scale, only fifty-five commissions being granted between 1689 and 1697. However, with the start of the War of the Spanish Succession in 1701 there was a notable increase in the scale of the islanders' privateering activities. Between 1st June 1702 and 29th September 1711 Guernsey privateers took 608 prizes, recaptures and ransoms; during the same period Jersey privateers took 151. In fact, the Channel Islands' privateers were "more numerous than those of any other English or colonial base but also, if the number rather than the value of prizes be a criterion, more successful than all the rest put together".

The islanders, of course, continued to pursue their more conventional means of livelihood—agriculture, cidermaking, knitting and fishing. In addition, many of the islands' men were sailors, particularly in the merchant marine. John Poingdestre records that the making of cider reached a peak in 1681 and that "There were not found in all ye Island Caskes for much above halfe that was made". Knitted goods, especially stockings, were made in large quantities, some 6,000 pairs being produced each week. A special allowance of wool was permitted to be imported by each island every year through the port of Southampton. The principal fishing was that carried on off the east coast of North America.

Despite all this activity the bulk of the islanders were by no means rich. The Civil War had depressed trade. Dumaresq in his *Survey* writes of Jersey as having "become poor, over what it was heretofore, and consequently the Islanders so unable to pay their rents, where with most part of the Island is overcharged, which causes such multitudes of Law Suits, that, few amongst them are free from, who have any Estates", and blames this situation upon a shortage of wool brought about by various causes. The poverty of the island and its inhabitants was no new problem, and it is no wonder that the States were looking to emigration to the New World as a means of disposing of the indigent poor.

From early times Channel Islanders were to be found beyond the confines of their native shores. At home there was little scope for able men, whether of learning or of commerce, to find an outlet for their talents. In fact, in the seventeenth, eighteenth and nineteenth centuries it was difficult for many people to find work in the islands and so some looked beyond the seas for an opportunity to earn their daily bread. At first, they emigrated to the newly founded colonies and plantations in North America, but later, as the British Empire expanded, they went also to more distant lands, and, in particular, to Australia and New Zealand.

In 1666 the States of Jersey were so concerned at the large number of poor that they were considering resettling such persons either in Ireland, in New England, in New Jersey or other parts of the King's dominions. On 21st February 1669 Captain Nicholas Ling, Lieutenant-Governor of Alderney for Sir George Carteret, issued an ordinance approved by the Court, which ordered poor people who had no means of feeding and clothing their family and had several children over the age of seven years to deliver them to be sent to Guernsey and from there to New England on the understanding that they would be well fed and clothed and sold or hired in the English manner.

Jersey had early connections with Salem, Massachusetts, which was founded in 1626. Jersey names such as Bailhache, Balleine, Cabot, Messervy and Poingdestre, abound in the local records, although in many cases the way in which they are spelt makes them difficult to recognize. In some cases the names were translated into English, for example the surname Langlois became English.

In fact, a Jerseyman Philip Langlois (1651–1736), known in Salem as Philip English, a godson of Sir Philip de Carteret, became involved in the witchcraft delusion which erupted in Salem Village in 1692. He was born at Trinity, Jersey, and in 1666 emigrated to Salem, where he lodged with William Hollingsworth, a merchant, whose daughter, Mary, he married in 1675. Hollingsworth died the same year and English inherited his father-in-law's fortune and became a merchant and shipbuilder. In 1676 he visited Jersey and took back with him to Salem a number of Jersey boys and girls as indentured apprentices.

Two of the twenty-seven ships which he owned traded regularly with Jersey. Their outward cargoes comprised of cod, molasses, rum and spermaceti and the inward cargoes of Jersey-made shoes and stockings and French brandy and wines. English prospered greatly and owned two wharfs and warehouses and a fine mansion, known as the Great House which stood in English Street. His ties with Jersey were renewed when his daughter, Susannah, married one of his captains, by name Touzel. In 1692 there was an outcry against witchcraft, which, it was alleged, was being indulged in in Salem and both English and his wife were suspected of being witches. She was arrested and subsequently a warrant was issued for his arrest. Fortunately he was warned of what was afoot and fled from the state. As it proved just in time for his house was sacked by the mob and his goods and property were arrested by the sheriff. After a month he gave himself up as he thought that his absence might prejudice his wife's trial. Before being sent to Boston both English and his wife were locked up in The Cat and Wheel Tavern as the prison was already filled to overflowing. Some 125 people were arrested of whom twenty were executed while English and his wife lay in Boston jail. The Sunday before their trial, on the advice of the Reverend Joshua Moody, they managed with the help of a few friends to effect their escape by carriage to New York. The Englishs returned to Salem when the trouble had died down and Philip managed to re-establish his business and survived to the ripe old age of eighty-five.

It was to Salem that Francis, George and John Cabot, the sons of Francis Cabot and Susanna Cabot (*née* Gruchy), emigrated from Jersey about 1700. Francis (born 1668) returned to Jersey prior to settling in Southampton in 1701, where he became a rich merchant. George (1678–1717) moved from Salem to Boston, where he settled and became a builder and merchant. In 1700 he built, at the corner of Crombie and Essex Streets, the first brick house in Salem of which there is any record. John (1680–1742) married Anna Orne of Salem in 1702 by whom he had nine children. He prospered greatly and was the founder of one of the leading families of the United States.

Another Jerseyman who made his mark in Salem was John Bertram (1796–1882), the merchant adventurer and philanthropist. Like John Cabot had before him, Bertram lived in Essex Street and his house is now the public library. In 1807 Bertram's parents John Bertram (1773–1825) and Jeanne Bertram (*née* Le Gros) (1773–1842) emigrated from Jersey to America with their six children; a seventh child was born in Salem. John Bertram, Snr, had letters of introduction to another Jerseyman, a Captain Pirrel, who was living in Salem.

As early as 1680 a number of Jersey families were established at Fortune Bay, Newfoundland.

In the newly settled lands across the Atlantic a new way of life, an American way of living, was slowly evolving. Back home in the Channel Islands the old ways persisted and feudalism was very much alive at the beginning of the eighteenth century as is well illustrated by the revolt of the St Ouen's tenants against their Lord, Sir Charles de Carteret, Bt (1679–1715). He was the only son of Sir Philip de Carteret, Bt (1650–93) and Elizabeth de Carteret (died 1717). Sir Philip was Lord of St Ouen and Lord of Sark and Bailiff of Jersey (1682–93), as well as being a very wealthy man who kept a coach with six horses. In 1683 he and his wife bought Hillingdon House, Middlesex, which remained in the family until 1725. Charles was baptized at St Margaret's, Westminster, his sponsors being King Charles II and the Duke of Monmouth. He was knighted by the King at Whitehall when eight years old. His father, the bailiff, whom he was destined to succeed in that office, died when he was fourteen. However, as he was too young to be appointed to the office, his uncle, Sir Edward de Carteret (about 1630–98), was appointed bailiff until he became of age. When in 1701 his St Ouen's tenants revolted against the performance of feudal services de Carteret took them to court. The Royal

Court gave judgement in his favour on 4th September, and on 31st December 1702 the Privy Council dismissed the appeal which the tenants had made against the judgement.

Queen Mary II died in 1694; King William III survived her until 1702. He was succeeded by his sister-in-law Anne, whose consort was Prince George of Denmark.

The war, resumed by King William III in 1701, continued unabated after his death, and the allied armies under John Churchill, Duke of Marlborough won great victories, the names of which are emblazoned in the halls of valour.

The States of Guernsey were so delighted at the defeats suffered by the French and the outcome of the war that they were moved to send two addresses to the Queen. The first, passed on 14th June 1708, contained the following paragraph:

> Providence seems to have permitted your enemies should be so rash and unjust, that your wisdom in and right of governing your realm should shine the brighter, and convince the world that it is easier to proclaim an imaginary King at Paris, than to introduce him into Great Britain; easier to give a French sword than usurp a British sceptre.

The second, dated 29th July 1713, was prompted by the advent of peace and the Treaty of Utrecht, and concluded:

> May you, Great Queen, reign long, very long, in happiness and prosperity; and, when full of years, may you transmit, as you desire to do, to the illustrious House of Hanover, which is in perfect harmony with your majesty, the diadems you wear, to take possession of the Crown of Glory reserved for you by your Saviour.

A medal comparing in magnificence with the Tupper Medal was that awarded by Queen Anne to a Jerseyman, James Lemprière (born 1654), Captain, R.N., for services rendered in 1703 when he successfully conducted the squadron commanded by Rear-Admiral Dilkes to destroy a considerable number of French merchant ships which were in convoy off their own coast between Avranches and Mont St Michel. On the obverse of the medal appear the head and shoulders of the Queen and on the reverse an inscription stating the reason for the award and depicting the Lemprière Arms, with the inscription "True to my Trust" beneath them.

Queen Anne, the last of the Stuart sovereigns died on 1st August 1714. Her reign had been rendered glorious by Marlborough's victories, and was in happy contrast to that of King James I, the first Stuart monarch to rule over England.

CHAPTER NINE

The First Two Georges—1714-60

> The first two Royal Georges and their father, Ernest
> Augustus, had quite royal notions regarding mar-
> riage; and Louis XIV. and Charles II. scarce dis-
> tinguished themselves more at Versailles or St James,
> than these German sultans in their little city on the
> banks of the Leine.
>
> William Makepeace Thackeray (1811–63)

Although 'The Good Queen Anne' had had a number of children, none
survived her, and by a queer quirk of fate she was succeeded on the throne
by George Lewis, Elector of Brunswick–Lüneburg, generally known as
Hanover, as King George I. In 1727 he was himself succeeded by his son
as King George II. They and their two successors gave their names to the
Georgian period, which lasted until the accession of Queen Victoria in
1837. It was an important time in British history—a full-blooded, lusty
and robust age, with a bright and scintillating side as well as a murky and
squalid one. The elegance which existed on the one hand and the squalor
on the other are well recorded in the paintings of William Hogarth.

The Georgians numbered among their ranks some of the greatest men
in British history—statesmen, naval and military commanders, explorers,
writers, poets, artists and actors, and many others who contributed much
to the greatness of their country.

Channel Islanders played their part in this formulative and exciting
period of history. They participated in the upsurge of all things British.
More Channel Islanders than ever before left their native shores to seek a
livelihood and many of them achieved success. They were to be found in
the navy and in the army, which together added vast territories to the
Empire. They helped to colonize these newly acquired lands, including

Australia, Canada and New Zealand. They occupied their traditional front line position in the French wars. They were also active at home during this period developing the islands and founding a number of important insular institutions.

At the time of King George I's accession, General Henry Lumley was Governor of Jersey, an office to which he was appointed in 1704, and was to continue to hold until his death in 1722. He was succeeded in 1723 by Richard, Viscount Cobham, who also held office until his death in 1749. Among those appointed lieutenant-governor during his term of office were Colonel George Howard who was in command in the island at the time of the riots of 1729-30.

John Cavalier (1681-1740) was Lieutenant-Governor of Jersey 1738-40, one of the most colourful people to hold the office. He was the son of a Languedoc peasant. As a young boy he helped his father, who was a shepherd, mind his flocks and in due time was apprenticed to a baker. In 1702 he became a leader of the Protestant insurgents in the Cevennes. With Pierre Laporte, better known as Roland, he maintained a brilliant struggle against King Louis's troops until 1704 when surrender became inevitable. Roland was shot down, but Cavalier escaped to Switzerland and served under the Duke of Savoy. Robert Louis Stevenson in *Travels with a Donkey in the Cevennes* described Cavalier as "a baker's apprentice with a genius for war". Cavalier raised a regiment in Holland for English service in Spain in 1706. He was severely wounded at Almanza in 1707 and received a pension from the British Government. He died at Chelsea in 1740. The previous year he had been promoted major-general.

By a strange coincidence at the same time as Jersey had a French-born lieutenant-governor, Guernsey had a French-born governor in the person of Francis, Marquis de Montandre, who held the office from 1733 until his death in 1739.

Alderney continued to have hereditary governors. In 1713 Sir Edmund Andros died childless and bequeathed the government of Alderney to his nephew, George Andros, who died in 1714. George's heir was his sister Anne, wife of John Le Mesurier (1682-1722), son of Thomas Le Mesurier, lieutenant-governor of the island under Sir Edmund. Anne Le Mesurier died in 1729 and on her death her son Henry Le Mesurier (1713-79) became Governor of Alderney. In 1744 he exchanged the Patent of Alderney with his brother John Le Mesurier (1717-93) for lands at Old College and Plaisance in Guernsey. In 1763 John Le Mesurier took out a new Patent of the island for ninety-nine years.

In 1720 John, Lord Carteret, sold the Lordship of Sark to Colonel John Johnson bringing to an end his family's connection with Sark after 165 years. Johnson sold it in 1723 to James Milner, who held it until his death in 1730. For a short time the Bishop of Gloucester, who was Milner's executor, was Lord of Sark. The same year Susanne Le Pelley, widow of Nicholas Le Pelley, purchased the Lordship and remained Dame of Sark until her death in 1733 when she was succeeded by her son Nicholas Le Pelley.

Sir Charles de Carteret, who had been Bailiff of Jersey from 1703, died in 1715 and was buried in Westminster Abbey where an inscription on the memorial to his mother Elizabeth de Carteret, daughter of Sir Edward de Carteret, records that "by (his) decease June ye 6th A.D. 1715, in ye 34th year of his age, was extinguished the Eldest branch of the ancient family of the name of Carteret, Seigneurs of Saint Ouen in ye Island of Jersey". Charles de Carteret was succeeded in that office, which had become virtually hereditary in the family of de Carteret, and in the Lordships of St Ouen and Sark, by his cousin, John, Lord Carteret (1690–1763). Unlike previous bailiffs, he took the oath of office before the Privy Council. The same year Lord Carteret was appointed a Lord of the Bedchamber. Carteret was the most learned and distinguished member of his family. Jonathan Swift wrote of him that he

was educated in the University of *Oxford*; from whence, with a Singularity, scarce to be justified, he carried away more *Greek*, *Latin*, and *Philosophy*, than properly became a Person of his Rank; indeed much more of each than most of those who are forced to live by their learning, will be at the unnecessary Pains to load their Heads with.

In 1719 he was Envoy Extraordinary to Sweden where he negotiated peace between that country, Denmark, Hanover and Prussia. He was rewarded by being made a Privy Councillor and Foreign Secretary for the Southern Department, which included France, Italy, Spain and the Colonies. Because Carteret was the only Minister who spoke German he gained influence with the King. In 1724 Sir Robert Walpole dropped Carteret from the Ministry on a trivial pretext. The same year he was appointed Lord Lieutenant of Ireland, a position which he held with some success for six years, his first commission lasting until 1727 and his second until 1730. In the latter year there was published in Dublin *A Vindication of His Ex—————y the Lord C—————, from the Charge of favouring none but Toryes, High-Churchmen and Jacobites* by Swift "which was calculated to amuse and compliment the Lord Lieutenant". Elsewhere Swift wrote: "I believe my Lord Carteret, since he is no longer Lieutenant, may not wish me ill, and I have told him often that I only hated him as Lieutenant. I confess he had a genteeler manner of binding the chains of this Kingdom, than most of his predecessors." Carteret himself wrote: "When people ask me how I governed Ireland, I say that I pleased Dr Swift."

Carteret for the next twelve years lead the opposition against the Whigs in the House of Lords. When Walpole, who had for so long been Prime Minister, fell from office Carteret was appointed Secretary of State for the Northern Department. His knowledge of German gave him influence with King George II, as it had done with his father, and he was present with the King at the Battle of Dettingen in 1743.

In 1744, the year in which Carteret became Earl Granville on the death of his mother, he was forced to resign office. Two years later the King asked him and Lord Bath to form a ministry. They accepted the seals of office, but were unable to form a government. In 1749 Carteret was made a Knight of the Garter and two years later became Lord President of the Council, a position which he held until his death.

Although Carteret never visited Jersey, his duties as bailiff being carried out by a lieutenant-bailiff, he nevertheless took an active interest in the affairs of the island. He appeared before the Privy Council when matters affecting the island were under consideration and on occasion managed to secure privileges for it. In 1722 Carteret sold two of his Jersey manors.

Carteret had inherited from his father, his great-grandfather's share in Carolina. When the Crown purchased the other shares, Carteret asked for and was granted a large tract of land which became known as "Granville's Grant". Carteret County formed from Craven in 1722 in North Carolina and Granville County formed from Edgecombe in 1746 were both named after him.

Carteret married twice. First, Frances Worsley who died in 1743 and, secondly, Lady Sophia Fermor who died in 1745. Carteret and his wives are buried in General Monck's vault in King Henry VII's Chapel, Westminster Abbey. Carteret was the last of nine members of his family to be buried in that famous church.

Four Bailiffs of Guernsey span this period—John de Sausmarez (1714–28,) who succeeded Sir Edmund Andros, Joshua Le Marchant (1728–52,) Eleazar Le Marchant (1752–58) and Samuel Bonamy (1758–71).

In the eighteenth century the Channel Islands were beautiful and unspoilt. A large part of Jersey's countryside was covered in apple and pear orchards, and especially the former. Guernsey had in parts, as nowadays, a somewhat rugged and windswept coastline and Le Clos du Valle had not yet been physically united with the island; Alderney too was exposed and windswept as it is today. The second and enlarged edition of Falle's *Account of Jersey* published in 1734 gives a comprehensive, if somewhat rose-coloured, description of the island as it was at that time. Included in this edition of the *Account* is an article entitled *Remarks on the 19th chapter of the 2nd book of Mr Selden's Mare Clausum* by Philip Morant (1700–70), a Jerseyman and a friend of Falle's. Morant changed the spelling of his surname from Mourant 1734. He was a distinguished antiquarian and the leading historian of the county of Essex. For many years the Essex Archaeological Society has held a memorial dinner in his honour. *An Historical Account of Guernsey* by Thomas Dicey published in 1751 gives a somewhat less adequate description of that island.

In Jersey a number of important changes had taken place in the town of St Helier since the beginning of the previous century. Notable among these was the Royal Court House, rebuilt at the instance of Sir George Carteret in 1648, the Corn Market built in 1668 on the western side of the Market Place, and the Prison built at the western end of La Grande Rue in 1693. The Royal Court House, replaced an older Court House which possibly dated back to as early as 1309, if not earlier. St Helier was slightly larger than it had been, and most, if not all, of the thatch had given way to pantiles or slates as the result of an Act of the States forbidding the use of thatch in the town so as to reduce the risk of fire.

An important addition to the town was the public library which was built to house the fine gift of books presented to the island by Philip Falle. In 1722 he had presented to Durham Cathedral, of which he was a canon, his collection of music books, together with a catalogue of the collection written in his own hand. The gift comprised 266 works, one-quarter of which are unique in British libraries. Many of them were printed abroad— at Amsterdam and Utrecht, at Dresden and Venice—and were collected by Falle on his visits to Holland in his capacity of chaplain to King William III. It was now the turn of his native island to benefit from his generosity. As early as 1696 he had stated in a memorial to the Archbishop of Canterbury his intention of presenting a library to Jersey. However, it was to be many years before his plan was realized. The foundation stone of the library was not laid until 4th July 1737 and the building was not finished until 1741. Even then seven years were to elapse before the appointment of the first librarian, Jean Baptiste de Chateauneuf. Happily the building which housed Jersey's first public library, which institution numbers among the earliest of its kind in the British Isles, still survives. Falle's collection was augmented by another Jerseyman, Daniel Dumaresq (1712–1805), a clergyman, distinguished scholar and friend of Pitt, who presented his library to the island in 1800.

In 1751 the King contributed £200 towards the cost of the new harbour. Out of gratitude the States caused a statue of their royal benefactor to be erected in the Market Place, approximately where the Market Cross had once stood. The statue, which is of lead and gilded, represents the King in the costume of a Roman emperor, and stands on a granite pedestal on the front of which is carved the royal cypher. It was unveiled on 9th July 1751 with military ceremonial in the presence of the lieutenant-governor, bailiff and States, and the officers of the garrison and the gentlemen of the island. Following the unveiling the deputy viscount proclaimed that the statue was erected in honour of the King, after which seven cannons were fired from Elizabeth Castle, followed by a volley from a company of fusiliers, and then a further salvo and a further volley.

Outside St Helier, the buildings had changed somewhat since the beginning of the previous century. A number of farmhouses had either been built or rebuilt since the Civil War. Many if not all of them had a cider crusher and a cider press.

The town of St Aubin had grown up at the western end of St Aubin's Bay opposite St Aubin's tower. Some of the new houses had three storeys, which was unusual in the island at that time; happily a few of them still remain. The *raison d'être* for St Aubin was the pier, built at the tower between 1648 and 1700, when St Helier was virtually without one. Poingdestre described it as a "peece for Eternity". The harbour at St Aubin was built between 1754 and 1819. The foundation stone of St Aubin's Church, the first place of worship to be built in the island since the Reformation, was laid in 1735, but although completed the following year the church was not opened for services until 1749. St Brelade's Hospital was founded in 1757 by Thomas Denton (1701-70).

St Peter Port was still very small and was to remain so until the end of the century. It extended from the lower part of Hauteville on the south to the end of the Pollet on the north; the Contrée Mansell, including the Bordage and Mill Street, marked its western limits. Berthelot Street and the north side of La Rue des Forges, now called Smith Street, were also in being. High Street was very narrow, particularly at its southern end. Fountain Street was so narrow that, with the houses on either side projecting progressively with every storey, neighbours living on opposite sides were able almost to shake hands across it. An ordinance of 1st October 1683 provided that all thatched houses in the town were to be covered with slates in order to reduce the risk of fire; anyone who failed to comply was to be fined. The parish church was the only place of worship of any denomination. The principal streets were paved, but there were neither street lighting, nor paved footpaths, nor sewers. An important addition to the town was the Town Hospital, the first block of which was built in 1742. The splendid house, once the property of the Le Marchant family, which is now the constables' office, dates from about 1740.

The lawful currency of the Channel Islands was for many centuries the *livre tournois*, or pound of Tours, which was subdivided into *sols* and *deniers*. There were twelve *deniers* to the *sol* and twenty *sols* to the *livre*.

In the early years of the eighteenth century French coins known as *liards* were circulating in Jersey. One *liard* was worth three *deniers*, equivalent to four to the *sol*; in France the rate was six to the *sol*. The only coins in circulation in the island in 1720 were *liards*. Consequently the

States found it difficult, if not impossible, to repay sums of money to a number of persons who had made interest-free loans to them in connection with the harbour works. Thus it was that they resolved to issue paper money to a total value of 50,000 *livres tournois* to enable them to repay the loans, to build the harbour without cost to the island, and to perpetuate the banishment of gold and silver. In 1725 the States declared that the only coins in circulation were *deniers* and *liards*. The following year they prepared a representation to the Privy Council recommending that the number of *liards* to the *sol* be increased from four to six, resulting in one *liard* being worth two instead of three *deniers* as formerly, a devaluation of fifty per cent.

On 22nd May 1729 the Privy Council made an order approving the States' representation and which provided:

> That the French Siluer Coins should be Current in the s^d Island only according to their intrinsick value in proportion to the British Crown Piece.
>
> That the British Crown Piece should continue Current att seuenty one sols, the half Crown att thirty fiue sols and a half, the shilling att fourteen sols, and the six pence att seuen sols.
>
> That the French liards should be reduced to their old vallue of two deniers each, and that the British half penny be Current for seuen deniers, and the farthing for three & half.

However, having obtained the order for which they had asked, the States, as a result of the civil unrest caused in the island by the change in the value of *liards*, then petitioned the Privy Council to revoke the order. However, the Privy Council declined to do so and made a further order on 9th July 1730 confirming the original order and directing that it be put into immediate execution.

The insular authorities were unable to enforce the Order in Council and there were three days of serious riots of which the following contemporary account gives a vivid picture:

Saturday 29th August Some people going to pay their Rents to M^r Le Geyt, they were forced to pay at 6 a penny. Whereupon the people highly threatened & said, that rather than pay at 6 a penny, they would destroy all the Jurats: and proceeded so far as to throw stones & break the windows, & even had like to kill some of them. Upon that M^r Le Geyt goes & complains to the Lieutenant Governor, Col. Howard, and desired his protection, saying, That the people were ready to pull down his house & destroy him & his whole family. The Lt Govr answered that the fault was his own, & he was fallen into the pit which he had digged,—The mob followed M^r Le Geyt at the Governor's. To quiet them, they were told to come back again on the Monday & they should have justice done them. M^r Le Geyt swore before the Council, that it was Lt Govr Howard who bid the people come again.—Upon that they were satisfied & dispersed themselves.

Sunday 30th August   After evening Sermon, at beat of drum (it is said the drum was beat only at St Saviour's & that it was cried in the rest of the parishes) in the Churchyard of each parish, orders were given to all persons in general from 18 to 70 to repair the next day to the Town, with spades, pick-axes, forks, clubs & all other sorts of weapons, 'pour détruire les six au sou' & pull down their houses, if they would not reduce again the farthings to four a penny.

N.B. Most of them were at the Cyder-Houses from Saturday night to Monday morning; consequently drunk & mad.

Monday 31st August   According to the orders above, the People flocked into the Town from all parts & threatened that if the farthings were not brought again to 4 a penny, they would destroy all the Jurates.

On the Sunday the Jurates met in the Town to consider what was to be done in that exigency & agreed, that a Convention of the Estates should be called for the next day; which was accordingly done.

Monday morning the Estates met accordingly in the Town. But before they went into Court, they assembled at the Lt Governor's, viz: Part of the Jurates & part of the Ministers, viz: Mr de la Trinité, Mr John Pipon, Mr de Saval, Mr Patriarche, Mr Nicolas Dumaresq,—of the Clergy, M^r Le Couteur Senr & Junr & Mr Lemprière of Grouville.—Constables, Mr Commissary, M^r Ph. Le Couteur, of St Brelade, Mr Mattingley of St Clement's, Mr Anley of St Peter's: Where they agreed that it should be published that the farthings were reduced again to 4 a penny, in order to quiet the people. Before they went into the Court they published an Act declaring that the farthings were again at 5 a penny as they were before. But this not being thought sufficient, they were forced to publish two others with alterations. The people thereupon seeming to be well satisfied, dispersed for a little while. The Jurates took that opportunity to go into the Court. As soon as they were in, the mob assembled in as great a fury as ever, thinking the Jurates were going to undo again what they had done last, that is to make acts contrary to the last acts. Some forced the door open & numbers rushing in, threatened they would have the lives of all those that were for 6 a penny. Mr de Saval, the Dean, Advocat Marett & Mr John Hardy the King's Procureur, the most obnoxious, seeing the danger that threatened them, crawled under the Benches of the Court & got out at the back Door of the Court.

Mr Saval went round by the street called La Rue de derriére (King Street) to his own house, hired by the Lt Governor, & desired Miss Howard to shut the door.

The Dean went into Harper's house, who kept a Tavern behind the Court, & taking his Brother's great coat that was there, & Harper's cap, jumped out at a back window, ran up the Town Hill & made into the (Elizabeth) Castle.

Mr Advocat Marett seeing a horse which belonged to Mr Advocat des Augrès, got upon it & rid away likewise to the Castle. When he came there, the Guard refused to let him in without the Governor's order: so that a soldier was forced to ride away with the same horse & fetch an order from the Governor, Mr Marett standing all the while at the gate trembling. Some of the people saw the Dean get into Harper's House & thinking he was there, ransacked the whole house. They went likewise to a chamber he had at Mr Aire's imagining he might be there: but the bird was flown.

Mr John Hardy sheltered himself at his brother-in-law's house, Mr Richard Patriarche's.

When the mob found that the persons most obnoxious to them were thus escaped, they were so very much enraged, that a body of them went directly to pull down Mr Advocat Marett's house, which they effected in part.

To return to the rest of the gentlemen. One held a knife at M^r Le Geyt's, & offered to rip up his belly. So he went out of Court along with the Lt Governor. But Mr Dauvergne, his son-in-law, getting first out of Court, waved his whip about & said, "Mes garçons, ils sont a six au sou pour la vie". Whereupon one struck him across the legs with a stick to beat him down. But he not falling, another struck off his hat & wig, & broke his head. Upon that he took to his heels, & part of the mob after him, some flinging sticks at him: but he went through one Philip Le Fevre's house, which was opposite to his father-in-law's, M^r Le Geyt's, where he got in safe. The wife of Philip Le Fevre shut the door to, after he had come in, which so angered the Mob that they broke all the windows.

M^r Le Geyt being come out of Court along with the Governor, found himself insulted on every side, & even received one blow. And the Lt Governor, who extended his arm to save him, received likewise one. Seeing his danger he begged the Lt Governor's protection; but the Lt Govr replied that he could not protect him, but wanted protection as much as himself, & advised him to run for his life. They saw a man with a grappling iron ready to strike at him; Whereupon he mended his pace & got in safe at the Lt Governor's; where he & Mr John Pipon & Mr de Saval remained till ten at night. From thence they went to M^r Le Geyt's; & the next morning about ten o'clock to the Castle, & Mr de la Trinité & Mr Edward d'Auvergne with them; all with the Lt Gov$^{r's}$ consent; where they staid three days, till they could get a boat to carry them to Guernsey; whither M^r Le Geyt, Mr de Saval, Mr de la Trinité, Mr John Hardy, & the Dean, also went, & from thence came to England to complain.

Upon their complaint Col. Gordon's Regiment of Invalids was sent to Jersey & staid from Novemb. 29, 1729 till Febr. 28, 1731-2, being quartered upon the people in the Town, to their no small injury.

The intensity of feeling of the rioters is summed up in the answer which a Mrs Hocquard received when she asked an old woman why she was in such a passion and commented that it was quite wrong. "Wrong," said the old woman, "we will have their guts. Yes, I say, we will have them. And here is a Bag I have brought to put them in. And with their Brains which we dash out, we shall make ink to write the Acts [for four to the *sol*] upon parchment."

On 5th October 1730 a commission was granted by the King to Colonel William Hargrave appointing him Lieutenant-Governor of Jersey in replacement of Howard whom it was stated in the commission was "charged with having contrary to his duty, neglected to support, and assist the . . . Magistrates in the putting of our . . . Order in execution, and in the suppressing of the . . . Riots". On 1st October the Privy Council made a further order ordering that certain acts made by the States purporting to repeal the changes made in the value of *liards* be erased from the records of the assembly, and that the orders of 22nd May 1729 and 9th July 1730 be carried into immediate execution. The last words on the matter were contained in a letter dated 8th April 1731 sent by the Privy Council to the States, signed by Lord Carteret among others, expressing His Majesty's "high displeasure" at everything which had taken place in defiance of the Orders in Council, also that His Majesty was "well pleased with the dutyfull behaviour" of those who had acted in obedience to the orders.

As late as 1741 the States of Guernsey were faced with the problem of that island being flooded with French *liards*, and were regulating their value at thirteen for two *sols*.

The eighteenth century was a time of great expansion in Channel Islands' trade. Cod-fishing off the east coast of North America, shipping and privateering were all important, not to mention smuggling. The manufacture and export of woollen goods—principally knitted stockings —were still important, but were to decline with the coming of the Industrial Revolution to Britain.

Southampton was still the principal English port for shipping between England and the Channel Islands. In fact it was Channel Islands' trade which helped to keep the port alive during its years of decline. It was the sole port through which wool might legally be exported to the islands in accordance with the Act of Parliament of 1660. Each year the Channel Islands accounted for over 123 or approximately two-thirds of the overseas ship movements through the port. However, it should be borne in mind that the ships used in trade with the Channel Islands generally belonged to islanders and were on the whole smaller than those used in trade with more distant ports such as America, Italy, Norway, Portugal and Spain. The larger vessels engaged in the trade were between thirty and eighty tons; the smaller varied between ten and twelve tons.

At this period there were no scheduled services between Southampton

and the Channel Islands; sailings were frequent, but irregular. Shipping
was regulated much more by weather conditions than nowadays. It
followed that there were more sailings in the summer than in the winter.
The journey took anything from one to five days, and sometimes considerably longer. In time of war there was the added hazard of falling into
the hands of the enemy and ships sailed in convoy, which sometimes
caused considerable delay.

Every type of commodity was imported into the Channel Islands
through Southampton, the most important being wool of which much
more was sent to Jersey than to Guernsey. Wheat was also shipped to the
islands in fairly substantial quantities.

The principal export to the United Kingdom was knitted goods. Other
exports were cattle, horses, untanned hides, agricultural produce, cider,
oysters and rags. French and Iberian wines were also re-exported,
principally, if not exclusively, through Guernsey.

Guernsey entered the world of banking with the establishment of
Messrs Samuel Dobrée and Sons in that island at least as early as 1720,
although it is known that a banking business was carried on in London
by William Dobrée in 1721, which may have dated back to the reign of
King William and Queen Mary. Messrs Samuel Dobrée and Sons transferred their business to London in or about 1770.

It was during this period that La Maison d'Eaux-de-Vie Martell, the
famous brandy firm, was founded by Jean Martell (1694–1753), a Jerseyman, born at St Brelade of an old island family. The design of the ancient
family seal depicting three hammers (martels) and a bird is now used as
the firm's trademark; it is also to be seen in the Martell window above
the nave aisle doorway of St Brelade's Church. Martell spent seven years in
Guernsey in the counting house of Laurence Martin before establishing
himself in business in France.

Channel Islanders, like most islanders, make good seamen and many
of them have served in the Royal Navy and in the Merchant Navy. In
the former service a number of them reached the highest ranks. Among
such were Vice-Admiral Sir Charles Le Hardy (1680?–1744) and Rear-
Admiral Sir Thomas Le Hardy (1666–1732). Charles Le Hardy came of a
Jersey family, although he was born in Guernsey, where his father was
Commissioner of Garrisons. Although he saw no active service, he gained
steady promotion, ultimately becoming one of the Lords Commissioners
of the Admiralty. He was for twelve years from 1730 captain of the Royal
Yacht *Carolina*, used by King George II for travelling to and from
Hanover. Thomas Le Hardy's career was unlike Charles Le Hardy's in
that he was present at a number of naval engagements. In 1715 he was
dismissed the service for suspected Jacobitism, but was reinstated. He was
buried in Westminster Abbey where a monument (1732), by Sir Henry

Cheere, Bt, to his memory stands against the west wall on the south side of the Great West Door.

Less exalted naval officers were Philip de Sausmarez (1710–47) and his younger brother, Thomas de Sausmarez (died 1766), sons of Matthew de Sausmarez, a Guernseyman, and Anne de Sausmarez (*née* Durell), a Jerseywoman. Philip entered the navy in 1726 and reached the rank of captain in 1743. He had a distinguished career which ended in 1747 when he was killed while in command of the *Nottingham* cruising under Admiral Edward Hawke. Saumarez, as he chose to be called, was buried in St Andrew's Church, Plymouth, where there is a tablet to his memory. There is also a monument (1747) to him by Cheere in the north aisle of the choir of Westminster Abbey and he is mentioned on another in St Helier's Parish Church, Jersey.

Philip Dumaresq (died 1741), a Jerseyman, became a privateer. He emigrated to Boston, where he married Susanne Ferry in 1716. In 1739 during the War of the Austrian Succession he was given the command of the *Young Eagle*, a privateer. Michael Dumaresq was his second lieutenant and William Dumaresq was a member of the crew. Dumaresq was extremely successful as a privateer captain, so much so that the Spanish fitted out a ship to hunt him down. However, when it caught him up and there was an engagement, the Spaniard fled. Dumaresq was wounded and his ship damaged. In the spring he captured his last prize, a French ship. The following year he died.

A Channel Islander of this period who distinguished himself in the world of art was Peter Monamy (died 1749). He was a Jerseyman, although at what date or in which parish of that island he was born has never been established. Monamy is reputed to have learnt the first rudiments of drawing from a sign and house painter whose premises were situated on Old London Bridge. His work is so like that of Van der Velde the younger that it has often been mistaken for it, and he may have been a pupil of his. Numbered among Monamy's works are *The Embarkation of King Charles II of England at the Restoration, The Battle of Solebay, The Landing of William of Orange at Torbay 5th November 1688, The Taking of the* Princesa *by Captain Durell, The Capture of the* Mars *by Captain Saumarez* and *A Ship in Distress*, which depicts the loss of the *Victory* in the Race of Alderney. Two of his pictures have been reproduced on postage stamps. In 1970 the Republic of Ireland issued a 4p stamp to commemorate the one hundred and fiftieth anniversary of the foundation of the Royal Cork Yacht Club, the oldest yacht club in the world, on which was reproduced a picture showing yachts of the Club Fleet painted by Monamy in 1738. This picture is one of a pair belonging to the club which hang in the Cork Art Gallery. In 1971 Jersey issued a set of four stamps depicting the work of four of the island's artists. On the

2½p value is reproduced Monamy's *English Fleet in the Channel* from the collection of the Société Jersiaise.

Channel Islanders continued to emigrate. Tupper refers to an advertisement which appeared in Boston, Massachusetts, in 1752, which read: "To be sold, Guernsey boys and girls, for a term of time, on board the sloop *Two Brothers*." He tells how in those days children of poor families in Guernsey were told that if they were naughty they would be sent to Boston.

CHAPTER TEN

A Time of War—1760–1815

France can only attempt to seize these Islands at the outset of a war, before they have received their armament. So soon as the measures for defence are taken, the attack becomes too difficult; the expedition would cost more than it can well be worth.

General Charles François du Périer Dumouriez
(1739–1823)

King George II died in 1760 and was succeeded by his grandson George William Frederick, Prince of Wales, as King George III. The new King was to reign for sixty years, although, because of bouts of a kind of delirium, and, ultimately, blindness and senility, from 1810 until his death, his duties were to be discharged by his son George, Prince of Wales, as Prince Regent. The King's consort was Charlotte Sophia of Mecklenburg-Strelitz, whom he married in 1761. King Street and Queen Street in St Helier, Jersey, and Fort George, Guernsey, were named after them, and a portrait of the King by Philip Jean (1755–1802), the Jersey portrait painter and miniaturist, hangs in the Court Room of the Royal Court House in St Helier. The King "as a particular mark of condescension and favour, agreed to give Mr Jean one sitting to enable him to finish the picture". William Henry, Duke of Gloucester, brother of King George III, visited Guernsey in 1765. His son William Frederick, who bore the same title, visited both Jersey and Guernsey in 1817; Gloucester Street in St Helier was named after him.

In 1760 Lieutenant-General John Huske was still Governor of Jersey, as he had been since 1749. On his death in 1761 he was succeeded by Lieutenant-General the Earl of Albemarle, who held the office until 1772. Among those who were lieutenant-governor during his term mention should be made of Lieutenant-Colonel Rudolph Bentinck who played a major rôle at the time of the civil disorders of 1769 and 1770. In 1772 Albemarle was succeeded by General Henry Seymour Conway, a painting of whom by Thomas Gainsborough, R.A., hangs in the Court Room of the Royal Court House; Conway Street in St Helier was named after him. Conway was Commander-in-Chief of the British Army 1792–93 and made a field-marshal in the latter year. Among those who served as lieutenant-governor during his term was Major Moses Corbet (1728–1817), a Jerseyman, who was in command at the time of the Battle of Jersey in 1781.

Conway, who died in 1795, was succeeded in turn by Field-Marshal Sir George Howard (1795–96), Field-Marshal the Marquess Townshend (1796–1807) and the Earl of Chatham (1807–21). The outstanding lieutenant-governor of this period was Lieutenant-General George Don (1806–14), who previously had commanded in Jersey as Lieutenant-Colonel of the 59th Regiment. Don Road and Don Street in St Helier were named after him and a statue of him stands in the Parade Gardens. Sir Tomkyns Hilgrove Turner was lieutenant-governor 1814–16. He was of Jersey descent on his mother's side. He is principally remembered for the part he played in securing the Rosetta Stone, now reposing in the British Museum. His name appears on the order of release depicted in the painting called *The Order of Release* by Sir John Everett Millais in the collection of the Tate Gallery. Turner purchased Gorey Lodge close by Gorey Village to which he retired in 1835. His grandson, Sir Adolphus Hilgrove Turner (1846–1911), was Attorney General for Jersey.

John, Lord de la Warr (created Earl de la Warr in 1761) was Governor of Guernsey (1752–66). He was the last holder of the office to visit the island. He was succeeded successively by Sir Richard Littleton (1766–70), Sir Jeffrey Amherst (later Lord Amherst) (1770–97), Charles, Lord Grey de Howick, Earl Grey (1797–1807) and George, Earl of Pembroke (1807–27). Among the lieutenant-governors of this time was Lieutenant-Colonel Sir Paulus Æmilius Irving (1770–84), whom it is believed was the first person to have a carriage in Guernsey. Another to hold the office was Major-General John Small (1793–96), who features prominently in John Trumbell's painting of the Battle of Bunker's Hill in 1775. Sir Hew Dalrymple (1796–1803) was the first lieutenant-governor to live at Government House (now Old Government House Hotel), which was bought as an official residence from Nicholas Le Mesurier in 1796. Sir John Doyle (1803–16) was an active and popular lieutenant-governor and was to Guernsey what Don was to Jersey. Fort Doyle in Guernsey and Fort Doyle in Alderney were named after him and a column was erected to his honour at Jerbourg.

John Le Mesurier, the Governor of Alderney, took out a new Patent of the island in 1763 for a term of ninety-nine years and remained in office until 1791, when, through illness, he was obliged to hand over the duties of the office to his son Peter Le Mesurier (1753-1803). On the death of his father Peter succeeded to the governorship which he retained until his death, when he was succeeded by his son John Le Mesurier (1781-1843).

Nicholas Le Pelley remained Lord of Sark until his death in 1742 when he was succeeded by his brother Daniel Le Pelley. He in turn was succeeded by his son Peter Le Pelley in 1752, whose son, also called Peter, followed him in 1778.

John, Earl Granville, the Bailiff of Jersey, died in 1763 and was succeeded in that office by his son, Robert (1721-76), who in turn was succeeded at his death by his nephew Henry Frederick, Lord Carteret, second son of Lord Weymouth. Charles Lemprière (1714-1806) had been appointed lieutenant-bailiff in 1750, and was to dominate the local scene until 1781. For part of the time he was helped in maintaining his position by his brother Philip Lemprière (1718-87), who had been appointed attorney-general in 1758, and other members of his family. Charles was succeeded as lieutenant-bailiff by his second son William Charles Lemprière (1754-90), who remained in office until his death, which ended forty years of rule by the Lemprière family. Samuel Bonamy remained Bailiff of Guernsey until 1771. His successor was William Le Marchant who held office 1771-1800. He was succeeded by his son Robert Porret Le Marchant who held the office until his resignation in 1810 and was himself succeeded by Sir Peter de Havilland.

Charles Lemprière gave his name to a political party 'The Charlots', who represented the 'Establishment'. He was opposed by Jean Dumaresq (1749-1819), who gave his name to 'The Jeannots', later to be known as 'The Magots', who represented 'the People'. These political parties, renamed respectively 'Laurel' and 'Rose', existed throughout the nineteenth century, and the last traces of them lingered on into the present century.

The Lemprières were hated by a considerable part of the populace. One of their bitterest opponents was Nicholas Fiott (1704-86), a merchant who nursed a grievance against Charles and Philip Lemprière. Another Jerseyman, Charles William Le Geyt (1733-1827), who at the end of the Seven Years War in 1763 was a captain in the 63rd Regiment and was to become Jersey's first postmaster, married Elizabeth Shebbeare, eldest daughter of John Shebbeare (1709-88), a political writer, whom he introduced to Fiott. There resulted from this introduction a series of publications written by Shebbeare, all of which attacked the Lemprières in a most vitriolic way. In 1771 there appeared *The Oppressions of the Islanders of Jersey* to be followed by *Six letters to Philip Le Hardy, An Effectual Remedy to the Complaints of the Islanders of Jersey* and *Tyranny of the Magistrates of Jersey and the Enslavement of the People*, all published in 1772. One sentence out of these four works may be taken as the theme for them all: "The world shall perish before a Lemprière shall perform a deed of goodness".

On 28th September 1769 the proceedings of the Royal Court were interrupted by armed rioters who compelled the court to pass six acts purporting to annul certain Orders in Council and for other purposes. Charles Lemprière, the lieutenant-bailiff and Philip Lemprière, the attorney-general, among others, were obliged for their safety to take refuge in Elizabeth Castle. This was the culmination of unrest which had been simmering in Jersey for some years. The people's principal grievances were summarized under thirty articles at the end of *Griefs de l'Isle de Jersey contenus dans une Requeste présentée à Sa Majesté* by Moses Corbet (later to be lieutenant-governor of the island) published in London in 1770. The first article demanded that the export of corn be forbidden, the following three articles, like the first, related to the preservation of food supplies. These demands were inspired by a fear of starvation among the population brought about by the passing of an act of the States on 29th August 1769 recalling an act of 21st April 1768 forbidding the export of corn from the island. A ship was loaded with corn for France, but was forcibly unloaded by women of the island protected by their menfolk, and the corn distributed among the people. Other articles covered a wide variety of matters, the most important of which demanded that the court be denied the power to tax rents above the market price, that the price of the Crown rents be taxed and not left to the whim of the receiver, that no member or officer of the court hold either the office of Receiver or be farmer of the royal revenues, and that there be a code of laws.

A series of orders were made by the Privy Council on 27th October 1769 following reports of the riots which had taken place in Jersey. The first order required the bailiff and jurats to erase the six acts which had been made under compulsion by the rioters; the second offered the royal pardon to any rioter who brought about the arrest of any other rioter, and a reward of £100 to any person not being a rioter who would do likewise, the third ordered five companies of the 1st Regiment of Foot to be sent to Jersey immediately to assist the insular authorities, who were to be responsible for their quartering.

On 15th June 1770 Lieutenant-Colonel Rudolph Bentinck who had been sent to Jersey with the five companies of infantry was sworn in as deputy-governor. On 7th July he was sworn in as commander-in-chief and lieutenant-governor in virtue of a royal commission which charged him to investigate the troubles there had been in the island and report to the Privy Council. He was also charged to select:

. . . a proper Collection of the most useful & necessary Political Laws and Customs of this Island, out of that immense Chaos of them, which are now found confusedly scattered through the many Books of the States of all the different Courts and even in the most Ancient Records of the Island, in Order that such a Collection having been examined and considered by such persons of Learning and Judgement as His Majesty shall be pleased to appoint, may receive the Royal assent and Confirmation; So as for the future with the addition of any regulations, which from the circumstances of the times shall be found requisite to be added to it (being also first approved of by His Majesty in Council) to be established by way of a permanent System for the Political government of this Country; after which this Code of Laws (with any provisional Political regulations, you may find requisite to establish upon different exigencies, being besides this Code of Law severally and particularly mentioned at your Courts of Heritage) may only be hereafter renewed instead of all those Political Laws and Ordinances indiscriminately, tho' never so obsolete, contradictory, and inconsistant with the ways of thinking in the present age, as is now practised here three times a year at those Courts of Heritage, and that all former Political Orders and regulations not inserted in the present Collection, save also such provisional Political regulations as above mentioned, may be then no longer in force in this Island, By which means every individual will be able to know how to regulate his Conduct conformable to the Laws of his Country and be no more obliged to live in a continual dread of becoming liable to punishments, for disobeying Laws it was morally impossible for them to have the least knowledge of.

Thomas Pipon (1736–1801) was charged with the task of making the compilation which was to be entitled *A Code of Laws for the Island of Jersey*. The *Code* was presented by the lieutenant-governor to the States on 6th September 1770. It was approved by the assembly and sent to the Privy Council for the royal assent. Pipon appeared before the council as deputy of the States to explain the code. The royal assent was given by Order in Council of 28th March 1771 and at last Jersey had its first written code of laws. The order is important as it recognized the States Assembly as the sole legislative body within the island and the Royal Court was deprived of the power to make ordinances as it had done in the past. Pipon was rewarded for his work by being appointed attorney-general in place of Philip Lemprière who by this time had had his fill of abuse and vilification and resigned the office. Lemprière retired to Woodbury, Devon, where there is a memorial to him in the parish church.

It is not known where the *Code* was printed. It could have been in Jersey for printing was introduced into the island at least as early as 1765 and into Guernsey in 1776. To start with the printers confined themselves to the production of miscellaneous publications as well as jobbing printing. It was not until 1784 that the first newspaper to be printed in Jersey

Le Magasin de l'Ile de Jersey made its appearance, and seven more years were to elapse before the start of the first Guernsey newspaper *La Gazette*. *Le Magasin* was short-lived, only lasting until 1785. However, a new paper *La Gazette de l'Ile de Jersey* was started in 1786 and lasted until 1797. It then continued under different ownership and with its name twice changed until 1814. Another newspaper called *La Gazette de l'Ile de Jersey* made its appearance in 1799 and continued until 1835. In Guernsey *La Gazette* was more fortunate and survived until 1936. When it ceased publication it was the oldest French language newspaper outside France.

In Jersey *Le Magasin* and its successor *La Gazette* were both Magot newspapers. It was because of a virulent attack on the Lemprières in the tenth issue of the former that that newspaper ceased publication.

This was indeed an age of war for between 1760 and 1815 Great Britain was at war for a total of thirty-six years, and if account is taken of the fact that during that time two wars, the Second American War and the Second French War, were being carried on concurrently for two years, the total may be increased to thirty-eight years. Throughout these hostilities the Channel Islands were much affected, not only because they formed part of the British nation and shared its destiny, but also because during the French Wars, being geographically so close to France, they were vulnerable to attack, their shipping was liable to be captured or sunk and their trade to be disrupted.

It is therefore not surprising that in the late eighteenth century and early nineteenth century, from about 1780 to 1814, a considerable number of fortifications were built in the Channel Islands, many of which still survive. These defences varied from modest towers (often wrongly described as martello towers although they much resembled them) to vast fortifications, like Fort Regent in Jersey, built 1806–14, and Fort George in Guernsey, built 1782–1812. With the timing all too common-place with 'government' Fort Regent was completed when the need for it had gone, and over a century and a quarter was to elapse before it fired a gun in anger.

When Don was Lieutenant-Governor of Jersey and Doyle was holding a similar office in Guernsey, a number of roads were constructed in both islands for military purposes as the existing roads which had remained unchanged since time immemorial were totally unsuitable for the rapid movement of troops and artillery.

In 1780 the Royal Court of Guernsey passed an ordinance requiring militiamen to wear uniforms—red coats with ornamental facings and collars and white stockings. Those who were able to afford it were to provide their own uniforms; those who were unable to do so were to be provided with uniforms by their respective parishes. The same year the militia was divided into four infantry regiments—the First or East Regiment drawn from the parish of St Peter Port; the Second or North Regiment drawn from Castel, St Sampson's and the Vale; the Third or South Regiment drawn from the Forest, St Andrew's and St Martin's; the Fourth or West Regiment drawn from St Peter-in-the-Wood, St Saviour's and Torteval—and the Regiment of Field Artillery. The first Regiment's facings were white; the Second's green; the Third's blue and the Fourth's black. The ordinance brought vigorous opposition, but the Royal Court refused to repeal it. A strongly supported petition against the ordinance was then sent to the Privy Council, but no ruling was given. Ultimately the difficulty was resolved by the King making a gift of uniforms and accoutrements to the militia.

In 1777 Peter Le Mesurier reorganized the Alderney Militia which hitherto had been an ill-disciplined force without officers, arms or uniforms. During the Napoleonic Wars the Sark Militia was re-equipped and all able-bodied men were enrolled for service.

The French considered from time to time the possibility of capturing the Channel Islands. On 1st May 1779 there was an attempted invasion of Jersey by the French under the Prince of Nassau, but it was not pressed home and no landing was effected. Less than two years later, on 6th January 1781, the French made their last attempt to capture the island. An expedition under Philippe Charles Félix Macquart, Baron de Rullecourt, soldier of fortune, landed at La Rocque by night. Two actions were fought, one at Platte Rocque, where the invaders were opposed by a party from the 83rd Regiment, and one in St Helier. The lieutenant-governor, Moses Corbet, was caught in bed by the invaders at his home, Le Manoir de la Motte, and believing them masters of the island signed a capitulation. Major Francis Peirson, the senior officer under Corbet, disobeyed the order to surrender and led the 95th and 78th Regiments, assisted by the militia, against the French, who were defeated. Both Peirson and de Rullecourt were killed. Peirson was buried in the Parish Church of St Helier on 10th January. His death at the moment of victory has been immortalized in the magnificent painting *The Death of Major Peirson* by John Singleton Copley, R.A., in the collection of the Tate Gallery, London.

Corbet was arrested on 25th January and tried by court martial held from the 1st to 5th May at the Horse Guards, Whitehall, London, the charges being:

That Moses Corbet, Esq; being Lieutenant Governor of the Island of Jersey, and by virtue of his commission as such, having, in the absence of the Governor, the command of the forces stationed there, for the defence of the said island, was, on the 6th day of January last, surprized and taken prisoner by a body of French troops, who landed in the island early in the morning of the said day; and that the said Moses Corbet, on the same day, soon after his being taken prisoner, did, contrary to his duty, and the trust reposed in him, take upon himself to agree upon and to sign, with the Baron de Rullecourt, commander of the said French troops articles of capitulation, whereby it was stipulated, that the militia should be disarmed, that Elizabeth castle, and all the other forts and castles of the island, should be evacuted, and that his Majesty's troops should be withdrawn from the island, although the enemy had become masters only of the town of St Hillier, and of one or two posts near the place where their landing had been made; and the said Elizabeth castle, as well as the other forts and castles, were still possessed by and in custody of his Majesty's troops; and further, that he the said Moses Corbet, on the said 6th day of January, soon after he had signed such articles of capitulation as aforesaid, did, as well verbally as by writing, endeavoured to induce others, and particularly the officer on whom the command had, by the Lieutenant Governor being made prisoner, devolved, and also the officer or officers who had then the command of the garrison of Elizabeth castle, to submit to the said articles of capitulation, and thereby shamefully to abandon and deliver up to the said French commander the said island of Jersey, and the several forts and ports committed to their respective charge.

Corbet admitted that he had been taken prisoner by surprise and had signed articles of capitulation and orders to the troops.

The court decided against Corbet and ordered that he be superseded in his commission of lieutenant-governor. The blow was softened somewhat by the grant of a pension of £250 a year.

A curious incident occurred in Guernsey on 24th March 1783, when a mutiny broke out in the 104th Regiment quartered at Fort George. The trouble seems to have been sparked off by the arrival from Portsmouth of some discharged men from the 83rd Regiment. Six days earlier the officers and men demanded that the gates of the fort remain open so as to allow them to go and come at their pleasure. Irving, the lieutenant-governor, gave way to this demand, but by doing so he did not pacify the mutineers for long. Early in the evening of the 24th the soldiery started firing on their officers and thus compelled them to withdraw from the fort. Directly what had happened became generally known, the lieutenant-governor, supported by the 18th Regiment, the militia artillery and the town regiment marched to Fort George, and the mutineers surrendered when they saw the strength weighed against them.

Methodism was introduced into the Channel Islands in 1784, although it took some years to become firmly established. Its adherents underwent a period of trial during the early years of the movement from which they emerged triumphant. Methodists were to play a considerable part in the affairs of the islands, and even today they have a strong influence, particularly in Guernsey. Among those associated with the early days of Methodism in the islands are Robert Carr Brackenbury, John de Quetteville and Adam Clarke. John Wesley gave a great boost to the movement by his visit to Jersey, Guernsey and Alderney in 1787. The matter of militia drill on Sundays became a sore point with the Methodists, and those who refused to attend met with the displeasure of the authorities in both bailiwicks. However, largely through the influence of William Wilberforce, they were eventually successful in their opposition and were permitted to drill on weekdays instead of Sundays.

The French Revolution began in 1789. It was the most momentous occurrence in Europe since the Reformation. The latter had freed part of Europe from the domination of the Church; the former freed the French people from the domination of a hereditary ruling class and from the considerable influence and power which the Roman Catholic Church retained in their country. The slogan *Liberté, Egalité, Fraternité* was to be a resounding battle cry for the revolutionaries of Europe in the years ahead.

As they had been in the past, the Channel Islands, and on this occasion Jersey in particular, were places of refuge for Royalists, both laymen and clergy, fleeing from the terrors of the Revolution. They fled to Jersey not only in hundreds but in thousands; as early as May 1791 they numbered 400 and by 1793 there were 4,007 aliens, mostly French refugees, living in the island, which was equivalent to one-fifth of the local population. The Royalist laymen included persons of every rank from the highest to the lowest; similarly the ranks of the clergy included bishops, Church dignitaries and many parish priests.

Most of the refugees were in straitened circumstances. Some travelled to England and others remained in Jersey. The first boatloads of clergy arrived on 16th and 17th September 1792. They and those who were to follow were principally from the Norman Dioceses of Bayeux, Coutances and Mans, and the Breton Dioceses of Dol, Rennes, St Brieuc, St Malo and Tréguier, but others came from as far afield as the Dioceses of Paris, Bordeaux, Poitiers and Tours. Among them were the bishops of Bayeux and Tréguier. The lay refugees wore a white cockade in their hats; the clerical refugees wore white ribbons through two buttonholes of their coats.

Initially the refugees were well received, but as time went by the native population regarded them with some suspicion. It must be remembered that the French were the hereditary enemies of the Channel Islanders over many centuries; they were also principally Roman Catholic while the islanders were resolutely Protestant. Furthermore, the influx of so many people put a strain on the supply of food and forced up prices. On 12th September 1792 the French National Assembly passed a decree forbidding the export of cattle and provisions to the Channel Islands, which cut off what was an important source of supply in time of peace. The refugees also started arming themselves which gave both the authorities and the inhabitants at large some cause for concern.

On 21st January 1793 King Louis XVI of France, having been tried and condemned as Citizen Capet, was guillotined. François René Vicomte de Chateaubriand tells in his memoirs how, when living as a refugee in Jersey in the house of his uncle, Marie Antoine Bénigne de Bedée, one morning late in January his uncle entered his room dressed in deep mourning and told him of the King's death. M de Bedée's house was in La Rue des Mielles, now Parade Place, St Helier.

As a direct result of the influx of French Royalist refugees Roman Catholicism returned to the Channel Islands. Five oratories were established in Jersey: de Saint Malo (ceased 1801), St Louis or du Port (ceased 1801), des Saints Anges (ceased 1803) and du Sacré Coeur (ceased 1801), and Saint Pierre at St Aubin with possibly another at Gorey. All these oratories served the refugees and it was not until 1803 that a permanent chapel, dedicated to St Louis, was opened in Castle Street, St Helier. It was closed in 1842 and replaced by St Thomas', New Street, St Helier, now incorporated in The Playhouse, which itself has ceased to be a theatre.

It is appropriate at this point to mention Matthew de Gruchy (1761–97), a Jerseyman, who while prisoner in France had turned Roman Catholic and become a priest. He returned to live in Jersey in 1792. He was trained at the seminary at Luçon, being ordained sub-deacon in 1787 and priest in 1788. He obtained a commission from the Bishop of Tréguier as Vicar-General in Jersey for the Bishop of Coutances to receive the recantations of heretics and schismatics in the island. His zeal to obtain converts caused him to earn the indignation of the local people and he ran into difficulties with the authorities. The limit was reached when, as a consequence of de Gruchy's activities, the Bishop of Tréguier was summoned before the Royal Court. As a result de Gruchy left the island and went to England where he became Chaplain at Southampton to the Irish soldiers in hospital there. Ultimately he returned to France in the Royalist interest and was arrested at Nantes and condemned to death. He was executed by a firing squad between 11 am and midday on 28th November 1797. He knelt down in front of the firing squad. After the first discharge he rose up saying that they had not killed him. He was commanded to kneel down again and he obeyed without hesitation. He was not killed at the second discharge and a gun was put to his head and fired. De Gruchy was dead, a martyr to his religion, a victim of bloody revolution.

In 1794 the Committee of Public Safety in France ordered the invasion of the Channel Islands between 19th and 28th February. The attack was to be carried out on a large scale involving 20,000 infantry, 200 to 300 cavalry and 200 artillery, all of whom were to assemble at St Malo. As late as 19th February General Rossignol wrote to the Minister of War, with a postscript dated the following day, in which he stated that he would be ready to embark on 22nd or 23rd February. For some unknown reason the attack never materialized. Perhaps at the last moment the French realized that their countryman General Dumouriez was right and that such an expedition would cost more than it would be worth.

The Quiberon Expeditions were despatched to France in 1795. They were intended to support the Royalist guerillas in La Vendée and Brittany. Some 3,600 *émigrés* and released French prisoners escorted by a British naval squadron landed at Quiberon on the 27th June. The members of the expedition were joined by a large number of Royalists known as *Chouans*. Divided leadership, timidity and treachery ensured defeat by General Lazare Hoche. On 19th July it was all over. The French republican forces took 6,000 prisoners, including 1,000 *émigrés*, of whom between 700 and 800 were shot. Some 1,800 were re-embarked and made their escape. A further expedition in September also proved a fiasco.

An Act of Parliament established post offices in both Jersey and Guernsey in 1794. Before then there were no regular British post offices in the Channel Islands. Letters were entrusted to the care of travellers or to the captains of ships and were deposited for collection and despatch at coffee houses, with merchants and others. Jersey's first postmaster was Captain Charles William Le Geyt, who was appointed in 1794 and held the position until 1815, when at the age of eighty-two years he retired in favour of his son, George William Le Geyt. The first postmaster in Guernsey was in fact a postmistress, Mrs Ann Watson, who was also appointed in 1794. She was a relative of Paul Le Mesurier, Lord Mayor of London. Like Le Geyt she was succeeded by her son, Nicholas Watson. A post office was established in Alderney in 1843, in Sark in 1857 and in Herm in 1925.

A result of the Channel Islands being incorporated in the British postal system was the establishment of a regular service of packet steamers between Weymouth and the islands. The following notice appeared in *The London Gazette*.

General Post Office
February 3, 1794

Notice is hereby given, that a Packet will sail every Thursday from Weymouth for the Islands of Guernsey and Jersey, and a Mail with the Letters for these Islands will be made and sent from this Office every Wednesday Night. The First Mail is to sail if possible on Thursday the 6th Instant.

The Course the Packet will take, and the Times of her Stay and Return, will be in general, and, unless in Cases of particular and occasional Orders to the contrary, the same as in the last War, namely, to sail to Guernsey, and drop her Letters there, to proceed immediately to Jersey, there to deliver her Letters, and to stay Three Days for the Answers, then to return to Guernsey, deliver her Letters, stay there Two Days, and return to Weymouth.

By Command of the Postmaster General. Anth. Todd, Sec.

In 1799 a combined force of British and Russian troops landed in Holland hoping to cause a diversion and draw troops away from Austria which was under pressure from the common enemy the French. Unfortunately, owing to the incompetence of the Duke of York, who was commander-in-chief of the allied force, the expedition proved a complete failure and ended in capitulation at Alkmaar. The allied troops were evacuated, but the Russians were unable to return home because all the Baltic ports were frozen up. It was not possible for them to winter in England because of a clause in the Bill of Rights (1684) which forbade foreign troops to land in England. At first the possibility of sending the Russians to Ireland was considered, but when this was dropped because of the opposition of Charles, Lord Cornwallis, the lord lieutenant, it was decided to send them to Jersey and Guernsey, which was done. They stayed in various barracks, some of them makeshift. Some of the Russians died during their stay and were buried in special cemeteries.

Peace with France came in 1802 with the Treaty of Amiens; but it did not last for long and hostilities were resumed later the same year.

On 21st October 1805 the British fleet under the command of Vice-Admiral Lord Nelson won the Battle of Trafalgar and Great Britain became the undisputed mistress of the seas. It is known that one Jerseyman and one Guernseyman served on board Nelson's flagship H.M.S. *Victory* during the battle; it is possible that other Channel Islanders were also present at the engagement. Great was the rejoicing in the islands and throughout Great Britain when the news of the battle become known. The victory meant that the Channel Islands' sea communications were no longer subject to sudden and violent disruptions resulting from the activities of the French navy and privateers.

Napoleon's defeat at sea had been decisive, but ten years were to elapse before his final defeat on land at the memorable Battle of Waterloo.

Ferdinand Brock Tupper in a footnote in his excellent work *The History of Guernsey and its Bailiwick* gave his account of how the news of the battle reached Guernsey, which reads:

I well remember seeing the packet from Weymouth—in 1815 a sailing cutter—as she appeared about noon at the head of the Small Russell, covered

(*above*) View of Herm from the sea, from a nineteenth-century lithograph

(*below*) The brig *Patruus* (206 tons) belonging to Robin & Co. of Jersey, during a squall, 24th October 1844

The Queen's visit to Jersey, 2nd September 1846: the royal
procession in Vine Street, St Helier—from a lithograph after
P. J. Ouless published in 1847

(*above*) The Jersey Races, 25th July 1849—from a lithograph after
P. J. Ouless

(*below*) The Prison, Sark—1856

with flags and firing guns, so that it was evident that she brought the news of some important victory. The wind and tide being adverse, a fast rowing boat was dispatched from the pier, which was crowded with anxious spectators, and in an hour or so the boat returned with the glad tidings of the Battle of Waterloo.

The brilliant dictator who had tyrannized over Europe was at last defeated and would soon be in exile. The "nation of shopkeepers" and her allies had triumphed; the weary wars with France were over and peace had come at last.

Work, coupled with service in the honorary system and the militia, and churchgoing occupied most of the waking hours of the male population; the female population was almost totally committed to child-bearing, domestic chores, other work of various kinds and, of course, to churchgoing. Entertainments were not for them. Such amusements as there were were of a homely type and public entertainment was virtually unknown until the arrival of the theatre and the Assemblies. These new-found forms of diversion were patronized by the local gentry, the English gentry and the officers of the garrison and their ladies, but found little support among the native islanders of the middle and lower orders until well into the nineteenth century. Plays were certainly being performed in Jersey as early as 1778, because in November of that year the States passed an act requiring that all theatrical performances should be licensed by the chief magistrate, hence the words "By permission of the Bailiff" which still sometimes appear at the head of advertisements announcing plays or other theatrical performances and on theatre programmes. Little is known of the early years of the local theatre, but the titles of some of the plays performed in the late eighteenth century are known. *The School for Scandal* by Richard Brinsley Sheridan and *Richard III* by William Shakespeare were among the plays performed during 1792, the list for 1793 included *Romeo and Juliet*, *Macbeth* and *Henry IV*, all by Shakespeare and *The Beggars Opera* by John Gay.

In 1802 James Shatford opened Jersey's first permanent theatre, the Theatre Royal at what is now known as Regent Road, St Helier. Plays were also being performed in Guernsey. In 1788 *The School for Scandal* was performed in St Peter Port and resulted in a riot, an incident referred to in the *Diary* of Elisha Dobrée. A theatre was built in Manor Street about 1793 or 1794.

In the winter of 1782 subscription assembly rooms were opened in Guernsey. The original subscribers and their families together with the naval and army officers stationed in the island were dubbed the 'Sixties'; those with newly acquired wealth and who aspired to social position but who were not of the 'Sixties' were dubbed the 'Forties' and excluded from the rooms. As a result of this, great bitterness was engendered similar to that which existed between the supporters of the Laurel and Rose political parties in Jersey in the following century. Some of the rules observed in the Assembly Rooms at St Peter Port, now part of the Guille-Allès Library, were worthy of Beau Nash, the uncrowned King of Bath and make amusing reading:

RULES OF THE PRIVATE ASSEMBLIES

1st. The Assemblies to take place every Tuesday (now altered to every other Tuesday) during the season; to open at seven, and to close at half-past eleven. The drawing of tickets to commence at half-past seven, the first numbers to be drawn by the ladies present, the remaining numbers to be drawn indiscriminately as the ladies come in.

2nd. No exchange of numbers permitted. Ladies losing tickets, stand at the bottom; if more than one, they draw for places.

3rd. As soon as drawing has taken place, dancing to commence with a quadrille, not exceding five figures, which, with an English country dance, compose one set.

4th. Ladies sitting down during a dance, to stand at the bottom during the remainder of the evening.

5th. Officers in uniform are admitted in boots, but must not dance in spurs.

7th. No native inhabitants, whose parents have not previously subscribed, to be admitted, unless proposed by the Master of the Ceremonies, and approved of by two-thirds of the ladies and gentlemen subscribers present. None but native inhabitants entitled to vote.

9th. Every native inhabitant subscriber is liable to serve the office of Master of the Ceremonies, or find a deputy, under the penalty of 10s. 6d.

Not all Channel Islanders stayed at home. Many continued to leave their native shores as they had done in years gone by and in ever increasing numbers would continue to do in the years ahead. More islanders than ever before were making names for themselves in many ways and in many lands.

Five Channel Islanders who reached the height of their naval careers in the latter part of the eighteenth century and the first half of the nineteenth century and who stood out from their compatriots were Sir Charles Le Hardy, Junior (about 1716–80), Philip de Carteret (1733–96), Philip d'Auvergne, Duke of Bouillon (1754–1816), James, Lord de Saumarez (1757–1836) and Thomas Le Marchant Gosselin (1765–1857).

Sir Charles Le Hardy was the son of Sir Charles Le Hardy, Senior. In 1731 he entered the Royal Navy. In 1737 he was promoted lieutenant and in 1741 captain. Three years later he commanded the *Jersey*, the fourth vessel to bear that name, the second and third being launched in 1694 and 1698 respectively. In 1755 Le Hardy was knighted and appointed Governor of New York. Two years later he was appointed Rear-Admiral of the

Blue. The same year he was ordered to escort the transports that were to attack Louisburg. In 1758 he was promoted Rear-Admiral of the White and ordered to prepare for a second attack on Louisburg. During this second attack Le Hardy's flagship sank four French men-of-war. The next year as Vice-Admiral of the Blue he was second in command of the Channel Fleet and for three years his squadron helped to blockade Brest. Ultimately, Le Hardy was made Commander-in-Chief of the Channel Fleet. He was Member of Parliament for Rochester 1764–68 and for Plymouth 1771–80.

Philip de Carteret, known as Philip Carteret, was the youngest son of Charles de Carteret, Lord of the Manor of Trinity and Frances Marie de Carteret (*née* St Paul). He entered the Royal Navy in 1757. Four years later on the death of his elder brother, Francis, he inherited Trinity Manor in Jersey. While he was away at sea his sister Anne looked after the property for him. In 1764 he was first lieutenant of the ship *Tamar*, one of the squadron sent by the Admiralty to carry out exploration in the South Pacific. On the outward voyage the expedition annexed the Falkland Islands for Britain. After the squadron passed through the Strait of Magellan Carteret was moved from the *Tamar* to the *Dolphin*. It was a fruitless voyage as the commander did not possess the attributes of an explorer. The squadron arrived home in 1766 having achieved nothing.

The first expedition having proved unsuccessful, the Admiralty sent a second. Captain Samuel Wallis was given command of the *Dolphin* and Carteret, now a commander, was given command of the *Swallow*. The two ships together with a supply ship, the *Prince Frederick* left England in August 1766 and arrived in the Strait of Magellan in December, where in January Carteret wrote an account of the Patagonians.

The *Swallow* proved herself a poor ship and when the three vessels left the Strait of Magellan she was soon left behind and never caught up again. On 2nd July 1767 Carteret discovered Pitcairn Island. This was the first of many discoveries which he made as he proceeded on his way to the Philippines and the Dutch East Indies. On 28th November 1768 Carteret reached the Cape and on 20th March 1769 he dropped anchor at Spithead. In 1770 he returned to Jersey and resumed residence at Trinity Manor. It was the time when the island was in a state of revolt. Carteret supported the anti-Lemprière rebels and gave a dinner party to their leaders to which he invited Colonel Bentinck.

The American War of Independence and the war with France brought Carteret back into active service. He finally retired in 1794 with the rank of rear-admiral, although for a number of years previous the Admiralty had denied him a command. He settled in Southampton, where he died and was buried in All Saints' Church, which was destroyed during World War II.

D'Auvergne was the youngest son of Charles d'Auvergne. In 1770 he was gazetted to the Royal Yacht and two years later was made a midshipman. With the other officers of his ship he was presented to the Empress Catherine of Russia while on a cruise in the Baltic and was offered a post in her service, which he declined. In 1773 he was transferred to the *Racehorse*, one of two ships being sent by the Admiralty to find the North Pole. During the voyage he kept the astronomical observations and the meteorological register, drew the charts and made the sketches, published in Captain Phipps' *Voyage towards the North Pole*. He later served as first lieutenant on the 'saucy' *Arethusa*, the exploits of which became famous. In March 1779 the ship was wrecked and d'Auvergne was taken prisoner.

At this point it is necessary to digress and to mention that at this time there existed on the continent of Europe in the Belgian Ardennes, just over the French border, the tiny independent Principality of Bouillon, eighteen miles long and fifteen miles wide. This small state was ruled over by His Serene Highness Godefroi Charles Henri de la Tour d'Auvergne, Duke of Bouillon, whose only legitimate son Jacques Leopold was scarcely capable of succeeding him. The duke did not want to be succeeded by cousins whom he heartily disliked and had consequently decided upon adopting a son. Just when his choice was about to be made he heard of a young Jerseyman Philip d'Auvergne who had been taken prisoner by the French. The duke obtained d'Auvergne's release on parole and invited him to his castle at Navarre. He was impressed by d'Auvergne and ordered researches to be made to ascertain whether there was any connection between the ducal house and the Jersey family of d'Auvergne. In due course the duke was satisfied that Philip d'Auvergne's family was connected with his own and he decided to adopt the young Jerseyman as his heir. In 1783 peace was declared and Philip attended Dorpat University and became a Doctor of Law in 1785; the following year he was elected a Fellow of the Royal Society. He also paid long visits to the Duke at Navarre. In August 1786 the duke officially recognized Philip's family as his cousins. The following year Major-General James d'Auvergne (1726–99) and his brother Charles d'Auvergne, Philip's father, obtained for themselves and their descendants a grant from the College of Arms exemplifying and confirming to them the Family Armorial Ensigns of the Duke of Bouillon. In 1791 the Duchy's General Assembly petitioned the duke to decide as to which branch of his house he intended to convey the sovereignty should his son die without issue. On 25th June 1792 the duke replied to the petition declaring his adopted son Philip his heir should his son die without issue and his son ratified his father's decision. On 4th August the General Assembly took an oath of loyalty to Philip as Prince Successor and ordered a Te Deum to be sung and bonfires to be lit in every village. On the same day the duke presented

Philip as his heir to his tenants and retainers. Philip was girded with the jewelled sword of Marshal Turenne and all the officials of the duchy knelt and kissed his hand. On 27th February 1792 King George III granted his royal licence and permission to Philip to accept and enjoy his nomination and succession to the sovereignty of the Duchy of Bouillon and to unite the arms of the duchy to his own provided that the relative documents were recorded in the College of Arms. The French Revolution began to make itself felt in the duchy. The reigning duke threw in his lot with the Sansculottes, called himself the Citizen Prince and even invited the National Guard to dinner. The duke died on 3rd December 1792 and was succeeded by his son. In the following February England was once more at war with France and Philip d'Auvergne was again on duty.

D'Auvergne was given command of the Jersey Naval Station with headquarters at Mont Orgueil Castle, where he commanded until 1812. He was charged with four definite tasks: the security of the islands, the maintenance of communications with Royalists in Western France, the obtaining of information about enemy movements, and the distribution of British government relief among French refugees in the island. D'Auvergne organized La Correspondance, a secret service composed of a hotchpotch of men and women of all types—aristocrats, priests, smugglers, heroes and villains—who wore no uniform and who went to and fro between Jersey and France giving succour to the Chouans, the Royalist guerilla bands in Maine, Brittany and Normandy who had taken up arms against the First Republic, and returning with intelligence for the British Government. They travelled like purposeful shadows moving stealthily on dark nights, often travelling long distances and sometimes having to carry their despatches in their teeth when they swam a river. Death was constantly at their heels. Arms and ammunition were smuggled from Britain to France via Jersey. D'Auvergne also provided a channel for funnelling forged assignats into France with a view to undermining the economy. The French retaliated through their own counter-espionage service.

D'Auvergne enjoyed steady promotion ending in him becoming Vice-Admiral of the Red in 1814. He was also Knight of the Prussian Order of St John of Jerusalem and a Grand Commander of the Equestrian Order of St Joachim.

James, Baron de Saumarez, was born in St Peter Port in 1757. He entered the Royal Navy and in 1776 was lieutenant in Victory, the Channel flagship. He was at the Battle of St Vincent in 1797 and the Battle of the Nile in 1798. He was created a baronet and promoted Rear-Admiral of the Blue in 1801. He commanded the Channel Islands' naval station based on Guernsey 1803-07. He was promoted vice-admiral and appointed second in command of a fleet off Brest in 1807. He commanded a squadron in the Baltic 1808-13. His promotions continued and he achieved the rank of Vice-Admiral of the United Kingdom in 1821. He was Commander-in-Chief at Plymouth 1824–27. He was created a peer of the United Kingdom in 1831 with the title Baron de Saumarez of Saumarez in the Island of Guernsey and made a General of Marines in 1832.

In June 1794 Saumarez, then Captain Sir James de Saumarez, Bt, was at Plymouth when he was ordered to proceed with his squadron of three ships to Guernsey and Jersey to discover the French naval strength at St Malo and Cancale Bay. A few days prior to sailing de Saumarez met John Breton and discovering that he was awaiting a passage to Guernsey offered to take him across. A day after setting sail the British squadron encountered a considerably superior French force some miles north-north-west of Guernsey, and, as it was impossible to engage the enemy at such a numerical disadvantage, de Saumarez wished to withdraw his own ships to safety. He first covered the escape of the *Eurydice* and the *Druid* to Guernsey and then made as though to ram his own ship, the *Crescent*, on to the rocks. In fact he was relying on Breton to pilot the vessel through the dangerous rocks by a passage never before negotiated by a ship of that size. Those who watched from the Guernsey shore did so anxiously for they thought that the *Crescent* would inevitably strike the rocks, not knowing that such a skilful pilot was aboard. The hazardous manœuvre was successfully accomplished, and the *Crescent* and her gallant commander and crew were soon safely out of the enemy's reach. At the most dangerous moment of the exploit de Saumarez asked Breton if he was sure of his marks, to which he received the now famous reply, "Quite sure, for there is your house and yonder is my own!" For his services on this occasion Small, the lieutenant-governor, presented Breton with a medal.

General Sir Thomas Saumarez (1760–1845) was Lord de Saumarez's younger brother. In 1812 he was commandant of the garrison at Halifax, Nova Scotia; and in 1813 was President of the Council and Commander-in-Chief of New Brunswick. At the coronation of Queen Victoria in 1837 as senior lieutenant-general he was advanced to the rank of general. Another brother, Richard (1764–1835), was a surgeon and writer on medical education. One of Lord de Saumarez's uncles was Philip de Saumarez to whom reference has already been made. Another uncle Thomas Saumarez (died 1766) was also a captain in the Royal Navy.

Thomas Le Marchant Gosselin (1765–1857) was another Guernseyman who attained distinction in the Royal Navy, which he entered in 1778. The following year he was captured in the *Ardent* off Plymouth. In 1799 he assisted at the reduction of Surinam and in 1808, with Sir Harry Burrard and other general officers as his guests, convoyed a large body of troops to Portugal, and, after their disembarkation at Maceira, proceeded to the River Tagus. The following year Gosselin covered the embarkation at Corunna for which service he received the thanks of both Houses of

Parliament. In 1825 Gosselin was made a vice-admiral and in 1841 he was promoted admiral.

Sir Harry Burrard, Bt, (1755–1813) was the son of George Burrard and Magdelaine Anne Burrard (*née* Durell). He was born at Vinchelez de Haut Manor, Jersey. He joined the Coldstream Guards in 1772, but in 1777 exchanged into the 60th Regiment and saw service in the American War. He became Member of Parliament for Lymington in 1780, which constituency he represented until 1806. He returned to America in 1781 and became a captain in the Grenadier Guards in 1786 and, finally, a lieutenant-general in 1805. He received a vote of thanks from the House of Lords in 1807 for services rendered in the raid on Copenhagen made that year; he was also created a baronet and made Governor of Calshott Castle.

Sir Hew Dalrymple, a former Lieutenant-Governor of Guernsey, with Burrard as his second in command, were sent to replace Sir Arthur Wellesley, the future Duke of Wellington, who was in command in the campaign in Portugal, which began the Peninsula War. Burrard refused to press home the victory won at the Battle of Vimeiro and as a result was recalled and his command was given to Sir John Moore. In 1810 Burrard was given command of the Guards Brigade in London. One of his sons, Paul Harry Durell Burrard, aide-de-camp to Sir John Moore, was killed at Corunna. Sir Harry Burrard gave his name to Burrard Street, St Helier, which was built on land given by him for the purpose.

The Channel Islands produced a number of other high ranking military men. Tupper rightly points out that of the five British generals killed in action in 1812 two were Guernseymen, Major-General John Gaspard Le Marchant, 6th Dragoon Guards (1766–1812) and Major-General Sir Isaac Brock, K.B., 49th Foot (1769–1812).

At school Le Marchant was considered a dunce and his youth was full of escapades. However, he joined the army and attracted the notice of King George III, with whom he became a great favourite. He interested himself in the introduction of a better cavalry sword and for his services in this connection he was presented with two swords, one by Charles, Lord Cornwallis, Master-General of the Ordnance, and one by Mr Osborne of Birmingham, a sword-cutler with a European reputation. Le Marchant was appointed Lieutenant-Governor of the Royal Military College at High Wycombe (later transferred to Sandhurst). He fought in the Peninsula campaign and was killed on 22nd July 1812 at the Battle of Salamanca, where his brigade, supported by Anson's Light Dragoons and Bull's troop of horse, made a famous charge which resulted in a French infantry division being routed and 1,500 prisoners being taken. A memorial (1812) to Le Marchant by Rossi, designed by J. Smith, is in the north transept of St Paul's Cathedral.

Sir Isaac Brock started his army career in 1785 as an ensign in the 8th Regiment. He served in the West Indies 1791–1803, in North Holland in 1799 and was second in command of the land forces in the attack on Copenhagen by Lord Nelson in 1801. Brock was in Canada 1802–05 and from 1806 commanded in Quebec and in 1810 Upper Canada. In 1811 he was promoted major-general. He received the surrender of General Hull's forces at Detroit. In 1812 he was made an extra Knight of the Bath and was killed on the 13th October of the same year at Queenston Heights, his troops having defeated the Americans and thus saved Upper Canada.

Earl Bathurst wrote in a despatch to Sir George Prevost:

... The Prince Regent is fully aware of the severe loss which his Majesty's service has experienced in the death of Major-General Sir Isaac Brock, in whom his Majesty has lost not only an able and meritorious officer, but one who in the exercise of his functions of Provisional Lieutenant-Governor of the Province displayed qualities admirably adapted to awe the disloyal, to reconcile the wavering, and to animate the great mass against successive attempts of the enemy to invade the Province, in the last of which he unhappily fell, too prodigal of that life of which his eminent services had taught us the value ...

In St Paul's Cathedral is a monument to Brock by Westmacott and on Queenston Heights stands a column (a replacement of the original) erected to his memory by the Provincial Legislature.

A special grant of arms was made to Brock and his brothers in 1813. In the Pension List for 1818 Brock's brothers Daniel de Lisle Brock, John Savery Brock, Irving Brock and William Brock were each awarded £200 in consideration of their late brother's distinguished merit and services, as displayed in the defence of Upper Canada. In 1969 to mark the bi-centenary of Brock's birth a plaque was affixed to the High Street side of St Peter Port Parish Church and the Guernsey Postal Administration issued a commemorative set of four pictorial stamps.

Another Channel Islander who distinguished himself in the Army, although not on the field of battle, was William Lemprière (died 1834). He entered the Army Medical Service and in 1789 was Regimental Surgeon's Mate in the 11th Regiment of Foot at Gibraltar. In September of that year Lemprière volunteered to attend one of the Sultan of Morocco's sons who was having trouble with his eyes. In return for such help the Sultan offered to release ten shipwrecked British sailors who were being held in slavery. Once inside the country Lemprière was virtually a prisoner despite the fact that his treatment had benefited the Sultan's son. Eventually, by a ruse, he managed to leave Morocco and arrived back from his mission in March 1790. He recounted his adventures in a book entitled *A Tour from Gibraltar to Tangier, Sallee, Mogodore, Santa Cruz, Tarudant, and thence over Mount Atlas to Morocco, including a particular account of the Royal Harem* published in 1791. The book was a success and reached a fifth edition by 1815; there were also German and Portuguese editions. Subsequently, Lemprière had a number of other works published. He left the army with the rank of Inspector-General of Hospitals and died at Bath in 1834.

Two Guernseymen were Lord Mayor of London during this period—Paul Le Mesurier (1793–94) and Peter Perchard (1804–05). Le Mesurier (1755–1805) was the brother of Peter Le Mesurier, Governor of Alderney and Commissary-General Havilland Le Mesurier (1758–1806). He was Member of Parliament for Southwark 1784–96 and Colonel of the Honourable Artillery Company 1794–1805. He was also Governor of the Irish Society 1798–1805, Director of the East India Company 1784–1805 and Prime Warden of the Goldsmiths' Company 1802–03. Le Mesurier's only son the Reverend Thomas Le Mesurier was Archdeacon of Malta for thirty-four years. Perchard was President of St Bartholomew's Hospital 1804–06 and Prime Warden of the Goldsmiths' Company 1786–87. He was buried in the church of St Mary Abchurch, London, in the same grave as his wife Martha, daughter of Henry Le Mesurier and their four children. He bequeathed £1,000 to his native parish, St Peter-in-the-Wood, Guernsey. Perchard's daughter, Martha, married Le Mesurier's nephew, John, in 1804.

The Channel Islands continued to produce scholars. Among those from Jersey were Daniel Dumaresq (1712–1805), Richard Valpy (1754–1836), Head Master of Reading Grammar School, his brother Edward Valpy (1764–1832), High Master of Norwich Grammar School, and John Lemprière (1765–1824). Lemprière was author of *Bibliotheca Classica, a Classical Dictionary, containing a full account of all the Proper Names mentioned in Antient Authors,* published in 1788, which was a very successful work and ran into a number of editions. The same year he became Assistant Master at Reading Grammar School under Dr Valpy (1788–91). In 1791 he became Master of Lever's Grammar School, Bolton. Two years later he was appointed Head Master of Roysse's Free School of the Blessed Trinity, Abingdon. In 1809 he became Head Master of Exeter Grammar School, a position which he resigned in 1823. Lemprière's daughter Susan married Philip Chilwell de la Garde (1797–1871), son of Philip de la Garde, Rector of St Martin, Jersey. He was Mayor of Exeter 1834–36. Among scholars from Guernsey or of Guernsey descent were Osmond Beauvoir (1720?–89), Head Master of King's School, Canterbury, which he himself had entered as a King's Scholar in 1732, and Peter Paul Dobrée (1782–1825), Fellow of Trinity College, Cambridge, and Regius Professor of Greek in that university.

A Guernseyman who distinguished himself in the world of commerce was Thomas de la Rue (1793–1866), the founder of the firm which bears his name. He was born at Forest and at the age of ten was apprenticed to Joseph Antoine Chevalier, a master printer. In 1811 he completed his apprenticeship and was then engaged by Tom Greenslade as editor of a new newspaper called the *Publiciste ou Journal Politique et Litteraire* which first appeared in September 1812. The two men parted company in December of the same year. With financial help de la Rue started his own newspaper *Le Miroir Politique* in 1813, a venture which only lasted two years. He then settled in England where he set up business as a straw hat manufacturer. In 1830 de la Rue with two partners went into the stationery business and the next year saw the first de la Rue playing card. The manufacture of straw hats was given up by the de la Rue firm in 1835, and thereafter they devoted their attention to their stationery and printing business which in due time became world famous.

In the world of art there are few names to mention. In addition to Philip Jean to whom reference has already been made, there were only two who come to mind, Isaac Gosset (1713–99), modeller of wax portraits, and Thomas Le Hardy (1771–1813), miniaturist.

Gosset was born in Jersey of Huguenot parents. He joined his uncle Matthew Gosset, a modeller of wax portraits, and learnt the art of modelling from him. Isaac was an apt pupil and excelled his uncle in his skill as a modeller and many distinguished people sat for him including members of the Royal Family. Among his 'royal' portraits are those of King George II, King George III and Queen Charlotte. Gosset exhibited with the Incorporated Society of Artists 1760–78.

Le Hardy was a Jerseyman. He went to London and was helped in his chosen profession by his fellow countryman Philip Jean. Among those whom he painted were Philip d'Auvergne, Duke of Bouillon, and Dr Daniel Dumaresq. Although Le Hardy was primarily a miniaturist, he painted some portraits.

War had brought prosperity to the Channel Islands; trade was booming. In February 1768 the Jersey Chamber of Commerce, the oldest Chamber in the English-speaking world was founded. The first recorded meeting of the founders was held at the 'King's Head', St Helier; three days later a general meeting was called to ratify their recommendations. In 1808 a similar institution was founded in Guernsey.

Privateering and smuggling were at a premium. In addition, there were the cod fisheries and the trading consequential upon them. Cider was being exported from Jersey, as well as oysters; stone was being exported from Guernsey. There were also the first stirrings of the potato trade, which was to bring prosperity to Jersey. The only industry which was in a state of decline was that of knitting. Regrettably it should be mentioned that some Jersey ships appear to have been engaged in the slave trade.

Privateering was to come to an end so far as the Channel Islands were concerned in 1815, although it continued to be recognized until its abolition in 1856 by the Treaty of Paris. Smuggling underwent a slow lingering death. In 1709 Guernsey received an Order in Council which repeated previous orders made at the behest of the commissioners of customs with the object of establishing their officers in the Channel Islands. In 1717 the British Government was desirous of establishing a customs house in Guernsey but the States resisted its endeavours to do so. Between 1720 and 1767 the Government continued its attempts, and in the latter year it succeeded in establishing customs houses in both Jersey and Guernsey. In 1800 the British Government sent Mr Stiles to Guernsey as a commissioner with the object of suppressing the long-established smuggling trade then carried on extensively from Guernsey and Alderney with England and Ireland. The Government pursued its purpose by further legislation in 1805 and 1807 which met with continued resistance from the Guernsey authorities. Ultimately, however, the Government triumphed resulting in the loss of a considerable amount of trade to Jersey, Guernsey and Alderney, and particularly the last two.

In 1797 important oyster banks were discovered between Jersey and France, a few miles north-west of the French-owned Island of Chausey. After their discovery the banks were exploited by Jersey fishermen, until in 1810 a regular fishery was established to supply the chartered companies of Kent and Sussex. For fifteen years the fishery prospered before going into a decline.

There is a great deal of granite in the Channel Islands. Granite has been quarried in all the islands, including Herm, Jethou and even the Ecréhous and Minquiers, and used in the construction of the islands' buildings. Its colour varies considerably, from pink right through to grey and blue. In course of time what was an industry producing stone solely for local requirements became, especially in the case of Guernsey, an important export industry. It is believed that the export from that island started about 1760. In 1819 2,666 tons of paving-stones were exported; two years later the amount had been increased to 6,390 tons. The introduction of macadamization in England between 1810 and 1816 gave a great boost to the trade. In 1841 between 300 and 400 vessels left Guernsey with cargoes of stone. Ten years later 82,593 tons were being exported annually, in 1861 the annual tonnage was up to 142,866 tons and by 1913 it had reached 500,000 tons. The stone was shipped principally from St Sampson's Harbour. Granite from Herm was used fairly extensively in London, and the steps of the Duke of York's column in Waterloo Place are believed to have been made from it.

The name of Charles Robin (1743–1824) will for ever be associated with Jersey's codfishing industry. The firm which he established in 1766, three years after the signing of the Treaty of Paris, at Paspébiac on the peninsula of Gaspé in the Gulf of St Lawrence River, Canada, continues to trade, although now known as Robin, Jones and Whitman Ltd. The Gaspé peninsula is in the Province of Quebec; it is 170 miles long and has an area of 11,400 square miles compared with Jersey's 45. Robin kept a diary which commences in 1767 in which are recorded the early years of the firm. One gathers from the diary that Robin was both hard working and extremely careful with money which was the reason for him remaining in business when most of his competitors had gone to the wall. Robin wrote of the Indians, civilized by Catholic missionaries who had been at work among them for 150 years. In 1768 two 'Robin' ships were seized by British naval patrols. These arrests resulted from the failure of the firm to observe the provisions of the Navigation Act which provided that Jersey ships sailing for America should clear outward from an English port. The firm protested to the British Government and in 1769 Parliament restored to Jersey shipowners the privilege of clearing direct from Jersey for America. Despite many difficulties, not least of which was the American War of Independence (1775–82), the firm prospered. For nearly 150 years apprentices left Jersey for the cod fisheries, which with everything associated with them became part of the island's way of life. The Robins introduced the truck system, which meant that the fishermen were paid half in cash and half in goods supplied by the firm. In 1778 Robin returned to Jersey where he remained for five years. He was a captain in the South-West Regiment of the Militia and took part in the Battle of Jersey. In 1802 he returned to Jersey where he settled at St Aubin. He died in 1824 and left £2,000 to build a new wing for the General Hospital and £1,000 to provide a chaplain.

Charles Robin brought a William Fruing to Canada from Dr Barnardos Orphanage in England. Robin taught him to read and write and he did so well that eventually he became Robin's Chief Agent at Paspébiac. Ultimately he established his own business with branches on the east and north of the Peninsula; also in the Straits of Belle-Isle, at Blanc Sablon and Greenley Island.

John Le Boutillier, Honourable John as he was known, was born on 23rd April 1797 at St John, Jersey. He was the son of John David Le Boutillier and Mary Le Boutillier (née Baudains). Following the death of his wife, John David Le Boutillier married Mary Coutanche. John went to Gaspé in 1812.

John Le Boutillier married Elizabeth Robin. About 1840, after a long career in the service of the Robins, he opened his own business in La Gaspésie with his sons.

Long experience in business enabled Le Boutillier to establish a successful company to exploit the fishing and he exported to Portugal, Spain, Italy, Brazil and to Antilles. He owned ships which sailed between Jersey and La Gaspésie.

John Le Boutillier was Member of Parliament for the County of Gaspé in the parliament at Quebec from 1833 to 1838, from 1844 to 1847 and from 1854 to 1867, the year of his nomination to the Legislative Council. David Le Boutillier was a Member for the County of Bonaventure from 1851 to 1854.

Another family of Le Boutilliers were carrying on a fish business at Paspébiac, New Carlisle, Bonaventure and Magpie on the north coast. This business belonged to the family of Victoria Sutton of Jersey. Her uncle, Amy Le Boutillier, managed the business. Victoria Sutton's mother was Mary Ann Le Boutillier, Amy's sister; she had married Charles Thomas Sutton, an Englishman.

Another Jerseyman, John Fauvel, who came to the Gaspé Coast for Robin's and eventually became their Chief Agent at Paspébiac, established his own firm at Point Saint-Pierre in the County of Gaspé. He had three sons, John, George and William. The latter after spending some time in Norway training the Norwegians to dry cod fish returned to Canada and became Chief Agent at Paspébiac for the Le Boutillier Brothers. He also became Federal Member of Parliament for the County of Bonaventure. He died at Paspébiac in 1897 and was buried at New Carlisle, where there is a monument to him in front of the Town Hall.

Other Jersey firms on the Gaspé Coast were John and Elie Collas, E. and E. Le Marquand, de la Perelle Brothers, Valpy and Le Bas, and Alexandre and Le Marquand.

In Newfoundland Jersey houses started business at Blanc Sablon, Forteau and other places in the straits. Poingdestre and Robinson were established in 1784. The Fortreau Great Room and the establishment at Admiral's Point were bought by Thomas Falle and de Quetteville in 1795. In 1802 de Quetteville bought both rooms. The firm of Richard Falle and Co. was founded at Point George, Little Burin, about 1830 by two brothers, Richard and Eli Falle. In 1838 they took their nephew Joshua George Falle (1820-1903) into partnership and when his uncles were drowned at sea at different times when trading with cod fish to Oporto he took control of the firm.

In 1806 a number of Guernsey families emigrated to Prince Edward Island and each was made a grant of fifty acres of land. Today there are a large number of people of Guernsey descent living in the island. Some of the place-names such as Amherst Cove, Fort Amherst, Carey Point, Crapaud, St Andrew's and St Peter's Harbour are attributable to the Guernsey settlers.

In the early 1800s a number of Guernsey families emigrated to the United States. They landed at Norfolk and sailed up the Chesapeake Bay to Baltimore where they spent several weeks fitting out waggons and preparing to go west to Chillicothe, Ohio. However, as it would have meant cutting a road nearly all the way, they decided to stop in the south-eastern part of Ohio and there founded the town of Cambridge, named after Cambridge Park in their native island.

CHAPTER ELEVEN

Peace and Progress—1815–37

I will venture to assert, that more is actually known, and more accurate information is to be gathered from authentic sources, respecting the smallest of the colonies which lie in the Atlantic or Indian Oceans, than respecting Jersey or Guernsey.

Henry David Inglis (1795–1835)

King George III died in 1820 and was succeeded by his son the Prince Regent, the First Gentleman in Europe, after whom Fort Regent, Regent Road and Regent Steps in Jersey were called, as King George IV. The new King reigned for only a decade and was succeeded by his brother, the Duke of Clarence, as King William IV, whose reign was even shorter. William Place and Adelaide Place (now part of Rouge Bouillon), St Helier, were named after King William and Queen Adelaide, his consort.

In 1821 the Earl of Chatham was succeeded as Governor of Jersey by William Carr Beresford, Viscount Beresford, who was the last to hold the office. He visited the island in 1821, but never after that; he died in 1854. Beresford Street in St Helier is named after him. Sir Tomkyns Hilgrove Turner was succeeded as lieutenant-governor in 1816 by Lieutenant-General Hugh Mackay Gordon. The latter was followed in 1821 by Sir Colin Halkett who gave his name to Halkett Place and Halkett Street in St Helier. Major-General Archibald Campbell who became lieutenant-governor in 1835 died in office and was buried in St Helier's Church.

In 1827 the Earl of Pembroke was succeeded as Governor of Guernsey by Sir William Keppel who held the office until his death in 1834. The governorship was abolished in 1835. Major-General Sir John Colborne (afterwards Lord Seaton) was lieutenant-governor 1825–28. He was appointed lieutenant-colonel at the dying request of Sir John Moore. He commanded the 52nd Regiment of Foot in the Peninsular War and at Waterloo. Francis Jeune, a Jerseyman, who later became Bishop of Peterborough, was Colborne's Secretary when he was Lieutenant-Governor of Upper Canada. Colborne gave his name to Colborne Road in Guernsey. When he was in Canada he named the most western harbour of the province Port Sarnia in honour of Guernsey.

In 1825 Major-General John Le Mesurier (1781–1843), Governor of Alderney, surrendered his grant of the island, said to be in consideration of a payment of £700 per annum for the remainder of the term, and retired to England. He took up residence at a property in Poole called Alderney Manor and remained there for some years. He died at Bradfield Place, Reading. In 1909 Alderney Manor became the residence of Augustus John, the painter, and was well known because of the large number of notabilities who visited him there. Ultimately the property was demolished and developed as a private housing estate the roads of which bear Channel Islands' names: Alderney Avenue, Corbière Avenue, Fermain Road, Gorey Road, Guernsey Road, Herm Road, Jersey Road, Plémont Close, Portelet Close, Sark Road, St Brelade's Avenue and St Helier Road.

Since 1825 Alderney has not had a separate governor, but has come under the Governor and, after that office was abolished, the Lieutenant-Governor of Guernsey. From then until 1949 the principal official of the island was the judge, an office dating back to 1583, although the first use of the title does not occur until 1612.

Peter Le Pelley, who became Lord of Sark on the death of his father in 1820, was to remain so until 1839.

Henry Frederick, Lord Carteret, was still Bailiff of Jersey and remained so until his death in 1826 at the age of ninety years. He and his two predecessors had held the office of bailiff for 123 years, an average of forty-one years each. Carteret was succeeded by Sir Thomas Le Breton, the first bailiff to reside in Jersey since the appointment of Sir Charles Carteret in 1703. The three bailiffs who held office from 1703 to 1826 never visited the island and were represented by lieutenants. Le Breton was succeeded on his retirement in 1831 by Sir John de Veulle, who was appointed during pleasure.

Sir Peter de Havilland was still Bailiff of Guernsey. He was succeeded in 1821 by Daniel de Lisle Brock, brother of Sir Isaac Brock, who held the office until 1842.

During the previous seventy-five years St Helier had undergone many changes, although it had not increased much in size, except for a limited amount of development at its east and west ends. A hospital was built in 1765 through the generosity of Marie Bartlett (*née* Mauger) (1677–

1741) to whom the States caused a monument to be erected in St Brelade's churchyard. Unfortunately, the hospital was severely damaged in 1783 when it was being used as a barracks and it was not until 1793 that the building was reinstated and in use once more as a hospital. A new Court House was completed in 1768. The building was of two storeys, surmounted by a belfry and had the Royal Arms above the entrance. It is depicted in the painting *The Death of Major Peirson*. In 1800 the site of the market was moved from in front of the Court House to a new site in Halkett Place. A theatre was opened in 1802 and a new prison built 1812-15. The construction of Merchants' Quay (now called Commercial Buildings) was started in 1811. The height of the buildings bordering this new thoroughfare was limited so as not in any way to restrict gunfire from Fort Regent.

St Aubin had also undergone some development. The harbour at the town, as distinct from that at the fort, was built between 1754 and 1819. St Aubin was a more important port than St Helier until about 1820, but with continuing harbour improvements at St Helier, its importance declined.

There were also changes in the countryside. A large number of farmhouses had been either built or rebuilt; in addition, a number of English-style country houses, with formal gardens, had been built.

Red-legged partridges were still to be found, but their numbers had sadly diminished from the days when they had been so numerous in the island that a partridge was nicknamed 'A Jerseyman'.

The roads had been considerably improved as a result of the efforts of Don, the lieutenant-governor, and were to be improved still further as the century advanced. It is surprising to discover that macadamization—the method of surfacing roads invented by J. L. McAdam and first used in England between 1810 and 1816—was employed in the western parishes of Jersey as early as 1824. The first road to be so surfaced was near Le Pont Duval, St Brelade.

The same period brought changes to St Peter Port. Among notable additions to the town were the Assembly Rooms (1780), referred to as the 'New Rooms' to distinguish them from the Old Assembly Rooms in The Pollet, Trinity Church (1788-89), the Royal Court House (1799) and the prison (1811). In addition to the demolition and rebuilding of old buildings, development took place which increased the size of the town. The newly built area was known as the 'New Town'.

In 1764 the Parish of St Peter Port purchased L'Hyvreuse or the New Ground as a promenade; it served for the garrison in time of war and for the militia. It was the scene of military parades and reviews, of demonstrations, and, on one occasion, of a duel. The name 'New Ground' was changed to 'Cambridge Park' to commemorate the visit of the Duke of

Cambridge to Guernsey in 1862. The same year the Duke visited Jersey and Alderney.

The greatest change outside St Peter Port was the reclamation in 1806 of La Braye du Valle, the shallow stretch of water covering 300 acres and extending from St Sampson's Harbour on the east to Grand Havre on the west, which separated the northern extremity of Guernsey, known as Le Clos du Valle, from the rest of the island.

St Sampson, the second town of Guernsey, developed from the time of the reclamation of La Braye du Valle and it was to prosper mightily with the growth in the export of granite.

In Alderney the clock tower was added to the church in 1767 and a Court House was built across the end of what is now New Street in 1770. The Georgian house which had been built on the site of Captain Ling's house was rebuilt and enlarged in 1763 to become Government House, now the Island Hall. Les Mouriaux House was built close by in 1779.

Mathias Finucane, a minor artist at one time resident in Guernsey, painted two attractive pictures of local interest, one of the Market Place, St Helier, with caricatures of Jersey celebrities in the foreground; the other of the Market Place, St Peter Port, and it, too, had caricatures of Guernsey celebrities in the foreground including W. Le Marchant, the bailiff, Philip d'Auvergne, Duke of Bouillon, Doyle, the lieutenant-governor and Billy Robin, the public crier. The figures are depicted in a manner slightly reminiscent of Thomas Rowlandson's.

During this period and in the 1840s two series of prints were published, one by P. Falle, bookseller of Jersey, and the other by Matthew Moss, bookseller of Guernsey, from the work of various artists which depict the islands in a very delightful manner.

Bad drainage and sanitary conditions existed in both the towns of St Helier and St Peter Port and resulted in outbreaks of cholera. There was an epidemic in both Jersey and Guernsey in 1832. The worst affected area in the former island was the town, notably Cabot's Yard, Sand Street. In all there were 806 cases in Jersey of which 348 proved fatal; in Guernsey there were 787 cases of which 341 proved fatal. There was a further outbreak in Jersey in 1849, when nearly 300 people died, and another in 1867. Tupper records how at one time the drains of the town of St Peter Port "discharged themselves into the old harbour, and at low water the effluvia from the deposit were so offensive as to engender disease and to render the houses in the High-Street almost unhabitable". Proper sewers were installed in the town of St Helier during the 1840s.

Private carriages became more commonplace as the century advanced. The first omnibus service in Jersey had been opened by Richard Monck in 1788. It operated on Saturdays between 'The Swan', St Aubin and 'The Bunch of Grapes', Water Lane (now Wellington Road), on the outskirts of St Helier. Horse buses are known to have been in operation between St Peter Port and St Sampson as early as 1837. The same year William Coleman started a bus service from St Helier to St Aubin. The fare was a shilling. As the century advanced many new types of horse-drawn vehicles made their appearance. The first cabs were introduced into St Helier in the early 1850s, excursion cars were used to carry visitors on tours, and in Jersey the Jersey-van made its appearance.

If communications within the islands were improving so were they between the islands and the outside world. The introduction of the mail packets in 1794 had been a great advance; so had the coming of peace which allowed shipping to proceed on its way without fear of attack by the enemy. Now the ships themselves were being improved. They were becoming larger, more comfortable and faster. The first packets of 1794 were in the order of sixty-seven tons; the *Chesterfield* built in 1812 was 107 tons. In 1823 the *Medina*, a 130-ton paddle-steamer, was the first steamship to visit the Channel Islands. It arrived at Guernsey on 10th June and at Jersey on the 11th and caused a sensation among the inhabitants. In 1824 the *Ariadne* a three-masted paddle-steamer of 132 tons went into service. She was commanded by John Bazin, a well known Guernsey captain. Only thirteen days after the *Ariadne* made her appearance the *Lord Beresford*, named after the Governor of Jersey, a two-masted schooner-rigged paddle-steamer of 155 tons also went into service. Each of these vessels was owned by a group of businessmen, principally Southampton merchants. As the years went by the Post Office began to lose heavily on its Weymouth packets and the responsibility for running them was transferred to the Admiralty on 16th January 1837. As is nearly always the case, the competition provided by private enterprise was too strong for the government-owned packets and in March 1845 they were withdrawn from service.

It must have been with a tremendous feeling of relief that most islanders learnt of the final defeat of Napoleon. Throughout long periods since 1204 England and later Great Britain had been warring with France, with the Channel Islands in constant danger of invasion and possible capture by the enemy. The French had made attempts on Jersey as recently as 1779 and 1781, and even since then the thought of capturing the islands had more than once entered their minds. Now peace had come at last. Not a few years of uneasy truce, but peace for good, for as long as the eyes of men were able to see into the future. Although there would be wars throughout the remainder of the century, the islands were not to be directly involved in them and the islanders were able to give their full attention to their own affairs, constitutional and domestic, without having at the back of their minds the thought that a hostile and powerful enemy lay but a few miles across the sea.

Peace, which had gladdened the hearts or so many, was the cause of ruin to Philip d'Auvergne. In 1814 he went to Paris to claim the Duchy of Bouillon and the King recognized him as Duke. He then went to Bouillon where he was warmly welcomed by the inhabitants. He was acknowledged as Duke by the General Assembly. The Supreme Court was reopened, state officials were appointed and the tiny army reorganized. Even a plot in favour of the Duke of Rohan, the late Duke's cousin, was a failure. All seemed set fair for d'Auvergne, but it was not to be. Napoleon escaped from Elba and after his defeat at Waterloo the Congress of Vienna continued its deliberations over the destinies of Europe. Among the matters which the Congress considered was the future of the Duchy of Bouillon. D'Auvergne's entitlement to the Duchy was questioned and on the grounds of expediency the Congress awarded the title to the Duke of Rohan and the Duchy to the Netherlands. D'Auvergne's world was shattered. On 18th September he died at Holmes Hotel, Westminster, a ruined and disappointed man, and was buried in St Margaret's, Westminster.

With the coming of peace virtually all the *émigrés* who remained in the islands returned to France. Their place was taken by British naval and army officers who began settling in Jersey and Guernsey owing to the cheapness of living and the climate, which compared favourably with that enjoyed by the mildest parts of the South of England. These new phenomena of island life moved in their own social circles, which were largely distinct from those of the native inhabitants. In 1834 it was estimated that there were 3,000 British residents in Jersey, exclusive of tradespeople settled in the island, three-quarters of whom consisted of officers on half-pay and their families; the remaining quarter was made up of either individuals with large families to educate or with limited incomes or a few attracted by the mildness of the climate.

A few celebrated people were among the many who settled in the islands during this period and later in the century. Among such was Gilbert Imlay, soldier and author who formed an association with Mary Wollstonecraft [1793–95]. He died at St Brelade in 1828.

Some of 'the residents' took a hand in Jersey politics. Hitherto, there had been two factions which, broadly speaking, corresponded to the Tories and the Whigs, but both of which were of the island. After 1815 there was to be added to these two factions a third, inspired by 'the residents', which had as its objective the alteration of the island's institutions and laws to bring them more into line with what they had been used to in Britain. This new faction had as their vociferous protagonist Abraham Jones Le Cras (1798–1869), A Jerseyman dedicated to the destruction of the island's ancient institutions, rights and privileges. He was indefatigable in his outpourings against the local establishment and bombarded the British Government and the public of Jersey at large with an almost endless stream of books, pamphlets, almanacs, newspapers and letters denigrating almost everything which the true Jerseyman held sacred.

French people too began to settle in the islands, especially Jersey. So much so that there was a French quarter of St Helier centred on Hilgrove Street, which came to be known as French Lane, and Halkett Street. These new settlers and their successors followed a variety of occupations, and a number of them became hotel proprietors.

These years following the coming of peace saw the beginning of the tourism industry which was to become increasingly important as a source of revenue to the islands in the years ahead. From early in the nineteenth century guide-books to Jersey, Guernsey and all the islands had begun to make their appearance. One of the earliest was *A Picture of Jersey* by J. Stead, published in London in 1809, another was *A Summer Stroll through the Islands of Jersey and Guernsey* published in Jersey in the same year. William Plees' *An Account of the Island of Jersey* appeared in 1817 and went into a second edition in 1824. The first important guide-book to all the islands was *The Channel Islands* by Henry David Inglis, first published in 1834, which ran into a number of editions. In fact, it was directed more to intending 'residents' than to tourists.

The islands first became well known because of the large number of 'residents' who had settled there; they had also become much more accessible because of greatly improved sea communications as a result of a regular service of mail packets and the cessation of hostilities. The residents were visited by friends and relations and this resulted in the islands becoming still better known, until they were finally recognized as tourist resorts in the late 1820s or early 1830s. At first only a trickle of visitors made its way to the islands, but as the century advanced this trickle became a steady flow.

Some of the visitors stayed in lodgings either in town or country; others stayed at hotels a number of which were already established in the islands. In 1830 there were in St Helier 'The British', 'Deal's', 'London and Royal Yacht Club', 'Old London', 'Union' and 'York', and in St Peter Port 'The British', 'Cole's', 'Crown', 'Payne's', Royal Yacht Hotel and 'Tozer's'. In course of time more hotels were opened to accommodate the increasing number of visitors. In Jersey a number of them were French owned, notably: Hôtel de la Pomme d'Or, Grand Hôtel de l'Europe, Hôtel de la Boule d'Or, Hôtel de Calvados and Hôtel Palais de Cristal.

Having written of 'the residents' and the visitors it is time to say something of the local inhabitants. It is interesting to read what Inglis, as an experienced travel writer, author of *Tales of the Ardennes, Spain in 1830* and *Ireland in 1834*, and as an outsider had to say about them, particularly as from now on the islanders would marry more and more with non-islanders thus over the years inevitably changing their traditional characteristics.

He wrote at length about the Jerseymen of the time, starting with the country people of the lower and middle classes whom he described thus:

It must always happen, that where men cultivate their own land, and labour for their own profit, a certain independence of character will be engendered,—an independence, whose foundation is natural and just,—and which is in itself, honourable to the possessor. In Jersey, other things contribute to foster this spirit among the inhabitants,—particularly, the possession of certain political rights and privileges, of which I shall afterwards have occasion briefly to speak; and the isolated position of the island which they inhabit. The spirit indeed, which animates the mass of the people,—more especially, the inferior classes, is strongly republican; and the blunt independence of character and manner, as well as other evidences of this spirit, bear no small resemblance to the traits which attach to our brethren across the Atlantic. The surplus labour required upon the soil, beyond that which the possessors and their families can give,—or upon those properties which are in the hands of English residents, is performed by English, Irish and French labourers; for, Jersey labourers are not to be obtained for hire, though there is no difficulty in obtaining an exchange of labour, which is more consonant with their notions of independence. Among female servants too, there is a good deal of the American "help." There is no absolute rudeness among them; but there is much of the free and easy; and the same treatment which would be acceptable to an English servant, would speedily offend the sensitiveness of a Jersey born damsel.

It is a fact, that in all countries where we find a love of independence, and where that independence of character, is generated by independence in worldly circumstances, we also find a strong disposition towards avarice, and its natural accompaniments,—parsimony, and excessive frugality. The origin of this, is not difficult to account for: independence in worldly circumstances, is absolutely essential towards independence of character and action; and men therefore, naturally employ the means by which this independence may be secured. With acquisition too, grows the love of it; and thus, we may easily comprehend how, in an isolated community, its members, gradually enriching themselves, and perceiving yearly, the certain results of frugality, should acquire habits which border upon the niggardly and sordid.

That this love of acquisition, and a strict frugality, form with independence, another strong trait of Jersey character, is undeniable; and although it be true, that these traits are sometimes offensive, we scarcely can quarrel with that, which presents to us a population without paupers; and amongst which, there is no man who does not feel himself above the contempt of the proud, and the sneer of the rich.

The love of acquisition, and the economical habits which accompany it, are incapable of being separated; and the same traits afford proof of both. Of these characteristics, abundant evidence may be found in the habits and manner of life, among the country people of Jersey.

I have heard it said, that a Jerseyman will do anything rather than put his hand in his pocket . . .

Inglis went on to say that the upper classes had "all the characteristic traits" of the lower and middle classes "only, in a milder form". Of the middle and lower orders in Guernsey he wrote:

It is scarcely to be supposed, that there is any very marked distinction between the characters of the people of Guernsey, and of Jersey. Love of acquisition distinguishes both; and perhaps, in nearly an equal degree; although I confess I have not observed, nor have been able to obtain such glaring proofs of extreme parsimony in Guernsey, as in Jersey. It is certain, however, that they are a thrifty, and a saving people; but it is equally certain, that among the more substantial farmers, the manner of living has considerably swerved of late years, from the old, and generally prevailing style; and that although "soupe à la graisse," is not exploded, a meat dish is creeping in; and foreign luxuries, and modern usages, are more prevalent among the country people, than in Jersey. That such should be the case, will appear quite natural, when I come to speak of the upper classes; among whom, in comparison with Jersey, little or nothing of the old island domestic economy prevails; and whose tastes, and example have had their effect, in the production of new and improved habits throughout the island.

Inglis was more impressed by the Guernsey upper classes than those of Jersey and wrote of them:

There is a marked difference in the state of society in Jersey and in Guernsey: and my object being, to speak truth, without any interest in pleasing the one—or any fear of offending the other—I am bound to say, speaking with reference to those classes which, from station or wealth are usually denominated the upper classes, that it will require at least another generation, before the general level of civilization in Jersey, can be raised so high as it is at this moment in Guernsey. To the most cursory observer, this must be obvious. Guernsey, and its localities, though far from indifferent to a Guernseyman in the educated classes, do not wholly engross his thoughts, or form the theme of his conversation. The world at large has a share in both: and if this were the only distinction between Jersey and Guernsey, it would be sufficient to establish the superiority; for it is, in fact, the best evidence that could be adduced, of a higher state of civilization.

That there should be this superiority in Guernsey, is no way wonderful; though I believe it has been the product of but late years. The absence of that party spirit, which in Jersey, so divides society, is perhaps of itself, sufficient to account for it; but only because it has allowed a freer inter-course; but more especially, because the absence of those topics of local politics, which in Jersey are the fulcrums upon which party spirit hangs, permits the mind to be employed in more useful, and more humanizing speculations; and leaves conversation at liberty to be a means of mutual instruction. In Guernsey, I have never heard conversation turn upon any question of local politics. I make a distinction between questions of local interest, and questions of local politics. It would be a poor compliment, to say, that the agriculture, the commerce, the improvement of the island, formed no theme of conversation in Guernsey; but such themes are very dissimilar from the angry discussions, or the engrossing colloquies, on matters of party politics, which are so inimical to the progress of civilization.

I may state as another reason of the higher standard of civilization in Guernsey, the greater wealth of the upper classes.

There is little doubt that Jerseymen and Guernseymen, being largely of Norman stock, were thrifty and hardworking. In addition, the islands were by no means rich, although no doubt in the eighteenth and early nineteenth centuries they were richer than they had ever been. However, for the most part the islanders were generally far from well off and if there were few paupers there were many who were poorly off. There is little doubt, therefore, that some at any rate of the "parsimony" which Inglis describes was attributable rather to necessity than to inclination.

Of the people of Alderney Inglis had this to say:

In the other islands, few are either very rich or very poor; but in Alderney, for the word, "few," nobody, may be substituted. Scarcely any one possesses more than thirty vergées of land; and the owners live almost exclusively, on the produce of their soil. There is one striking difference in the character of the inhabitants of Alderney, and of the other Channel Islands. The parsimony of Jersey and Guernsey, is no where to be seen. Indeed, in place of parsimony improvidence, rather, is a characteristic of the people. This, I should think, is a characteristic of the people. This, I should think, is to be ascribed to the effect of the smuggling trade. "Light come light go," is the rule of action; and the pound that is easily earned—easily at least, to those who are accustomed to a sea life—is spent on any holiday afternoon. This regardlessness of expendi-ture, certainly enters into the general character of the people; for although all are not smugglers, yet many have been at one time or another, indirectly connected with the trade; and besides, the example of profuseness is conta-gious; and I learnt from undeniable authority, that nothing is so rare, as to find the country people grow rich by saving, as they are wont to do in the other islands. The great occasion for spending, is at weddings. As much is spent at such time in one day, and would support the new married pair for a year. All relations are bidden to the feast; and when I mention, that an individual lately died, leaving behind him, four hundred and sixteen nephews, nieces, grand nephews and grand nieces, it will easily be credited that such entertainments are not given for nothing.

(*above*) Elizabeth College, Guernsey—from a lithograph after T. Compton
published by Moss in 1830

(*below*) Victoria College, Jersey—about 1870

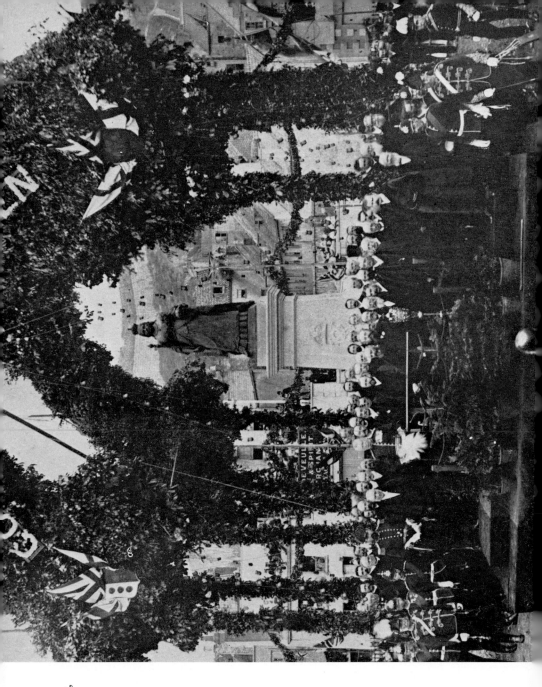

Unveiling of Queen
Victoria's statue, St Helier,
on 3rd September 1890

Inglis wrote at some length about the people of Sark. He said that "the life of a fisherman has more attractions for a Serkman, than that of an agriculturist", and "to ask him, there is an indescribable pleasure in sitting idly in his boat, basking in the sun, and waiting God's luck". He went on to observe that "This preference of sea to land, imposes upon the women, the necessity of performing much outdoor labour" which "leads to the neglect of children . . . Labour and exposure to the sun, have produced their usual effect on the appearance of the women, who are, with few exceptions, remarkably plain; while, on the other hand, the men may be called a good looking race". Inglis also remarked that "Drinking to excess is not . . . a vice of the Serk people" and that they "have few temptations to immorality; and are rather a religiously disposed people".

One of the results of so many 'residents' coming to live in Jersey was the establishment of two English language newspapers, the *British Press*, established in 1822 and the *Jersey Times and Naval and Military Chronicle* in 1832. The two publications merged at the beginning of 1860 becoming the *British Press and Jersey Times, Naval and Military*. In 1881 the words *Naval and Military* were dropped from the name and in 1889 the name was changed to *Jersey Times and British Press*.

There were of course a number of French language newspapers. Mourant's *Gazette* lasted until 1836. There were also the *Chronique de Jersey* 1814–1917, *Le Constitutionel* 1820–76 and *L'Impartial* 1831–46. There were, in addition, less important papers, some in English and some in French. Guernsey had many fewer newspapers than Jersey. Its first English language paper was *The Star* which lasted until 1965. Another long-lived newspaper in the same language was *The Comet* which existed from 1828–97. Among the French language newspapers were *La Gazette* and *L'Independance* 1817–35.

In 1832 Inglis had this to say about Jersey's newspapers:

Almost every grown-up person, man or woman, reads one or other of the Jersey newspapers. On Saturday morning, when three of the French papers are published; one is seen in every market person's hand, or lying on almost every market stall. The fish-woman, the fruit-woman, the butter woman, has each her newspaper; and lays in, for another week, a stock of knowledge to the affairs of Jersey. The circulation of the island papers is very considerable. There being no stamps on the paper, their price is extremely low, and the absence of duty also on advertisements, encreases their number, and consequently gives to the newspaper another attraction. I have counted, in the "British Press", which is published twice a week, as many as a hundred and thirty advertisements; and I have counted one hundred and forty in the "Chronique". I scarcely think any district will be found in Britain, containing a population of no more than 40,000 inhabitants in which eleven newspapers are published.

Most of the newspapers owed allegiance to one or other of the two political parties, the Laurel and the Rose, and the editors abused each other in the most vitriolic manner reminiscent of the editors of *The Eatanswill Gazette* and *The Eatanswill Independent* in Charles Dickens' *Pickwick Papers*.

During the summer of 1818 Dr John Fisher, Bishop of Salisbury, acting in the name of the Hon. Brownlow North, Bishop of Winchester, who was old and infirm, visited the Channel Islands, the first Anglican bishop to do so. He made the journey in the *Tiber*, a forty-six-gun frigate. He carried out numerous confirmations and consecrated two churches in Guernsey, St James-the-Less and Torteval. John Jacob in his *Annals of some of the British Norman Isles* (1830) recalls how the bishop visited Alderney aboard the *Vigilant*, the yacht belonging to the governor of the island, and received a thirteen-gun salute both on his arrival and departure. Dr Charles Richard Sumner, who visited the islands in 1829, was the first Bishop of Winchester ever to set foot in that remote part of the diocese. The bishop, Mrs Sumner and the episcopal party travelled to and from the islands in *The Lightning*, a steamer placed at their disposal by the government. Following this visit to the Channel Islands, the bishop visited them regularly at intervals of about four years until 1867, the year of his last visit. In 1865 in a speech made in the Upper House of Convocation Bishop Sumner expressed the view that the Channel Islands "should be erected into a separate see". However, in a letter written the following year he expressed the view that "There would be serious obstacles, even if funds were provided, in finding a see for the Channel Islands . . .".

In passing, it is interesting to note that Bishop Sumner in the autumn of 1850 paid a visit to the Bishop of Coutances in which diocese the Channel Islands were until they were transferred to that of Winchester some 300 years earlier. The account of the meeting in the *Life of Richard Sumner, D.D.* by George Henry Sumner runs thus:

Crossing, with his eldest son as chaplain, to Granville, they drove thence to Coutances. The Curé of Granville, a very handsome and courteous man, met them as they got out of the carriage, and said that the Bishop of Coutances would be ready to receive his English brother at three o'clock. At the time appointed the Bishop and his chaplain repaired to the episcopal palace, and were ushered into an oak-panelled library. They found the Bishop of Coutances evidently prepared to receive them, dressed in his purple cassock. One of the canons of the cathedral was by his side as chaplain. The French Prelate came forward and greeted the Bishop of Winchester most courteously, and an hour's conversation followed. He reminded him that Jersey was at one time in the diocese over which he presided, and asked a great many questions respecting the Church of England. The whole interview was of a very pleasant character, and at the close the two Bishops shook hands cordially, the Bishop of Coutances saying: "Nous sommes frères, Milord" ("We are brothers, My Lord"); to which the Bishop of Winchester responded heartily, "frères en Jésus Christ, j'espère" ("brothers in Jesus Christ, I hope").

In 1829 St Mary's, the first Roman Catholic church in Guernsey since the Reformation, was opened at Burnt Lane, St Peter Port. It was the only Roman Catholic church in the island until St Joseph's was opened in 1851. The roof of St Mary's Church was in the form of a boat's upturned hull, but this was lost inside because the ceiling was curved.

Whereas the Roman Catholic Church was undergoing a renaissance in Guernsey, Elizabeth College was in the last stages of decline. So much so that in 1821 Colborne, the newly appointed lieutenant-governor, received a letter from George Le Boutillier, a Jerseyman who had been in business in Guernsey since 1804, containing proposals for the reorganization of the school. As a result the lieutenant-governor took a hand in the matter, but, although the college did show signs of improvement, he was not satisfied and a committee under the chairmanship of Lieutenant-Colonel Thomas Fiott de Havilland was appointed to conduct an inquiry into its running. In due course the committee reported to the States, who themselves appointed a committee of Public Instruction to consider and report. This second committee largely endorsed the recommendations of the first, and in due course the States prepared proposals for the future of the college which were submitted to the Privy Council. On 30th September 1825 an Order-in-Council was made agreeing the States' proposals almost *in toto*. The foundation stone of the new college was laid on 19th October 1826:

> After the ceremony the boys of Elizabeth College were regaled in a most splendid manner under marquees erected upon the lawns in front of Government House, and in the evening Lady Colborne gave a grand ball and supper. The Royal Court, part of the Clergy, the Directors of the College, and the Militia officers, who had assisted at the ceremony—to the number of fifty-nine—dined together at Rosetti's Assembly Rooms at five o'clock. The expense of this dinner was defrayed by subscription. The Douzaines from the country parishes dined together at Coles' Hotel, the cost being met by a grant from the States Lotteries Fund, at the disposal of the Royal Court. Wine and biscuits were distributed as refreshments to the troops after the procession upon the New Ground; and the workmen were presented with a good solid dinner and a hogshead of wine by the Royal Court.

Le Boutillier (1783-1867) was born at Trinity, Jersey. He settled in Guernsey in 1804 where he established a drapery business. He is chiefly remembered for the building of Le Boutillier's Arcade, now called Commercial Arcade, which he caused to be lit by gas. He took part in local politics, but became so financially embarrassed as a result of the arcade scheme, which was never completed, that he emigrated to the United States in 1838. With his sons Charles, George and James, all of whom were born in Guernsey and attended Elizabeth College, Le Boutillier founded a business with branches at Cincinnati, New York and Philadelphia, and in 1864 he returned to Jersey a very wealthy man.

Lieutenant-Colonel de Havilland (1775–1866) had retired to his native island of Guernsey in 1825 after a successful career in the Madras Army, which he had entered as a cadet in 1791. As Architect of Madras he built the cathedral, St Andrew's, Presbyterian Church, the Mount Road and the bulwark or sea-wall, known as The Groins. In Guernsey he built Havilland Hall in 1829. He was elected a jurat in 1842.

In 1832 an attempt was made to extend the Habeas Corpus Act to the Channel Islands. On 1st June of that year the Parish of St Pancras, Middlesex, presented a petition to the House of Commons relating to one John Capes, a beadle of the said parish. The petition set out at length how Capes had gone to Guernsey taking with him James Streep, his wife and children and William Locker, all paupers, with the intention of leaving them in the island, Streep and Locker having been born there, and how Capes had been detained by the insular authorities because he refused to take Streep and the others back with him to England. The petition went on to recount how a writ of habeas corpus had been obtained from the Lord Chief Justice and served on the Deputy-Sheriff of Guernsey in March 1832, how, when that official had made no return to the writ, the Lord Chief Justice had issued a warrant for his arrest, and how, when the tipstaff went to execute it, he too had been detained for a short time. As a result of the flouting of his authority, His Lordship was instrumental in the issuing of an Order in Council dated 11th June 1832 requiring the registration both in Jersey and Guernsey of an Act of Parliament passed in the fifty-sixth year of the reign of King George III entitled *An act for more effectually securing the liberty of the subject*. Registration of the Order was suspended in both Jersey and Guernsey and Deputies from the States of both islands were sent to London to argue against its registration. Capes was imprisoned in Guernsey from the 3rd to 7th August because he withdrew the pledge he had given in March that he would not attempt to leave the island. Ultimately Capes, together with his charges (Guernsey made no demands for the refund of the cost of their keep while in the island), returned to England and the Order in Council was not registered in the islands.

Banking in the Channel Islands was developing during this period.

The first bank in Jersey was founded by Hugh Godfray in 1797 which came to be known as "The Old Bank", and lasted until 1891 when it was amalgamated with the Channel Islands Bank. After Samuel Dobrée and Sons, who were merchants and privateers, transferred the banking side of their business to London about 1770 there were no banks in Guernsey until the foundation of Bishop, de Jersey and Co., a few years after the turn of the century, and of Macullough, Allaire, Bonamy and Co. in 1808. Both banks went into liquidation in 1811. Hugh Godfray's bank was the first of about a hundred banks to be founded in Jersey during the next century. Numbered among the islands' banks were the savings banks established in Guernsey in 1822 and in Jersey in 1834; the Post Office Savings Bank opened branches in Jersey, Guernsey and Alderney in 1861.

Most, if not all, of the local banks issued notes. In Jersey prior to 1813 local notes were issued in denominations ranging from one shilling to one pound, but in that year legislation was passed which forbade the issuing of notes in denominations of less than one pound.

In the early years of the century tokens were issued in both Jersey and Guernsey. Three of these were in silver as follows: Guernsey—a 5s token issued by Bishop, de Jersey and Co. in 1809, which was forbidden to be circulated by Ordinance of 2nd October of the same year; Jersey—a 3s token and an 18d token issued by the States in 1811, both of which were withdrawn in 1834. In addition to the silver tokens there were a number of copper ones. All these tokens were issued because of the shortage of coinage in circulation.

In Jersey a change was made from French to English currency in 1834. The pound sterling was equated to twenty-six *livres tournois* of twenty sous, each sou equal to one half-penny, thus resulting in a Jersey penny becoming one-thirteenth of a shilling.

The States of Guernsey had for some time been desirous of having their own copper coinage. When they had asked the Privy Council in 1813 for Matthew Boulton of Birmingham to be permitted to strike coins for the island, it was stipulated that the coins would have to be struck by the Royal Mint. Seventeen years later the States issued their own coinage and had it struck not by the Royal Mint but by R. Boulton and Co. of Birmingham. On the obverse of the two coins issued, the four double piece and the one double piece, appeared the arms of the bailiwick; and on the reverse the denomination. Ever since, with only one exception, the ten shilling piece of 1966, the sovereign's head has never appeared on any Guernsey coinage. A possible explanation may lie in the fact that the States defied, albeit it seventeen years later, the Privy Council's prohibition on the use of a private mint for the production of the coinage, and consequently they hesitated to include the sovereign's head in the design of the coins struck at a private mint in defiance of that prohibition.

On 6th January 1831, the fiftieth anniversary of the Battle of Jersey, the insular militias were made 'Royal' by King William IV, and, in future, the facings of the militia uniforms were blue. In 1830 the King had appointed a militia aide-de-camp in both Jersey and Guernsey. John Le Couteur, later to be knighted, was the first to hold the appointment in Jersey, and Colonel John Guille, later to be bailiff, was the first to hold it in Guernsey.

John Le Couteur (1794–1875) was a distinguished son of Jersey with many and varied interests. In 1808 he entered the Royal Military College where he came to know George Fitzclarence, the illegitimate son of the Duke of Clarence, later King William IV. In 1810 when Henry, the Duke's second son was ignominiously dismissed from the Navy, he was placed in Le Couteur's care at the Royal Military College. The same year Le Couteur was commissioned ensign in the 96th Regiment, then stationed in Jersey. The next year he was promoted lieutenant in the 104th Foot, then in New Brunswick. He fought in the American War. In 1815 he was retired on half-pay and returned to Jersey, where he set up home and took an active part in island life. In 1836 he persuaded the King to donate a cup to the Jersey races; the King also donated a cup to the Guernsey races which had been established since 1828. Le Couteur was re-appointed militia aide-de-camp on the accession of Queen Victoria and in 1842 was made viscount (sheriff), an office which he held until his death. Le Couteur was a keen agriculturist and horticulturist and founded the Royal Jersey Agricultural and Horticultural Society in 1833. He was elected a Fellow of the Royal Society for his work *On the Varieties, Properties and Classification of Wheat* first published in 1836. In 1872 he was knighted. His elder son, John Halkett Le Couteur, who became Lieutenant-Colonel in the Coldstream Guards, was named Halkett after the lieutenant-governor. Sir John's daughter, Mary, married John Maunoir Sumner, eldest son of the Bishop of Winchester. Le Couteur's copious diaries and papers form the basis of a book entitled *Victorian Voices* by Joan Stevens.

It would appear that during the latter part of the eighteenth century and until about 1815 Guernsey's shipping and trade were more important than those of Jersey, but from then on the position was reversed.

Cider continued to be made in the islands, especially in Jersey, where at one time a large area of the island was covered with apple orchards and most farms had a cider trough and press. In 1806 cider was one of Jersey's principal exports and it continued to be so for a number of years. In 1832 no fewer than 564,768 gallons were exported. The quality of Guernsey cider was equal to that of Jersey, but little, if any was exported. Like many other of the islands' industries, cider-making declined and by 1893 cider ceased to be listed among Jersey's exports, although it continued to be made in the islands for local consumption. A Jerseyman, Francis Le Couteur (1744-1808) was an expert on cider-making and wrote a book about it which was recognized as a standard work and adopted as such by the British Board of Agriculture, forerunner of the Ministry of Agriculture.

Shipbuilding was carried on in Jersey and Guernsey, and there is little doubt that from the earliest times Channel Islanders built small fishing boats for use in local waters. The first mention of a boat being built in Jersey occurs in 1468 and the second not until 1789. The first permanent yard appears to have been that of George Deslandes, established in 1821. The industry prospered and some twenty-six shipyards are known to have existed at one time or another. The ships which were built were very small by modern standards. The *Matilda Wattenbach* (955 tons) launched in 1853 is believed to have been the largest built in Jersey; the largest built in Guernsey was the ship *Golden Spur* (656 tons), launched in 1864. The industry had declined in Jersey by 1880 and was almost non-existent by 1890. The subsidiary trades of blockmaking, mast and oarmaking, ropemaking, sailmaking and ship- and anchor-smithing were also carried on in the island. The first steamer built in Jersey was the S.S. *Don*, launched in 1851; the first, if not the only one, built in Guernsey was the S.S. *Commerce*, launched in 1874. The Guernsey industry was similar to that of Jersey; it lasted from 1815 until 1895 and brought with it the same allied trades as in the sister island.

Among the reasons for the decline in shipbuilding in the Channel Islands were the introduction of steamships and ironclad ships as well as the increase in the size of vessels.

Silver-mining in Sark started in 1834 when John Hunt located a vein of silver at Le Pot. A company was formed and a three-years' lease was taken from the Lord of Sark, Peter Le Pelley, which was later extended for a further eight years. Operations were carried out at Le Pot until 1836, when another vein was discovered and two existing galleries from the original shaft were extended into it. Subsequently, no less than four new shafts were sunk. Many thousands of ounces of silver and some lead were extracted from the mine, but unfortunately, the venture proved a failure, and in 1852 Peter Carey Le Pelley, who was then Lord of Sark, was obliged to sell the Lordship of Sark, owing to his financial involvement in the mine.

Most of the silver mined in Sark was exported to France, where the best price was to be obtained. None of it was used to make Channel Islands' plate, as by the time the mines were opened silver goods were no longer being manufactured locally.

In Guernsey silver was located at Mont Durand, St Martin's, and exploited by the Blanchelande Mining Corporation during the 1840s. This enterprise was even less successful than the Sark mine; furthermore, the company found itself involved in litigation as its mining operations had resulted in the drying up of wells at St Martin's.

In 1815 there was published in London a *General View of the Agriculture and Present State of the Islands on the Coast of Normandy, subject to the Crown of Great Britain* which was written by Thomas Quayle for the Board of Agriculture. It contains a number of statistics concerning exports from the islands. In 1812, the last year for which figures are given, 541 head of cattle were exported from Jersey, 225 pipes and 98 hogsheads of cider and 155 tons of potatoes; 6,390 tons of paving stones were exported from Guernsey for paving dockyards and streets, and 237 head of cattle.

Throughout the century there was considerable emigration from the Channel Islands. In the previous century it had been confined to other parts of the British Isles and North America, but now it was possible to go to Australia and New Zealand, which were newly discovered and gradually being opened up and settled.

Among early emigrants from the Channel Islands to these new lands were Thomas Lemprière (about 1757–1829), brother of William Lemprière, the Inspector-General of Hospitals, Thomas's son Thomas James Lemprière (1796–1852), John Alexander Gilfillan (1793–1864), son of Lieutenant John Gilfillan of the 83rd Regiment of Foot and Elizabeth Gilfillan (*née* Bridge), who was born at St Brelade, Jersey, and John Laurens (1821–94).

Thomas Lemprière was born in Portugal and married Harriet Allen. He was engaged in banking in Europe. In 1796 his son Thomas James was born in Hamburg. He was caught in Calais during the Napoleonic Wars and he and his family were interned at Verdun. His son Thomas James managed to get out of France on the pretence that he was only eleven years old, although, in fact, he was sixteen, and to get to England. Lemprière senior was released after the Battle of Leipzig and set up as a merchant in London.

In 1822 Thomas James Lemprière emigrated to Australia arriving in Hobart on 30th December. At first he went into business under the name of Lemprière and Co., and then went into partnership with John Weavell under the name of Lemprière, Weavell and Co. The partnership was terminated by mutual consent in May 1823, but Lemprière continued in business under the original name of Lemprière and Co. The business failed in 1825 and the following year he entered the Commissariat Department. Lemprière gained promotion and by 1844 was deputy-assistant-commissary-general. In 1849 he was recalled to England for transfer as assistant-commissary-general in Hong Kong, where after a brief period of service he was invalided home in 1851. He died during the voyage on 6th January 1852 and was buried with full military honours in the cantonment at Aden. Lemprière was an artist, a diarist and a naturalist. He wrote *The Penal Settlements of Van Diemen's Land*, published in part in the *Tasmanian Journal of Natural Science* during 1842 and 1846 and in full by the Northern Branch of the Royal Society of Tasmania in 1954. He was an artist of some merit and was commissioned to paint portraits and landscapes.

Thomas Lemprière and his wife Harriet followed their son to Tasmania in 1825. Lemprière set up practice as an accountant and obtained a grant of 1,000 acres of land at Mount Direction in Forbes District. Harriet died in 1826 and Thomas three years later.

Gilfillan learnt carpentry and engineering before emigrating to New Zealand in 1841. He was prominent in public affairs and painted many portraits. His wife and four children were killed by Maoris in 1847. He then went to Australia where he exhibited his paintings regularly until his death. Gilfillan's most famous picture is that which depicts Captain Cook landing on Possession Island, Australia. The whereabouts of the original picture are not known but an engraving by Samuel Calvert is in the National Library of Australia.

Laurens first went to Canada, where he worked as a blacksmith. In August 1853 he sailed from Nova Scotia for Melbourne arriving in December, bringing with him a dwelling house and a store which he erected in Spencer Street, West Melbourne. Six weeks later he opened a grocery business which thrived so well that by 1865 he was able to retire. He moved to the suburb of Hotham where he entered politics. In 1870 Laurens became a member of the borough council and was mayor in 1872 and 1873. He was elected to the lower house of the Victorian Legislative Assembly in 1877.

These men were some of dozens, soon to become hundreds and later thousands, of Channel Islanders, who were to seek new opportunities overseas. The increase in the population—in the case of Jersey from 28,600 in 1821 to 57,155 in 1851 and in that of Guernsey during the same period from 20,827 to 33,645—meant that work was scarce and many of those who emigrated were obliged to do so if they were to enjoy a tolerable standard of existence.

Tupper records that the failure of the corn harvest in Europe in 1816 because of heavy rains considerably increased the cost of bread causing distress among the poorer people in Guernsey and resulting in the formation of relief associations. In June 1817 the Douzaine of St Peter Port fixed the price of bread at 5½d per pound or 1s 10d per 4-pound loaf; in August the price was reduced to 3½d and 1s 2d respectively. For three or four years many people were compelled by financial necessity to emigrate to the United States of America in Guernsey vessels specially fitted up for the purpose. In 1822 there was a popular rising in Jersey owing to the high price of food and in 1828 there were bread riots.

CHAPTER TWELVE

Victorian Spring and the Queen's Visits—1837–61

> We passed between Alderney and the French coast—
> Cape de la Hague—and saw the other side of
> Alderney; and then, later, Sark, Guernsey, and the
> other islands. After passing the Alderney Race, it
> became quite smooth; and then Bertie put on his
> sailor's dress . . .
>
> Queen Victoria, 1819–1901

On 20th June 1837 Princess Victoria, the late King's niece, ascended the throne of the United Kingdom of Great Britain and Ireland at the age of eighteen. The Georgian age was dead and a new age had commenced to which the Queen was to give her name. On 28th June 1838 Thomas de la Rue printed a golden edition of the *Sun* newspaper to commemorate the coronation; the issue ran to 100,000 copies and such was the demand that some people were prepared to pay a guinea for a single copy.

In 1840 the Queen married Albert, Prince of Saxe-Coburg and Gotha; in 1857 the title and dignity of Prince Consort was conferred upon the Prince. Albert Edward, Prince of Wales, heir to the throne, was born on 8th November 1841.

The Victorian age is one which many people are wont to decry, but, in fact, it was a time of vast achievement in every sector of life; a time of industrial expansion and of tremendous urban development. Communications, both by land and sea, were considerably improved, largely as a result of the steam-engine. The Empire was ever increasing in size, and during the period was to reach its zenith; Britons and British goods were to be found throughout the world. At the end of the reign the British economy was more stable and prosperous than it had ever been or ever would be again. It was the time of large families, which caused a considerable growth in the population. Although there were wide differences between the various classes of society, the social conscience was awakening and a large amount of reforming legislation reached the statute book. In all, despite its faults and shortcomings, its failures and disasters, it was a time of which Britons could be justly proud—and most of them were.

The Channel Islands largely followed the pattern of the mother country. There too, but on a smaller scale, were to be notable achievements in every department of life, including considerable urban development, particularly in Jersey, where the town of St Helier had been expanding steadily since the beginning of the century. Improved communications encouraged more people to retire to the islands, as well as being of advantage to the new tourist industry. Channel Islanders were to be found throughout the world, especially in the rapidly growing Empire. Although the islands' economies suffered setbacks from time to time resulting in emigration to the colonies on a substantial scale, by the end of the century they were sound enough. The population of each island considerably increased during the period, especially in the case of Jersey, partly as a result of immigration by 'the residents' and the French. As the century advanced conditions of life improved for the generality of the population; for the vast majority life was tolerable, and for a considerable minority more than tolerable.

Lord Beresford was still Governor of Jersey, Major-General Campbell, his lieutenant-governor since 1835, died in Jersey in 1838. He was succeeded by Sir Edward Gibbs (1838–47), who died in office and was buried in St Saviour's churchyard, Major-General Sir James Henry Reynett (1847–52), Major-General Sir Frederick Love (1852–57), Major-General Godfrey Charles Mundy (1857–60) and Major-General Robert Percy Douglas (1860–63).

Sir James Douglas was Lieutenant-Governor of Guernsey 1837–42. He was succeeded by Major-General Sir William Francis Patrick Napier, Lieutenant-Governor 1842–48, the author of a number of books of which the best known was his *History of the Peninsular War*.

In 1852 the Lordship of Sark was sold to Marie Collings (*née* Allaire) in whose family it has remained ever since. Mrs Collings died in 1853 and was succeeded by her son the Reverend W. T. Collings.

There were three Bailiffs of Jersey during this period, Sir John de Veulle to 1848, Sir Thomas Le Breton, Junior, 1848–57, and John Hammond, who remained in office until his death in 1880. There is no doubt that de Veulle was a failure as bailiff, which office he secured through the influence of his wife's uncle Chief Justice Thomas Tindal. John de Veulle was unable to control the court and in 1832 he accepted a challenge to a duel which took place at Jardin d'Olivet. Later the same year he was committed to prison by the jurats for contempt of court as a result of his failure to attend the hearing of a case in which he had been summoned as a witness. Daniel de Lisle Brock was still Bailiff of Guernsey and remained so until 1843. He was succeeded by John Guille (1843-45). In 1845 Sir Peter Stafford Carey was appointed Bailiff of Guernsey, a position which he was to hold until 1883. He was the first of four members of his family to be bailiff.

On 31st May 1837 La Chevauchée de St Michel took place in Guernsey for the last time except for a revival held in 1966. La Chevauchée was the triennial inspection of the King's highways throughout the island, which generally took place in the month of June. It was without any doubt the most elaborate and picturesque custom there has ever been in the Channel Islands.★

In 1838 occurred the "Battle of the Oyster Shells" resulting from an Act of the States of Jersey of that year concerning the conduct of the oyster fishery and the laying down of new beds at Grouville. The fishermen defied the prohibition against dredging in the new beds, and the Constable of St Martin tried to enforce the law, but without avail. The military were called out and fired on the defiant fishermen, who at once submitted to the inevitable. The chief offenders were arrested, but were lightly dealt with. Campbell, the lieutenant-governor, who had gone to Gorey to supervise the operation, caught a chill from which he subsequently died.

The industry had prospered until 1835 when hostile French action resulted in a restricted area of the oyster banks being available to the Jersey-based fishermen, which caused an immediate halving of the quantity of oysters usually obtained. However, the fishery continued, and in 1857 it reached a peak when some 179,690 tubs worth £37,248 were dredged.

The Queen's head appeared on the obverse of Jersey's first coinage issued in 1841. The coins which were of copper were struck at the Royal Mint from dies engraved by William Wyon and were in denominations of 1/13th, 1/26th and 1/52nd of a shilling; they bore the arms of the island on the reverse. From and including the issue of 1877, the denominations were changed to 1/12th, 1/24th and 1/48th of a shilling. Farthings ceased to be issued after 1877.

In 1842 Major-General Napier whom Queen Victoria described as "a very singular-looking old man, tall and thin, with an aquiline nose, piercing eyes, and white moustaches and hair" was appointed Lieutenant-Governor of Guernsey. He received a particularly warm welcome and everything was set for His Excellency having a happy and successful term

★ For a description of La Chevauchée de St Michel see my *Portrait of the Channel Islands*.

of office. However, that was not to be because the appointment went to Napier's head. Of his reception in the island he said, "I smiled and bowed, and spoke my acknowledgments, conversed and did King". In 1843 Napier ordered Le Conte, a Frenchman, to leave Guernsey very much contrary to public opinion. The bailiff and the jurats waited upon the lieutenant-governor with a view to remonstrating with him regarding the expulsion. Napier received them in a most discourteous manner much to the indignation of the islanders in general. In 1844 the lieutenant-governor obtained a pardon for Fossey, a soldier of the 48th dépôt who had been sentenced to two months' imprisonment for having in the company of eight other soldiers violently assaulted an Englishman called Clark and his wife. Instead of presenting the pardon to the Royal Court Napier went to the prison with his staff and insisted upon Fossey being released immediately. When the gaoler hesitated to release Fossey the lieutenant-governor sent to Fort George for troops with a view to compelling Fossey's release. This was too much for the gaoler and he released the prisoner. Despite his ultimate compliance with Napier's demand the gaoler was prosecuted before the Royal Court for disrespect to the lieutenant-governor. However, the unfortunate man was acquitted.

Napier's high-handedness resulted in the Royal Court sending two petitions to the Queen, supported by a memorial from the islanders. The general tenor of these communications was that the lieutenant-governor should observe the rights, privileges, customs and laws of the island. Unfortunately Napier's reputation, as well as his friendship with the Duke of Wellington, were such that the pleas of the outraged Royal Court and people of a small and insignificant island went unheeded. Sir James Graham, the Home Secretary, sided with the lieutenant-governor. Lord Wharncliffe, the Lord President of the Council, over-ruled Graham's contention that all complaints from the islanders should first be submitted to his department and upheld their right to direct access to the Privy Council. The judgement went in Napier's favour. It was ruled that the lieutenant-governor had the right to deport aliens from the island without the consent of the Royal Court, but that the jurats were entitled to take part in any conference. It was decided that the gaoler should have released Fossey when ordered to do so by the lieutenant-governor, but that he should not have been threatened with the use of military force.

Relations did not improve between Napier and the civil authorities. However, nothing untoward happened until 1844 when in May of that year some 600 troops arrived in Guernsey much to the amazement of the islanders. There was considerable speculation as to the reason for this access of force. The actual reason for their being despatched to Guernsey was to quell a supposed insurrection of the islanders against the lieutenant-governor. There is no doubt that all this was Napier's doing.

Queen Victoria and Prince Albert visited Guernsey in 1846. They travelled aboard the Royal Yacht *Victoria and Albert*, which was accompanied by three other vessels, *Fairy, Black Eagle* and *Garland*. This small squadron anchored in the roadstead off St Peter Port on the evening of Sunday, 23rd August. With the Queen and the Prince were the Prince of Wales and the Princess Royal. This was a surprise visit, but despite this a royal salute was fired from Fort George. The news of the Queen's arrival spread rapidly and soon people began gathering at various vantage points in order to catch a glimpse of the royal yacht. The lieutenant-governor went aboard to receive the Queen's commands. Her Majesty indicated that she would land the next morning. When this news became known there was great excitement in the island. Next day from daybreak there was great activity among the population. The Royal Court met at 7.30 am to prepare a loyal address. It proved to be a fine day.

The Queen and the Prince with their suite left the royal yacht at a few minutes to 9 am and a short time later were stepping ashore at the harbour. Another royal salute was fired from Fort George. The flags fluttered, the ships were dressed overall, the church bells were rung, the streets were decorated and the royal route was lined with troops. The royal couple received a rapturous welcome. Even the militiamen who lined the route so far forgot themselves as to hold their muskets at the present with their left hand at the same time taking off their shakos with their right, cheering vigorously as they did so. The carriage procession proceeded from the harbour, through the town and after a small tour returned to the harbour where the royal party re-embarked in the royal barge at 10.30 am. The royal squadron set sail soon after 11 am.

The royal visit was commemorated by the erection of the Victoria Tower (1848—by William Collings) on an elevated site to the northwest of Elizabeth College.

The fact that the Queen did not receive Napier when he went aboard the royal yacht on Sunday evening was considered significant; as was her failure to visit him at Havilland Hall, then Government House. Napier was on the way out, although it was not until 1848 that he was finally replaced. With the change of government from that of Lord John Russell to that of Sir Robert Peel Napier's influence in high places was at an end. Sir George Grey, the grandson of Lord Grey a former Governor of Guernsey, who succeeded Sir James Graham as Home Secretary, sent a message to the Duke of Wellington, the Commander-in-Chief, insisting on Napier's removal. The bearer of the message was Sir Denis Le Marchant, Bt, a Guernseyman. Napier's dismissal was softened by the award of a K.C.B. and the colonelcy of the 27th Regiment.

Sir Denis Le Marchant (1795-1874) and Sir John Gaspard Le Marchant (1803-74) were the sons of John Gaspard Le Marchant. Denis was a politician. He became Under-Secretary for the Home Department in 1847, and Secretary of the Board of Trade in 1848. He was Chief Clerk of the House of Commons 1850–71. Jonathan Duncan dedicated his *History of Guernsey* to Le Marchant when it was published in 1851. John entered the Army in 1821, was promoted colonel in 1851, and held local rank as a major-general until fully promoted to that rank in 1858. He retired from the command of the 85th Foot in 1846 on proceeding to Newfoundland. He was Governor and Commander-in-Chief of the Colony from February 1847 to June 1852. His last speech to the House of Assembly before taking up his appointment as Lieutenant-Governor of Nova Scotia was attacked by a section of the local press in the most scurrilous terms, his devotion to agriculture and livestock being particularly ridiculed. Le Marchant was appointed Governor of Malta in 1857 and received the local rank of Lieutenant-General in 1859. He was awarded a number of Spanish orders which the Queen gave him permission to wear when she conferred the honour of knighthood upon him.

The Queen and the Prince visited Jersey on 3rd September 1846. They travelled on the royal yacht accompanied by the same three vessels as on their visit to Guernsey. Among the royal party was Lord Palmerston. At 11 am the Queen placed her foot for the first time on Jersey soil:

—the quick sharp report of the guns of the Militia Artillery echo and answer, as it were, to the heavier thunder from Elizabeth Castle—all assembled on the Pier rise from their seats—hats are waving in the air, and to nearer observers the Viscount may be seen handing her Majesty from the temporary bridge to the stairs, while the distinguished honour of handing her on shore devolves upon Lady de Veulle, Mrs. Major Simmonds, aided by Miss Le Maistre and Miss de Carteret—the Queen is advancing—the soft plaintive voices of the ladies appointed to sing the national anthem fall pleasantly and harmoniously on the ear as they, nearest to her Majesty, welcome her with song to their native land—the band stationed at the extremity of the pier strike up the air—the singers have begun—and as the Sovereign leans on the Prince's arm, graciously and with cheerful smile do they seem to acknowledge the brilliant reception and cordial welcome prepared for them—forming into two rows, the lovely train of ladies scatter rare and rich flowers upon her Majesty's path—but for a brief space does she remain seated in the Pavilion—rising with a dignified air, but with animated countenance, the Sovereign receives the addresses presented to her.

After receiving the loyal addresses, that from the States being presented by the bailiff and that from the militia by Colonel Thomas Le Breton of the Town Battalion of the Royal Militia, a procession formed up. It was led by Colonel Le Breton followed by the troopers of the Town Battalion, all mounted. Next came the bailiff, Thomas Flower Ellis and Thomas Bros, the two royal commissioners, and the States, all on foot, with the

The Quay, St Peter Port, about 1900

A Jersey Excursion Car—pre-1914—the type of vehicle from which many visitors viewed the island

Royal Mace and the ancient seal of the island borne before them. They were followed by Gibbs, the lieutenant-governor, Major-General Helier Touzel and the aides-de-camp. Then came the Queen's carriage and a second carriage containing Her Majesty's suite. The Queen's aide-de-camp for Jersey, Colonel John Le Couteur and Colonel Frazer accompanied the procession on horseback, as did Centeniers Le Bailly and Chevalier on foot.

The procession passed through the town of St Helier and then proceeded to Mont Orgueil Castle, passing Government House on the way. Colonel Le Couteur took the Queen on a short tour of the castle after which Her Majesty returned to St Helier and re-embarked for the royal yacht anchored in St Aubin's Bay.

The Queen wrote:

A splendid day. I never saw a more beautiful deep blue sea, quite like Naples; and Albert said that this fine bay of St Aubin, in which we lie, really is like the Bay of Naples. Noirmont Point terminates in a low tower to our left, with St Aubin and a tower on a rock in front of it; farther in, and to our right, Elizabeth Castle, a picturesque fort on a rock, with the town of St Heliers behind it.

The royal visit to Jersey was amply recorded in prose, verse and illustration. Lieutenant E. P. Bedwell, R.N., drew a picture of the landing of the Queen and Prince Albert, which was engraved. John Le Capelain (1812–48), a Jersey artist whose style is somewhat reminiscent of Turner's, was commissioned by the States to produce a commemorative album for presentation to the Queen. He painted twenty-five water-colours, six of the visit and nineteen of local scenery, which were bound in red morocco and accepted by Her Majesty. The pictures were lithographed and published in book form under the title *The Queen's Visit to Jersey* in 1847. The same year Philip John Ouless (1817–85), another local artist, who specialized in marine subjects, published *The Royal Jersey Album*, containing pictures of the royal visit. The royal visit was also commemorated by the issue of a large medallion depicting on the obverse the arrival of the Queen and the Prince at St Helier's Harbour.

In addition to Le Capelain and Ouless the Channel Islands produced a number of other artists during the century: Peter Le Lièvre (1812–78), a Guernseyman; Paul Jacob Naftel (1817–91), also a Guernseyman, who went to London in 1870 and exhibited at the 'Old' Society of Painters in Water-colours (1856–91) of which he had become a member in 1859; Maud Naftel (1856–90), Paul Jacob Naftel's daughter, who painted flowers in water-colour; Thomas Berteau (1819–1905), a Jerseyman; Walter William Ouless, R.A. (1848–1933), a son of Philip John Ouless, a portrait painter, whose daughter Catherine was also an artist; Charles Henry Poingdestre (1829–1905), who was also a Jerseyman and President

12

of the British Academy at Rome; Sir John Everett Millais, Bt (1829–96), who became President of the Royal Academy. Millais is thought by many to be a Jerseyman. Actually he was born in Southampton, his father being John William Millais, a Jerseyman of an ancient island family, and was taken to Jersey as a young child. He showed an exceptional talent for art at an early age, and his pictures were accepted at the Royal Academy when he was only seventeen. Millais became the most fashionable painter of his day and produced a quantity of paintings, including such famous works as *Christ in the House of His Parents, Ophelia, John Ruskin, My First Sermon, My Second Sermon, The Boyhood of Raleigh* and *Bubbles*. The last mentioned picture was a portrait of his little grandson, William James, which, much to Millais' horror, was purchased by a famous firm of soap manufacturers from the magazine proprietors who had originally bought it, and used for advertising purposes. The portrait of his daughter, Alice, entitled *The Picture of Health*, hangs in the Barreau Art Gallery at the Museum in St Helier. Millais was buried in St Paul's Cathedral, the Royal Academy undertaking the arrangements for the funeral, and among the pallbearers were Holman Hunt and Sir Henry Irving.

In May 1847 Reynett, the Lieutenant-Governor of Jersey, wrote to the bailiff of that island pointing out that the desire of King Charles II that 2,000 *livres tournois* per year be paid out of the duty levied on wines and spirits towards an island school for boys had not been complied with, that for some time there had been adequate funds arising from that duty for establishing a school, and suggesting that the foundation of such an institution would meet with the Queen's approval. The Assembly of Governor, Bailiff and Jurats, the body which administered the funds referred to in the lieutenant-governor's letter, agreed that the establishment of a school would be highly desirable and appointed a committee to go into the matter and report back. The committee after consultation with authorities in England, and, in particular, with Dr Francis Jeune, Master of Pembroke College, Oxford, an eminent Jerseyman, reported to the assembly. An architect was duly selected, and the States set up a committee. In August the Assembly decided to buy the present site of the college from Mr W. Le Breton for the sum of £5,070. The Joint Committee of the Assembly and the States disagreed with their first architect and he was dismissed. It was decided to erect a building to accommodate 300 pupils, and in May 1849 Mr J. Hayward was appointed architect and instructed to prepare plans. On 24th May 1850 the foundation stone of the school, which was to be known as Victoria College, was laid by the lieutenant-governor. On 29th September 1852 the college was opened in the presence of the States and of Reynett who by that time had ceased to be lieutenant-governor.

In 1855 a grant of £80 a year was made by the Crown for the establishment of an exhibition to the Universities, and three gold medals to be awarded annually. The medals were first awarded in 1856.

Francis Jeune (1806–68) was educated in Jersey, in France and, finally, at Pembroke College, Oxford. He graduated B.A. 1827, M.A. 1830 and D.C.L. 1834. He was Tutor of his College 1828–32 and Fellow 1830–37. In 1834 he was appointed Head Master of King Edward's Grammar School, Birmingham, a position which he held until 1838. Four years later he was made Dean of Jersey and Rector of St Helier. In 1844 he was appointed Master of Pembroke. He was Vice-Chancellor of Oxford University 1858–62. In 1864 he was appointed Dean of Lincoln and a few months later Bishop of Peterborough. He was succeeded as Dean of Lincoln by Dr James Amiraux Jeremie (1802–72), a Guernseyman. Jeremie was Dean of Haileybury 1838 and Regius Professor in the University of Cambridge 1850–70.

Jeune's eldest son, Francis Henry Jeune (1843–1905) was educated at Exmouth, Harrow and Oxford. He had a brilliant career at the University. In 1864 he was President of the Union. He was called to the Bar in 1868, and was Junior Counsel for the Plaintiff in the famous Tichborne case. In 1888 he was made a Queen's Counsel and in 1891 he was raised to the Bench and knighted. The following year he was made a Privy Councillor, President of the Probate, Divorce and Admiralty Division of the High Court and Judge-Advocate-General. In 1905 he resigned the Presidency of his Division and was raised to the peerage, choosing the title Baron St Hélier.

The ancient schools of St Mannelier and St Anastase were closed in 1863.

Jersey and Guernsey shared one small court at the Great Exhibition of 1851. It was the most western opening on the colonial side being the eighth department, 112 feet west of the Crystal Fountain on the north side of the nave under the main gallery, and forming the principal entrance to the Fine Arts Court. Jersey's thirty-four entries included such diverse items as a machine to stop railway carriages, specimens of artificial teeth, specimens of wheat classified and arranged, a paper model of the Victoria Pier at St Helier, knitted stockings, specimens of granite, boots used in the Newfoundland fishery, and specimens of hot-air baths for the feet and back. Guernsey's sixteen entries included manufactures of sea-weed into iodine, a Guernsey crab-pot, fishing-baskets and utensils made of willow used in fishing, salts, the produce of Guernsey, similar to 'Epsom', and raw silk also produced in the island.

Guernsey had a further interest in the exhibition through the firm of de la Rue which had 289 items on show in a first class situation in the central aisle of the English exhibition. The firm's outstanding exhibit was an envelope-making machine in full operation, which proved very popular with the public.

Colonel John Le Couteur received a prize for his entry of 194 specimens of wheat classified and arranged, seven of which bore the name 'Jersey'. He was so delighted with the exhibition that he visited it on numerous occasions, the first being on the 1st May, the opening day. By July he had made his fifteenth visit.

Le Couteur's exhibit formed part of two collections in the Bethnal Green Museum, opened in 1872. Unfortunately it no longer exists.

In 1855 the firm of de la Rue secured the contract for printing the Great Britain fourpenny carmine postage stamp to be followed four years later by a contract to print three denominations of currency notes for Mauritius. In 1862 the firm printed the United States of America Confederate Five Cents Blue postage stamp, the only American stamp to be printed abroad and remain current for any considerable period, and in 1862 secured the contract for Italian postage stamps.

Jersey continued its rôle as a place of refuge when some 200 political refugees went to the island following Louis Napoleon's *coup* in 1851. Two years later it was estimated that there were 226 of these exiles living in Jersey of which 108 were French, ten Italian, and eight German and Hungarian. Among them were a number of colourful figures, of whom Victor Hugo was pre-eminent. Another outstanding figure was Zéno or Zénon Boleslas Swietoslawski (1811–75), a Pole who had played a very active part in the revolution of 1830. He lived for many years in Jersey, where he founded *L'Homme*, a newspaper printed specially for the exiles. One of the island's most active and gifted refugees was Paul Harro Harring (1798–1870), a Dane, who claimed that for upwards of half a century he had worked for the cause of freedom. There was also Count Narcisse Achille de Salvandy (1795–1856). Positions held by him included those of Member of the Académie Française, Ministre de l'Instruction Publique (twice) and Ambassador to Spain. He refused to follow Napoleon III and lived for some time in Jersey. The house where he lived, 'Monaco', St Saviour's Road, St Saviour, still exists.

A number of these political refugees died in exile and were buried in a common grave at Macpéla Cemetery, St John, each burial being made the occasion for a funeral oration extolling liberty and freedom and condemning oppressors. Several of these orations were delivered by Hugo. Swietoslawski, who at one stage was obliged to leave Jersey, was eventually allowed to retire there and when he died he was buried in Green Street Cemetery, St Helier.

Hugo himself was expelled from Jersey in 1855. The issue of *L'Homme* of 10th October of that year had printed the text of a speech delivered in London by Félix Pyat to the Comité International de Commune Révolutionnaire on 22nd September, the anniversary of the founding of the First French Republic in 1792. Pyat had spoken in the strongest and most objectionable terms and had attacked Queen Victoria for her state visit to Paris. He said that she "had sacrificed everything, her dignity as a Queen, the scruples of a Woman, the pride of an Aristocrat, the feelings of an Englishwoman; her Rank, her Race, her Sex, all down to her Modesty, for Love of this Ally". The people of Jersey were not prepared to tolerate such criticism of their sovereign and a protest meeting attended by some 2,000 persons was held at the Queen's Assembly Rooms. Following the meeting the protesters, some of them armed with sticks, made their way to the Great Universal Printing Press in Dorset Street where the offending newspaper was printed, with a view to wrecking the premises, which in anticipation of such a move had been occupied by some of the political refugees. The Constable of St Helier, one centenier and two policemen managed to prevent a bloody encounter.

On Monday morning Love, the lieutenant-governor, ordered Piancini, an Italian, who managed L'Homme, Ribeyrolles, the editor and Thomas, who distributed it, to leave the island within a week, which they did. On the 17th the newspaper printed a justification for printing the offending report. The following day a revolutionary declaration concerning the expulsion, emanating from the Great Universal Printing Press, made its appearance on the walls of St Helier. The Declaration was signed by thirty-six of the political refugees. At the top of the list was Hugo's signature; at the bottom was the taunt translated as "And now expel us!" The lieutenant-governor accepted the invitation and signed an order expelling 'the thirty-six'.

The lieutenant-governor's order was delivered to Hugo at No 3 Marine Terrace (now incorporated in the Victor Hugo Hotel), St Clement, where he had resided since 1852, by the Constable of the Parish. On 31st October Hugo accompanied by his son François Victor, known as Toto, and Juliette Drouet, his mistress, left the island bound for Guernsey; Charles and the remainder of the family followed later. Hugo bought Hauteville House, St Peter Port, in 1856 and lived there for the remainder of his exile. After his expulsion from Jersey, Hugo returned there only once, in 1860.

Another distinguished writer who spent some time in Jersey during this period was Mary Ann Evans, known to the world as George Eliot, the novelist. She stayed in Gorey Village at the house known as Rose Cottage (now called Villa Rosa) for some weeks during 1857.

An event took place in Jersey in 1852 which secured for the island a niche in the postal history of the British Isles. By Act of Parliament of 1794 Jersey, together with the other Channel Islands, was incorporated in the British postal system and although being a part of that system conferred definite advantages on the inhabitants, there was nothing particularly remarkable in the matter. However, in 1852 through the initiative of

Anthony Trollope, a Surveyor's Clerk employed by the Post Office, but better known to the world as a novelist, the first pillar boxes in the British Isles were set up in Jersey. There were four original boxes, all in St Helier, located in David Place, nearly opposite the Rectory, New Street, Cheapside, at the top of the Parade and at St Clement's Road, at the corner of 'Plaisance'. They were made locally by Mr John Vaudin reputedly at Le Feuvre's Foundry in Bath Street, St Helier. None of the original boxes survives in Jersey, but it is believed that two of the first Guernsey boxes, erected in 1853, survive in that island.

It was a century of constitutional wrangles and of Royal Commissions. In Guernsey there had already been the 'Capes', 'Le Conte' and 'Fossey' cases; in Jersey the 'Daniel' and 'Prison Board' cases were yet to come. In 1811 royal commissioners were sent to Jersey to inquire into the system of electing jurats; they issued their report the following year, but the Privy Council did not implement their recommendations. In 1815 royal commissioners were sent to Guernsey to consider the laws relating to debtors and their creditors and other matters; their report was published the following year. In 1846 royal commissioners were again sent to Jersey and Guernsey to inquire into their Criminal Law.

On 11th February 1852 the Privy Council issued three Orders in Council for Jersey as follows: the first for the establishment of a court for taking preliminary proceedings in criminal cases, and of summary jurisdiction; the second for the establishment of a civil court for summary jurisdiction for the easier recovery of small debts; the third for the establishment in the town of St Helier and its vicinity of a paid police force in place of the honorary police.

The registration of these orders was suspended by the Royal Court and by the States as they had been issued without consultation with the insular authorities. The States addressed to the Queen in Council a petition with reference to the orders protesting that they were made contrary to the constitutional rights of the island and praying that they might be recalled so that the States might be at liberty to pass such legislation as they considered necessary. In addition to the petition, 6,750 people signed an address to the Queen praying for the repeal of the orders as unconstitutional. Furthermore, a deputation from the States waited upon the Lord President of the Council and the Home Secretary and it was arranged that the States would be given time to take such measures as they might deem appropriate.

On the 10th, 16th and 17th August, 1852, the States passed six Acts dealing with the same matters as were dealt with in the three Orders in Council. The Acts were transmitted to the Privy Council for the royal assent. In their train came a number of petitions. The matter was argued at length before the Judicial Committee of the Privy Council. Judgement went in favour of the States of Jersey, their lordships being of opinion that there were serious doubts whether the three Orders in Council purporting to legislate for Jersey without the consent of the States were consistent with the constitutional rights of the island. An Order in Council dated 29th December 1853 revoked the three offending Orders in Council and approved the six Acts of the States.

Royal Commissioners were once again sent to Jersey in 1859 to inquire into the civil and ecclesiastical law of the island. Their report was published in 1861.

Quite apart from constitutional wrangles, reports of Royal Commissions and efforts made through the British Parliament to bring about changes in the islands' legislatures and courts, prison reforms were carried out and changes made in the treatment of prisoners. In 1833 Elizabeth Fry spent some time in Jersey during which she visited the prison and made a report with recommendations to the *Authorities of the Island of Jersey, who have the Direction and Management of the Prison and Hospital.* The British Government sent Dr Bissett Hawkins to the island in 1836 to inquire into the state of the prison. The following year a Prison Board was established and the office of Public Executioner was abolished. The pillory was last used in Jersey in 1835; hanging was still carried out in public. In 1870 the transportation of prisoners was abolished and penal servitude substituted.

In 1854 a paid police force was established, particularly for night duty, in the town of St Helier. The police had to speak both English and French, devote the whole of their time to their duties and were disfranchised. The cost of the force was born in the ratio of one-third by the States and two-thirds by a rate on the householders of the Parish of St Helier. In 1856 a policeman received 18s a week.

In Guernsey paid police were first employed in the Parish of St Peter Port in 1853, when four men were appointed. Subsequently this number was increased to twelve. Some years later two further policemen were employed in the Parish of St Sampson and that of Vale and one in the Parish of St Martin.

During Victorian times Channel Islanders played their part in many naval engagements and fought in many land battles. It would be impossible to list the many daring exploits in which they took part. One of them John Le Feuvre, a Jerseyman, serving aboard H.M.S. *Algiers* in the Crimean War has left a vivid description of the Battle of Inkerman, part of which reads as follows:

The day mentioned happened on Sunday the 5th November 1854, a day of Glorious memory, a day which should never, no never, be effaced from the annals of Victory. The tale should be written with letters of blood. The brave defenders of England and France, should never allow the word Inkerman to part from their lips without offering a prayer of thanksgiving to the heavenly throne for their preservation, without shedding a tear in remembrance of those who fell victims on that great and glorious day . . . It is useless to state the whole day's trial for volumes would be filled to give a thorough and detailed account, but suffice it to say that the day dawned clear and bright . . . By 10 a.m. the heavens were overshadowed with clouds of smoke coming forth and discharging themselves from the muzzles of heavy guns, the report of which was as thunder. Volleys of musketry were fired; bayonets and swords were handled with dexterity. Dreadful to relate thousands were falling here and there in all parts of the battlefield on those plains of blood. At the moment of the heaviest of the battle Divine Service was held on board of the "Algiers". The Minister during his sermon mentioned part of the war of olden time as mentioned in Scripture and knowing at the moment there were thousands falling victims at the point of the sword he could no longer speak, and closing his book and falling backwards wept bitterly. Service being therefore ended the nine hundred persons composing the ship's company soon were seen in all parts of the rigging and mast heads. Shocking was the scene to behold. The Land appeared as if paved with human flesh of dead and dying. The British fought desperately and bravely. There were but eight thousand of them against forty thousand Russians. The British being weak in number the Russians advanced on them in great numbers. But the Almighty's hand being stretched forth to our aid a large and powerful French Army was seen plainly coming down rapidly over the hills and soon were seen relieving the British . . . who exhausted welcomed them with a hearty cheer of three times, three which was redoubled as the French formed their ranks and commenced opening a murderous fire upon the Russians and cutting them in a fearful manner. The Russians making their retreat were cut down with a dreadful slaughter.

A number of Channel Islanders saw service in the Crimean War, among them were Havilland John de Carteret, Philip Gosset Pipon (1824–1904), who was to become Colonel Commandant in the Royal Artillery and to attain the rank of general, and John Halkett Le Couteur (1825–73), son of Sir John Le Couteur, who was in the Coldstream Guards. Le Couteur arrived in the Crimea in December 1854 and remained there until the end of the war. He took part in the Battle of Sebastapol in 1855.

The same year another Jerseyman, Captain of the Mast George Henry Ingouville won the Victoria Cross at Viborg. He received it at the first investiture of the Victoria Cross which took place in Hyde Park on 26th June 1857 when the Queen decorated sixty-two recipients in the presence of the Prince Consort, Prince Frederick William of Prussia and a vast concourse of spectators. A painting by George Housman in the royal collection depicts the occasion. The recipient shown being decorated is Ingouville. The ribbon of his Victoria Cross is incorrectly shown as red instead of blue which was the correct colour for naval awards at that time. Ingouville was also one of the first to be awarded the Conspicuous Gallantry Medal. In addition, he was awarded the Crimea, Baltic and Turkish Crimea Medals.

The Queen and Prince Albert visited Alderney on 8th and 9th August 1854. They arrived within the breakwater aboard the Royal Yacht *Victoria and Albert*, accompanied by the *Dasher*, commanded by Captain Nicholas Lefebvre, a Guernseyman, the *Black Eagle* and the *Fairy*. Early in the evening of the 8th Colonel Le Mesurier, the town major and the commanding officer waited upon the royal party. Later that evening they received the Prince, the Prince of Wales and Prince Alfred when they made a brief shore visit to inspect the breakwater and the new fortifications. The following morning Judge Gaudion, accompanied by five of the jurats and the court officers, went aboard the royal yacht to present a loyal address from the States. At 9.30 am the Queen, Prince Albert, the Royal Princes and Princess Helena landed to an enthusiastic reception. They toured the island partly in a rail-car drawn along the railway lines by two horses and partly by carriage. P. J. Naftel painted a fine picture recording the royal visit to the island.

Captain Nicholas Lefebvre (1794-1884), was the son of George Lefebvre, H. M. Greffier, and Martha Lefebvre (*née* Gosselin). He joined the Royal Navy in 1811 and served under Captain Philip Dumaresq in H.M.S. *Victory* while she was Vice-Admiral Sir James Saumarez's flagship in the Baltic. Lefebvre was made a prisoner-of-war by the French, but managed to effect his escape. In 1826 he was promoted lieutenant and appointed to H.M.S. *Britannia*, Saumarez's flagship. In 1850 Lefebvre was given the command of H.M.S. *Cuckoo* whose duty was to protect the Jersey oyster fisheries. The following year he was given the command of H.M.S. *Dasher* which replaced H.M.S. *Cuckoo* on the Channel Islands' Station. In 1853 H.M.S. *Dasher* went to the help of the packet *Dispatch* and saved that vessel from almost certain destruction. At the end of 1856 Lefebvre's period of service in the Channel Islands ended. In 1864 Captain Lefebvre, as he then was, was placed on the retired list. However, he continued to obtain promotion and ultimately attained the rank of admiral in 1880. Lefebvre was responsible for the building of a fishermen's harbour at Saints Bay, St Martin's, Guernsey, where a granite obelisk erected to his memory was destroyed by the Germans during the Occupation.

In 1857 there took place in Scotland one of the most famous trials in Scottish legal history—the trial of Madelaine Smith for the murder by poison of her lover Emile L'Angelier, a Jerseyman. He was the son of Pierre L'Angelier, a seedsman of St Helier. In 1842 L'Angelier, Junior, moved to Edinburgh where he had secured employment. Ten years later he was in Glasgow where he entered the employment of Huggins & Co. In 1855 L'Angelier was introduced to Mrs Smith, a fatal introduction. They became friends and lovers. On 23rd March 1857 L'Angelier died of arsenical poisoning and Madelaine Smith was accused of his murder. Her trial opened on 30th June and closed on 9th July; the verdict was 'non-proven'. It could not be proved that she was guilty, but it is almost certain that she was. L'Angelier's name appears on the middle stone above the family grave in Green Street Cemetery, St Helier. In the same cemetery is a monument to another murder victim Centenier George Le Cronier who was murdered in the course of his duties in 1846.

The Queen and the Prince Consort paid a second visit to Jersey in 1859. The royal party landed twice, in the morning at St Helier when they saw Victoria College and again later in the day at St Aubin when they went for a drive up St Peter's Valley and then through the northern parishes to St Catherine's Bay where they re-embarked.

The following day the Queen and the Prince paid a visit to Guernsey where they landed at 3 pm. They made a tour of the island during which they viewed the Victoria Tower, which had been erected to commemorate their visit in 1846, and visited Castle Carey, then Government House, where they were received by Mrs Slade, the lieutenant-governor's lady.

Jersey's exports at the end of the period included apples, bricks, butter, cattle, cider, grapes and other fruit, oysters, pears, potatoes and confectionery. Guernsey's included stone, grapes and other fruit, and lobsters and crabs.

The population of the Channel Islands continued to increase during this period. In 1841 the population of Jersey was 47,544 by 1861 it had increased to 56,078. During the same period the population of Guernsey increased from 26,698 to 29,846 and that of Alderney increased even more dramatically from 1,038 to 4,932. The population of Sark increased only slightly in relation to that of the other islands. The population of Jersey was made up of 41,000 natives and 15,000 non-natives—English, Irish, Scottish and French.

Of the children born in Jersey in the 1850s, one-fifth died during the first year of their age, and one-half during the first 25 years of life. The average duration of human life in the island was 35 years. The expectancy of life in Guernsey was greater than that of Jersey.

The increase in the population of the islands was partly accounted for by immigration and partly by an increase in the native islanders. It led to shortage of work, and even those who had work did not always receive wages sufficient to enable them to live more than just above subsistence level. It was not surprising therefore that many decided to seek a new life with better opportunities in North America, Australia and New Zealand.

In 1847 there were serious riots in Jersey. The trouble started in January and culminated in May. In January the workers in the shipyards left their work complaining of the high price of food and seized several loads of potatoes without police interference. In February the States opened a bakery to supply bread to the poor at a price lower than the current rate of 1s for a four-pound loaf and 6d for a two-pound loaf. On 18th May the Constable of St Helier announced that the States' scheme would be discontinued and the next day a meeting of the constituents of St Helier was told to collect subscriptions for the relief of the working class. The following Monday the 150 men building St Aubin's Road between First Tower and St Aubin held a meeting at which they discussed their grievances. They sent delegates to their employers to ask for an increase. Their request was refused and so they enlisted the support of the men at George Deslandes & Sons' yard at First Tower and marched to the town. Now they were 200 strong and as they went along so men rallied to them. More support was gained from the men working in the shipyards at Havre des Pas and their numbers rose to about 400. On they went to the Harbour where they gathered still more support. Around 11.30 am the ranks of the marchers had increased to 700 and by the time they reached the Royal Square they numbered 1,000. Their leader at this stage was John Picot, a shoemaker, who was arrested by the police. George Sargent, a seaman, was also arrested for attempting to lead a rush on the Royal Court Building. Suddenly the crowd decided to head for the Town Mills and when they arrived there they tried to break in and Centenier Le Bailly and the other police were powerless to stop them. The garrison was called out and placed at the disposal of Peter Le Sueur, Constable of St Helier, and the Attorney General read the Riot Act in the Royal Square. Eventually, at about 2.30 pm with the aid of men of the 81st Foot from Fort Regent the crowd was confronted at the Robin Hood Inn and dispersed and order restored. The marchers continued to parade through the town for the rest of the day. Next morning many of the men returned to work. There was further trouble, this time from the quarrymen from Mont Mado. As a result of the riots the price of bread baked for the States was reduced to 2d per pound and the rate of poor relief paid by the constables was increased. A number of the rioters received varying terms of imprisonment.

This was the background against which many islanders took the decision to emigrate.

There were direct sailings from Jersey to Australia. These two extracts from the issues of the *Jersey Times* of the 25th and 29th August 1854 relate to the *Evening Star* one of the ships which carried the emigrants.

The new ship *Evening Star*, built by Mr Allen at St Aubin, and bound for Australia with about 200 emigrants, was towed out of Victoria Harbor into the outer roads on Tuesday evening by the mail-steam-packet *Courier*, Capt. James Goodridge, Jun. This task was beautifully performed by the *Courier*. She commenced it about 10 or 15 minutes before 6, and was safely at her harbor-moorings again at ½ past 6, o'clock. Several thousands of persons witnessed the interesting scene from the Victoria and Albert piers.

The fine new emigrant-ship, *Evening Star*, left Jersey-roads on Friday morning, at ¼ before 10 o'clock, for Melbourne direct, with about 230 passengers on board.

Another ship which had sailed earlier the same year with emigrants direct to Australia was the *Exact*.

The first direct sailing from Guernsey to Australia took place when on 3rd April 1841 the barque *William*, owners Moullin and Co., under the command of Captain Le Beir, left the island. It was the first of many such sailings to a land of opportunity. On 8th April of the following year the schooner *Veritas* left the island bound direct for New York with eighty-five emigrants, mainly from Guernsey.

The very strong connection which continued between Jersey and Newfoundland is well evidenced by a poster of 1841 offering for sale in Jersey on 1st January 1842 in one lot the properties of Frederick Janvrin at Gaspé, Lower Canada, comprising his principal establishment at Grand Grève, in Gaspé Bay, four miles from Gaspé Point, his property at the Basin of Gaspé, comprising a wharf and salt and fish stores, his property Malbay, comprising a dwelling house, stages and fish stores, to the south of Grand Grève, Cape Roziers, another fishing establishment with a dwelling house and spacious fish stores, in the River St Lawrence, and a new establishment at Griffin's Cove, six miles from Cape Roziers, comprising a dwelling house, stage, fish store, flakes and cook rooms.

In 1848 Joshua George Falle was elected Member for Burin in the Newfoundland House of Assembly. Some years later he returned to Jersey and in 1864 was elected a Deputy of St Helier. Nine months later he was elected Constable, an office which he held for nine years. In 1873 he was elected jurat in replacement of Jurat Joshua Le Bailly.

CHAPTER THIRTEEN

Victorian Summer—1861–81

Roads, steam-boats, and public works, have already
so far altered the peculiar features of the larger islands
and the national peculiarities of their inhabitants,
that we must now seek for many quaint and interesting characteristics, that, only a few years ago, openly
presented themselves in the streets and market places.
J. W. Hill & Co.
Historical Directory of the Channel Islands (1874)

In 1861 the Prince Consort died; the Queen was to survive him by forty years. A painting of the Prince, a copy of an original by F. Winterhalter, hangs alongside a copy of the painting of the Queen by the same artist in the Great Hall of Victoria College. The Albert Pier and Albert Street were named after the Prince. In Guernsey Prince Albert Road and the Albert Pier were named after him, and a statue of him (a copy of an original by Joseph Durham) was erected at the head of the Albert Pier in 1863. In Alderney Fort Albert was named after the Prince and the granite arch and wrought-iron gates at the main entrance of St Anne's Church were erected in his memory.

Five Lieutenant-Governors of Jersey span this period: Major-General P. Douglas until 1863, Major-General Burke Cuppage 1863–68, Major-General P. Guy 1868–73, Major-General W. Norcott 1873–78, after whom Norcott Road was named, and Major-General Lothian Nicholson 1878–83.

Major-General M. Slade was still Lieutenant-Governor of Guernsey and remained so until 1864. He was followed by Major-General Scott in 1869, who in turn was succeeded by Major-General Frome. His successor in 1874 was Major-General the Hon. St C. G. Foly, who was succeeded in 1879 by Major-General Nelson.

John Hammond was Bailiff of Jersey until 1880 when he was succeeded by Sir Robert Pipon Marett. Sir Peter Stafford Carey was still Bailiff of Guernsey and remained so for the whole period, as did the Reverend W. T. Collings as Lord of Sark.

Since 1815 there had been important changes in St Helier. A cattle market was built in Minden Place and a fish market in Cattle Street in 1841 and a vegetable market connecting Beresford Street with Minden Place in 1854. The General Hospital was destroyed by fire during the night of 18th–19th July 1859. The portraits of the foundress, Mrs Barlett, and her husband, as well as the communion plate were saved. The new hospital (1860–63—by Philip Gallichan) was erected on the site of the old. The Royal Court House was replaced by a new building (1863–66—by T. Gallichan), which itself was reconstructed (1877–79—by Philip Le Sueur and Philip Brée). In 1863 the Theatre Royal in the Crescent suffered the same fate as the General Hospital four years earlier. It was not rebuilt, but a new theatre, called the Royal Amphitheatre and Circus (later renamed the Theatre Royal) was built in Gloucester Street in 1865. The States ordered the posting up of street names in St Helier in 1843.

The town had also undergone very considerable expansion. Many new streets were built extending the town westwards towards Gloucester Street, northwards towards La Pouquelaye and eastwards towards St Clement's Road. At first the new houses were built in continuous rows either with small front gardens divided from the street by granite walls surmounted by railings or directly onto the street. Later the houses were built in select terraces some of them with carriage drives and grass verges planted with trees for the use in common of the proprietors. The Royal Crescent in Don Road was particularly attractive with the new Theatre Royal (1828) at its centre. Almorah Crescent high up on the north of the town was a fine new crescent; Windsor Crescent (1835) in Val Plaisant was another. There were also many substantial houses standing in their own grounds.

Many of these new houses were really very fine. The large houses usually had a basement or semi-basement, a storey of reception rooms and another of bedrooms with attics above. They were stuccoed and had sash windows, many of them with Venetian shutters. The front door was usually reached by a flight of granite steps and sometimes had a porch. These houses whether built before or after 1837 were in the Georgian tradition with good proportions and classical details.

In order to maintain these big houses it was necessary for the proprietors to have a staff of domestic servants, who generally lived in and worked long hours.

Extensive improvements were carried out to St Helier's Harbour in accordance with a plan prepared by James Walker. The foundation stone of the New Harbour, later known as the Victoria Harbour, was laid on 29th September 1841. The south pier was finished first and in 1846 work was started on the north pier, later known as the Albert Pier. In 1872 further substantial work was carried out to the harbour in accordance with a plan prepared by Sir John Coode, but it was ultimately discontinued in 1874 owing to considerable storm damage caused to the work which had already been done.

While earlier manor houses were generally little more than farmhouses a number of country houses had now been built to house the richer residents and local gentry. New farmhouses were also built.

Strange to relate, despite the fact that Britain was at peace with France eight martello towers were constructed in Jersey in 1834, the last of their kind to be built in Europe.

St Catherine's breakwater was built 1847–55. It was the north arm of what was intended to be a harbour of refuge, the south arm of which was to have extended out from Archirondel Tower. The work was abandoned before completion and "like the works at Alderney, it stands as a monument of human folly and waste of the British taxpayers' money".

There had also been considerable development in St Peter Port since 1815. Many new streets had been built and some fine buildings added to the town. Much of the new work had been designed by John Wilson. In 1822 alterations were made to the interior of the Royal Court House. The same year the States built a meat market and in 1830 they built the arcades. The Commercial Arcade and Fountain Street were built in the 1830s. A new vegetable market was erected and in 1876 the Queen's Weights were removed to premises immediately to the west of and adjoining the Assembly Rooms. The same year the Oddfellows erected a new hall, later to become St Julien's Theatre, in St Julien's Avenue.

Substantial improvements were made to the harbour for a number of years from 1853 when the foundation stone was laid by the bailiff in the presence of the States "amid much ceremony and rejoicing".

There was some development in the countryside. St Sampson grew considerably, especially the harbour.

In Alderney the British Government decided to carry out considerable works as a result of the establishment by the French of a strongly fortified naval base at Cherbourg. A huge harbour of refuge was planned at Braye Bay to provide an anchorage of 150 acres. The breakwater was built 1847–64, but its companion breakwater was never started. In addition a series of ten forts were built along the north coast from Fort Clonque to Fort Essex 1845–61. Many of those employed on these works were Irish, as was the case with the building of St Catherine's breakwater in Jersey.

In Sark, St Peter's Church was built in 1821; the chancel was added in

1878. The tiny barrel-roofed prison, containing only two cells, was built in 1856.

The Channel Islands did not escape the 'railway fever' of the nineteenth century. In both Jersey and Guernsey the first mention of a railway appears in the newspapers of 1845, but nothing resulted. In Jersey a small temporary railway was used by the contractors building St Catherine's Breakwater. On 28th September 1870 the Jersey Railway Co. Ltd opened its line from St Helier (Weighbridge) to St Aubin. In 1884 the line was extended to La Moye Quarries and in 1899 to Corbière. The latter extension was carried out by Jersey Railways and Tramways Ltd which was the successor to the Jersey Railways Co. Ltd, which itself was the successor to the original company. The Jersey Eastern Railway opened its line from St Helier (Snow Hill) to Gorey in 1873. Gorey Station was renamed Gorey Village when the line was extended to Gorey Harbour in 1891. In Guernsey the Guernsey Steam Tramway Co. Ltd opened a tramway between St Peter Port and St Sampson in 1879. Alderney's railway was opened as early as 1847 and is the only railway still operating in the Channel Islands. It has always been used in connection with foreshoring along the breakwater at Braye, where the foreshore is constantly being eroded by the considerable seas which build up there during strong easterly and north-easterly gales.

The red-legged partridge which had secured a small niche in the history of Jersey became extinct in the island in the 1870s. Joseph Sinel (1844–1929), a Jersey naturalist, writing in 1916 had this to say about the last days of the bird in the island:

> The Red-legged Partridge was fairly numerous in the Island of Jersey until about 1870. I have seen numbers of them at Bouley Bay and have seen them breeding near Moulin de Bas, Trinity. In the last locality a nest containing thirteen eggs was netted in by my father-in-law, Mr Charles du Feu (the parent birds were also enclosed). The whole brood was reared and kept in confinement until full-grown. Then, with the scientific tastes of that time (this was about 1856) the whole lot was duly cooked and served at table. In 1868 a pair nested on the lawn of a house occupied by my brother, at La Garenne, Trinity. Fifteen eggs were laid, but the nest was raided by boys and the old birds disappeared.

So ended the long history of the red-legged partridge in Jersey, a bird which had been mentioned as long ago as 1576 in letters by Sir Amias Poulett to the Earl of Leicester and the Lord Admiral; which had graced the table of the governors, lieutenant-governors and gentry of the island time out of mind; a bird which James, Duke of York, had enjoyed shooting on the wing while staying in Jersey; a bird which had been sent as a present by the bailiff to Mr Secretary Pepys with the suggestion that he might pass some on to the King "if he thought them worthy of his majesty's acceptance". What an ignoble end it was for such a bird to have its last nest plundered of its eggs by a pack of callous savage boys!

In 1871 the Channel Islands Exhibition was held at Victoria College. It was inspired by the Great Exhibition which had been held in Hyde Park in 1851. The Channel Islands Exhibition was an entirely local enterprise and all the exhibitors were from the islands. It was opened on 28th June 1871 with much solemnity by the Lieutenant-Governor of Jersey in the presence of the Bailiff and States of Jersey, the Bailiff of Guernsey and other civil and military dignitaries of both bailiwicks. Some 30,000 people visited the exhibition during its three weeks' duration.

The exhibition was divided into a number of departments: Agricultural, Horticultural, Dogs and Poultry, Natural Products, Art and Industry, Loan Collection and Musical. Her Gracious Majesty the Queen:

> . . . signified her royal pleasure and readiness to take part in the Exhibition, and though, not able from state engagements and other important arrangements to be Herself or any other member of the Royal Family, present at the opening, yet most graciously gave directions that a Marble Bust (after a design of Her Royal Highness the Princess Royal,) of the late Prince Consort, surnamed the Good,—and himself the founder and first promoter of these kind of peaceful and industrial congresses, together with a case of East Indian small arms, and a sword once that of the great and pious naval Commander and discoverer Christopher Columbus, should be forwarded from Her own private Collection at Windsor Castle, to grace the Channel Islands' Exhibition; a compliment which the Committee most highly appreciates and which it is confident will ever be gratefully remembered by all her Majesty's faithful and attached subjects—in this portion of her dominions . . .

Successful exhibitors received silver and bronze medals on one side of which were depicted the arms of the two bailiwicks and the date "1871" surrounded by the legend "Channel Islands Exhibition + Prize Medal +" and on the other a female figure, draped and crowned, against a background of sea and sky and surrounded by various objects signifying agriculture, industry, trade and seafaring.

1873 was a bad year for Jersey because of two bank failures. The first, that of the Jersey Mercantile Union Bank occurred on 1st February; that of the Jersey Joint Stock Bank occurred on 3rd July. Joshua Le Bailly, one of the jurats of the Royal Court and managing director of the Jersey Mercantile Union Bank was tried for fraud and embezzlement. Seven charges were preferred against him; the sixth and seventh were treated as one. After a trial lasting eleven days Le Bailly was found guilty on the first, second, fourth and fifth and not guilty on the third and sixth. He was sentenced to five years' penal servitude.

Elias Neel, the Chairman of the Board of the Jersey Joint Stock Bank, who had been a jurat at the time of the collapse and had subsequently resigned, Philip Ahier, an ex-manager, and P. B. Mourant, the manager, were arrested on 16th August. On 4th September Mourant was discharged. Neel and Ahier stood trial at the January Assizes of 1874 and were acquitted on all nine counts of the indictment.

On 6th January 1881 was celebrated the centenary of the Battle of Jersey. Triumphal arches were erected at Millbrook and First Tower and in the town from Cheapside to the Beresford Street, Bath Street, Peter Street junction. It was, however, the Royal Square which was the real centre of attraction. The royal arms above the entrance to the Court House and the statue of King George II were regilded in honour of the occasion. In the windows of Mr Gallichan's house in Peirson Place was the inscription "While fields bloom his name shall live", a tribute to the hero of the battle, Francis Peirson. In the morning the troops had assembled at the People's Park and from there they marched through the streets of the town to the Royal Square. Eventually the square was full of troops surrounded by a large crowd. Every window overlooking the square was filled with spectators. On the steps of the Court House facing the military were the bailiff, the jurats, the other States' members, Lady Marett, the Hon. Mrs Nicholson and Lord Chelmsford, one of the descendants of the hero's family. When the troops had taken up their positions and His Excellency had received the general salute he addressed the assembled company in English. His speech was followed by three hearty cheers for the Queen and the band played the National Anthem. Then there were three cheers for the *Entente Cordiale* between Jersey and France, for the bailiff and for Lord Chelmsford. The last named made a speech in reply. Then followed the church service at which the Reverend Mr Thomas Le Neveu, Rector of St Martin, preached the sermon. At the conclusion of the service one of the ladies of the choir sang the National Anthem. The States then returned to their chamber where an address was voted to the Queen in honour of the occasion. There followed three official banquets—the military banquet presided over by the lieutenant-governor at the Hotel de la Pomme d'Or, the municipal banquet presided over by the Chef de Police of the Parish of St Helier at the British Hotel and the States' banquet presided over by the bailiff at the Royal Yacht Hotel. A large peaceful crowd filled the town at night looking at all the illuminations. So were the exploits of the young and gallant Peirson remembered a century after the event when he won victory and honour in the moment of his death. This was the last appearance of the militia under the old regulations and in their uniform of scarlet tunic and white trousers. At the close of the year the militia was authorized to inscribe on its colours the battle honour "Jersey 1781".

The attitude towards work in the days of the golden sovereign was very different from today. Craftsmen took a pride in their work and were expected to show respect to their employers. The matter is well illustrated by this extract from the Indenture of a Jerseyman bound apprentice to a local shipwright on 7th February 1887:

. . . during the full term of years next ensuing, fully to be completed and ended. During all which time he the said Apprentice his said Master shall and will faithfully serve, his secrets keep, his lawful commands everywhere gladly obey, and diligently and carefully demean and behave himself toward him. He shall not do, or willingly suffer to be done by others, any hurt, prejudice or damage to the goods and merchandises, or other affairs of his said Master, neither will he waste or lend them unlawfully to others, but the same to the utmost of his power shall hinder or thereof forthwith warn. He shall not commit fornication, nor contract matrimony, within the said term. At cards, dice tables or any other unlawful game, he shall not play, whereby his said Master may be damaged, or lose any of his own or others' goods, during the said term. Without licence of his said Master he shall neither buy or sell. He shall not absent himself by day from his said Master's service, without his leave, on pain of making up every day he absented himself, at the expiration of the said term. He shall not haunt ale houses, taverns, play houses, or any other places of debauchery; but in all things behave himself during the said term, as a good and faithful Apprentice ought to do.

The Empire was vast and ever growing and fighting was constantly going on somewhere within or along its boundaries. The First Boer War broke out in 1880 and lasted into the following year. Where there was fighting Channel Islanders were to be found following in the tradition of men such as Brigadier-General Thomas Anquetil (1784–1842), a Jerseyman, who was listed in 1804 among the cadets of the Bengal Infantry, spent the whole of his military career in India and Afghanistan, and was killed during the retreat of the British forces from the latter country.

A distinguished fighting man of this period was Major-General George Jackson Carey (1822–72), a Guernseyman, who served in the Kaffir Wars 1846–47 and 1850–52 and in the Maori War 1863–65, in which latter campaign he commanded at the siege and capture of Orakau. On 27th May 1865 he accepted the surrender of William Thompson, the Maori Chief, and his submission to Queen Victoria. Another such was Hubert Le Cocq (born 1833), also from Guernsey. He was a second lieutenant in the Bombay Artillery in 1851 and obtained steady promotion, reaching the rank of general in 1895. He saw service in the Persian War 1856–57, in the Indian Mutiny 1857–58 and further active service in India 1858–59. He became a Jurat of the Royal Court of Guernsey in 1892 and was appointed Supervisor of the States in 1897.

Another Channel Islander, this time a Jerseyman, William Mesny (1842–1919) even went so far as to distinguish himself in the army of a foreign country, China. Mesny went to sea at an early age, and in 1860, when only eighteen, deserted his ship at Hong Kong. He learnt to speak Chinese and three years later entered the Chinese customs. When Gordon went to China Mesny served under him in the Chinese Army. When Gordon left China in 1865 Mesny remained in the army and was promoted colonel (1869), major-general (1873) and lieutenant-general (1886). He died at Hankow.

Exports from Jersey at the end of this period included cattle, fruit, potatoes and bricks; in the same year those from Guernsey included cattle, fruit, tomatoes, flowers and stone. The old industries of cidermaking, knitting, oyster fishing and shipbuilding, as well as the Newfoundland fisheries, were either dead or dying.

A stimulus was given to Jersey's potato industry around 1880 when Hugh de la Haye (1835–1906) introduced the Royal Jersey Fluke, commonly known as 'the Royal'. By 1881 the quantity of potatoes exported annually from Jersey had risen to 38,596 tons.

The growing of tomatoes in Guernsey started about the year 1874. There is little doubt that the tomato was grown in the island before then as a decorative plant which produced 'love apples'. From small beginnings the industry grew rapidly and by 1893 a writer on the Channel Islands stated that: "The cultivation of tomatoes under glass has lately become a large industry in Guernsey."

The flower growing industry is said to have started in Guernsey in 1864 when a single consignment of daffodils was sent to the London market by Charles Smith of the Caledonia Nursery; this was a few years earlier than the first consignment from the Scilly Isles.

The tourist industry was becoming steadily more important. Its success was partly attributable to ever improving sea communications. The London South-Western Railway Co. provided a service from Waterloo Station, London, to the Channel Islands, via Southampton; the Great Western Railway Co. and the Weymouth and Channel Islands Steam Packet Co. provided between them a service from Paddington Station, London, to the islands, via Weymouth. There were also minor services from the South of England. Among the L.S.W.R. steamers of the period were *Normandy*, *Brittany*, *Caesarea*, *Alice*, *Fannie*, *Guernsey*, *South Western*, *Diana* and *Caledonia*; among the steamers on the Weymouth run were *Aquila*, *Cygnus* and *Brighton*. The number of passengers who travelled to Jersey via Southampton during May, June, July, August and September 1879 was 12,588, in 1880 13,844 and in 1881 12,881; the number who travelled via Weymouth in 1879 was 4,413, in 1880 5,071 and in 1881 6,522.

The Channel Islands were good places to visit, at least that was the opinion of David Thomas Ansted and Robert Gordon Latham as expressed in Chapter I of their excellent book *The Channel Islands* published in 1862, which went into three editions, the last of which, revised and edited by E. T. Nicolle, a Jersey historian, was published in 1893. Ansted and Latham wrote:

> As a place to visit during summer and autumn, but especially in the late autumn, up to November, it may safely be said that these islands are, beyond comparison, superior to any of the ordinary resorts of tourists, unable to reach the south of Europe. Much more varied in the style of beauty, though much smaller than the Isle of Wight, we have in most parts of Jersey and Guernsey, conditions only found in the most sheltered parts of the Undercliff in the Isle of Wight.
>
> The winds blow, and may be troublesome, but in the latter half of the year they are seldom cold, and never treacherous; there are then no fogs, and night frosts are extremely rare. The flowers continue to bloom, the fall of the leaf has more of softness and tenderness than of sternness, and the approach of winter is so quiet and gradual, that it is almost unheeded. There may be better summers on the Continent, though they are pleasant enough here, and the spring is ungenial in all northern latitudes; but for late autumn, there is no rival to the Channel Islands within several hundred miles.

Many new hotels had been opened to cater for the influx of visitors. One Jersey directory published at the end of the period lists nearly a whole page, double column, of hotels and boarding houses. Means of communication within the principal islands had improved what with two railways in Jersey, a tramway in Guernsey, excursion cars and cabs. There were pleasure grounds, bathing machines for those who indulged in sea-bathing, and there were boat trips. There were also souvenirs to take home such as locally made eau de cologne, miniature milkcans and Jersey cabbage walking sticks. And if there was any doubt as to what there was to be seen and done there were numerous guide books from which to choose.

Although the number of visitors to the islands was steadily increasing the population of Jersey had declined between 1861 and 1881 from 55,613 to 52,455. During the same period the population of Guernsey increased from 35,365 to 36,351.

CHAPTER FOURTEEN

Victorian Autumn—1881–1901

A very happy day for the British people and not
least the Channel Islanders was 22nd June 1897, the
Queen's Diamond Jubilee, the glittering pinnacle of
the Victorian Era.

Sir Lothian Nicholson was still Lieutenant-Governor of Jersey and the
island was to see five more lieutenant-governors before the end of the
reign, the last two of whom were Lieutenant-General Edward Hopton
1895–1900 and Major-General Henry Richard Abadie 1900–04. The latter
was very unpopular.

Major-General Nelson was still Lieutenant-Governor of Guernsey.
The Reverend Collings died in 1882 and was succeeded as Lord of Sark
by his son William Frederick Collings. Prince Blücher von Wahlstatt
took up residence as Tenant of Herm in 1891.

Sir Robert Pipon Marett remained Bailiff of Jersey until his death in
1884 when he was succeeded by Sir George Clement Bertram who held
the office until 1899. In that year William Henry Venables Vernon was
appointed bailiff, a position which he was to retain into the fourth decade
of the following century.

Sir Peter Stafford Carey was still bailiff after nearly forty years and was
to remain so for a further two years until 1883. He was succeeded by
John de Havilland Utermarck, who in turn was followed by Sir Edgar
MacCulloch in 1884, who held office until 1895. His successor was
Sir T. Godfrey Carey.

The Victorians were great churchgoers. The Church of England had
become somewhat decadent during the eighteenth century and remained
so during the early years of the nineteenth century. However, two
churches, the Methodists and the Roman Catholics, were building up their

congregations in the Channel Islands. Queen Victoria on her accession changed the whole mood of the court from one of laxity to one of circumspection. The Queen's example was followed by the nation and the Church of England underwent somewhat of a renaissance; other churches also prospered. In the Channel Islands new churches were built by the Church of England, the Methodists, the Roman Catholics and a number of other denominations. The Methodists celebrated the centenary of their establishment in the islands in 1884. In 1871 their numbers in Jersey reached a peak of 2,619 representing 4.6 of the population. Their peak in Guernsey of 2,490 was not reached until 1911 representing 6.3 of the population; their peak in Alderney of 162 was not reached until 1861, although in percentage terms their peak was reached in 1841 when the number of Methodists reached 81 representing 7.8 of the population, including the military. The number of Roman Catholics in the islands would have been few but for Irish and French immigrants. In Jersey the Irish Mission was established in Hue Street, St Helier, in 1826, moving to Vauxhall in 1843; the Mission at Faldouet, St Martin, was established in 1847 to meet the needs of Irishmen employed in building St Catherine's Breakwater (1847–55), and Frenchmen living in the east of the island; St Matthew's, St Peter, was established in 1872. In 1860 priests from Rennes obtained permission to reopen St Mary's, St Peter Port, which had been closed in 1850 on the opening of St Joseph's, as a dependency of that church and under the patronage of Our Lady of the Rosary. The church regained its independence in 1868. The Roman Catholic church of St Anne and St Mary Magdalen was established at Crabby in Alderney in 1848. The Roman Catholic Hierarchy was restored in 1850 and the Channel Islands were included in the Diocese of Southwark. When the Roman Catholic Diocese of Portsmouth was created in 1882 the Channel Islands were transferred to it.

Sunday by Sunday the native islanders and those who had settled in the islands attended in their 'Sunday best' one or other of the many churches or chapels, which were everywhere to be found. They worshipped in the ancient parish churches, hallowed by the centuries. They worshipped in the beautiful Regency church of St James-the-Less in St Peter Port and in the prickly Victorian gothic church of St James in St Helier. They worshipped in great barn-like chapels with neo-classical pediments and porticoes. They worshipped in fine modern churches built by leading architects of the day—St Anne's, Alderney (1850—by Sir George Gilbert Scott), St Joseph's, Guernsey (1846–51—by Augustus Welby Pugin), St Stephen's (1864—by George Frederick Bodley) in the same island, and St Simon's, Jersey (1865–66—also by Bodley). A new Roman Catholic Church of St Thomas (1887—by the Reverend Father Michaux, O.M.I.) was built in Val Plaisant, St Helier, and consecrated on 5th September 1893 to commemorate the centenary of the re-establishment of the Catholic Church in the Channel Islands. Prayers went up to the Almighty in his blue heaven in the words of the Book of Common Prayer, in the words of the Roman Missal and the extempore outpourings of the nonconformist ministers. The Book of Common Prayer and the Psalms had been published in French for the use of the islanders, as had been the Methodist hymns, and to the end of the century and beyond, services were held in the French language.

On 11th January 1886 the Jersey Banking Company (generally known as 'the States' Bank') suspended payment owing to 'Unforeseen circumstances'. Many individuals and firms were gravely affected by these financial disasters.

Three Jersey firms engaged in the Newfoundland fisheries seriously affected by this bank disaster were Charles Robin and Co., Philip Robin and Co. and Le Boutillier Bros. Applications were made on their behalf to the Royal Court for their affairs to be placed in the hands of the Judge Commissioner in order to avoid bankruptcies and to enable agreements regulating their affairs to be made binding upon all parties.

The application to the court by Charles Robin and Co. disclosed a very serious state of affairs. It was stated that although the firm "had immense landed and shipping possessions at Cape Breton, New Brunswick, and elsewhere" they were "difficult of realisation, and its enormous actual value would be unavailing if the creditors acted with impatience..." The firm was probably the greatest debtor to the Jersey Banking Company, and "the interests of the two concerns were almost indisolubly connected".

The application went on to disclose the reason for the firm's serious financial state:

In obedience to laws of nature, recent fishing seasons had been sterile, fish having been comparatively scarce. Swedish competition had also caused prices to go down, and last summer was so wet in Canada that drying operations were seriously impeded, and through the prevalence of cholera at some of the best markets, the demand had been considerably diminished. All the floating capital of the firm had thus become exhausted, and advances had been obtained from the Jersey Banking Company. Hence the embarrassed condition of the firm although owners of extensive property.

The application then went on to explain how the firm's employees were dependent on it and the consequences that had flowed from the financial difficulties in which it found itself:

Messrs C. Robin and Co. employed some 2,000 persons at Canada, New Brunswick, Etc., mostly Jerseymen and their descendants, and large numbers of Canadians were also dependant upon their establishments. It was the custom during the winter, instead of giving the Canadians money, to distribute food and clothing among them daily or weekly. That distribution had now ceased since the suspension of payment by the firm eight or ten days ago, and telegrams have been received here to the effect that riots had already broken out and that it had been necessary to apply to the Canadian Government for protection . . .

The Attorney-General stated the Government at Ottawa had been immediately requested to despatch troops to preserve order and distribute relief as had been done in connection with Hudson Bay Company. The Canadian Government would probably order the firm's stores to be opened and distribution of food and clothing proceeded with as transport was impossible at this season, and afterwards indemnify the owners. The stores contained large supplies of provisions, but the great object now was to prevent pillage by rioters in danger of starvation.

Philip Robin and Co., were stated to be trading at Cape Breton and elsewhere, and Le Boutillier Bros, at Jersey, Canada, British North America, and elsewhere. The latter firm had some time previous amalgamated with Le Boutillier and Co.

The proprietors of C. Robin and Co., Philip Robin and Co., Le Boutillier Bros, Le Boutillier and Co., the Jersey Banking Co., Abraham de Gruchy and Sons, bankers, and Abraham de Gruchy and Co., made arrangements with their creditors. The two last named firms were two of the leading and most respected businesses in Jersey.

The Manager of the Jersey Banking Company was Philip Gosset, the States' Treasurer, which was the reason for the bank being called by some 'the States' Bank'. Gosset was arrested on 14th January. Two days later he and Joshua Mauger Nicolle, Treasurer of the Impôt, were declared bankrupt, as were a number of shareholders of the bank during the succeeding weeks.

Charges were preferred not only against Gosset, but also against three of the managing directors of the bank and the sub-manager. All were acquitted except for Gosset who was found guilty and condemned to five years' penal servitude.

In Jersey the Daniel Case of 1889-90 was to some extent a repetition of the Fossey Case, the Guernsey *cause célèbre* of 1844-45. On 1st November 1889 a woman by the name of Daniel who had been charged with a serious offence had been committed to prison pending Her Majesty's pleasure. On 27th December when it came to the notice of Bertram, the bailiff, that the viscount acting by virtue of a Royal Pardon had given orders to the gaoler of the prison to release Daniel so that she might be placed aboard a boat for France, he immediately instructed the gaoler not to release Daniel until such time as the Royal Pardon had been registered by the Royal Court, and informed Ewart, the lieutenant-governor, of the action which he had taken.

The 'Prison Board Case' occupied the attention of the Jersey public from the summer of 1891 to the summer of 1894. The dispute was really one between Ewart, the lieutenant-governor, and Bertram, the bailiff, as to which of them was by right the President of the Prison Board. The Order in Council of 1837 confirming the constitution of the board was silent on the matter of the presidency. At the time of the Daniel case Ewart had written to the Home Secretary urging that the appointment of the President should lie with the Home Office. Matters had come to a head on 15th February 1890 when, in the absence of the bailiff, the lieutenant-bailiff, Edward Charles Malet de Carteret, claimed the right to be chairman and the lieutenant-governor, the viscount, Gervaise Le Gros, and the receiver-general, Edward Mourant, had withdrawn. The lieutenant-governor thereafter declined to attend meetings of the board until Her Majesty's pleasure was known.

On 23rd June an Order in Council was issued laying down that whenever the lieutenant-governor was present at a meeting of the Prison Board he was to preside, and in his absence the bailiff. The States considered that the Order in Council constituted a violation of the Order of 1837 and postponed registration, at the same time asserting the right of the bailiff to preside at meetings of the Board. In November 1891 issue was joined when the Privy Council agreed to hear the case for the States. The outcome was an Order in Council of 27th June 1894 recalling the offending order of 23rd June 1891, thus restoring the *status quo*. One beneficial result of the case are the four substantial volumes containing the cases on both sides, with appendices, in which are printed *in extenso* many interesting documents relating to the constitution and history of the island.

A very happy day for the British people and not least the Channel Islanders was 22nd June 1897, the Queen's Diamond Jubilee, the glittering pinnacle of the Victorian era. Her Golden Jubilee of 1887 had been an outstanding event, but had not been quite like this. The Royal Jersey Militia was represented in the procession in London. It was a proud day for the small Jersey contingent when they marched with "Men from New Zealand, Queensland, South Australia; men from the Cape, Natal and other parts of South Africa; from the Crown Colonies; from all over the world". Within fifty years this ancient force would be disbanded and have passed into history, but on this glorious 22nd June its proud representatives were marching with a host of other 'Soldiers of the Queen' in honour of their sovereign.

When in May 1900, during the Second Boer War, the news that Mafeking had been relieved reached Jersey there was great rejoicing among the local people and the British residents. However, the French colony favoured the Boers and in the evening a move was made by the crowds towards the French quarter of St Helier. Unfortunately, Mme Cousinard, who lived at No 9 Hilgrove Lane, did not take kindly to the demonstrators and emptied some slops over the leaders of the procession. Pandemonium broke out and the windows of hotels and other premises owned by the French people, both in 'French Lane' and elsewhere, were smashed by the infuriated demonstrators. Disorder reigned and it was well after midnight before order was restored.

The most famous Jerseywoman of the time was undoubtedly Lillie Langtry (1853-1929), a beauty, woman of the world and actress. Emilie Charlotte Le Breton (Lillie was a nickname) was born at St Saviour's Rectory (now a private house called La Belle Maison), her father being the Very Reverend William Corbet Le Breton, Dean of Jersey and Rector of St Saviour and her mother Emilie Davies Le Breton (née Martin). Lillie Le Breton married Edward Langtry, a widower, who died in 1897. Her second husband was Hugo de Bathe, whom she married in 1899, and who succeeded to a baronetcy in 1907. John Millais painted a portrait of Lillie Langtry holding a lily and called it *A Jersey Lily*, which was the origin of the sobriquet by which she became widely known. He once described her as "quite simply, the most beautiful woman on earth". Mrs Langtry mixed in high society and her intimate association with Albert Edward, Prince of Wales (later King Edward VII), attracted widespread public comment. As an actress (not a very good one) she toured the British Isles, the United States and South Africa. She died at Monte Carlo and was buried in St Saviour's Churchyard, Jersey. Both John Millais and Lillie Langtry were depicted among a number of other celebrities in the picture *The Private View at the Royal Academy 1881* by W. P. Frith, R.A., which was exhibited in the Bi-centenary Exhibition of the Royal Academy.

A famous Jerseyman born during this period was Edward Seymour George Hicks (1871-1949), the actor-manager. He married Mary Ellaline Terriss (known professionally as Ellaline Terriss), in 1893 when they were both in Arthur Chudleigh's Company at the Royal Court Theatre, London. Hicks was considered the most versatile and brilliant comedian of his day. He played many parts including Scrooge in John Baldwin Buckstone's play of that name and Valentine Brown in Barrie's *Quality Street*. In September 1904 came his great Vaudeville success, *The Catch of the Season*, written by him in collaboration with Cosmo Hamilton, which ran until 1906. He built the Hicks Theatre (now called 'The Globe') in Shaftesbury Avenue, London, and opened it on 27th December 1906 with a production of *The Beauty of Bath*, which was also written by himself and Hamilton. Hicks was knighted in 1935.

During the last year of the period Jersey exported 51,750 tons of potatoes worth £320,901. All the island's other exports were insignificant by comparison. Stone, tomatoes and grapes were the principal exports from Guernsey. Cattle were also being exported from both islands.

The number of visitors to the Channel Islands had increased enormously since the beginning of the reign. In Jersey alone some 50,759 passengers arrived from England and France between 1st May and 30th September 1901 compared with 43,079 during the same period of the previous year.

The ships which brought the visitors from England were always improving. The L.S.W.R. ships included *Dora, Frederica, Lydia, Stella* and *Vera*; the G.W.R. ships included *Lynx, Antelope, Gazelle, Ibex, Roebuck* and *Reindeer*. The *Stella* struck the Black Rock on the Casquets Reef on the morning of 30th March 1899. One hundred and five lives were lost. Mrs Mary Rogers, a stewardess, gave her lifebelt to a passenger, refused a place in a lifeboat and was drowned. Her act of heroism is commemorated in a stained glass window depicting 'Noble Women' in Liverpool Cathedral.

Throughout the century there were changes in Jersey in connection with public elections and the States Assembly. In 1831 public elections were first held on a weekday and two years later the public were first admitted to meetings of the States. In 1856 a law was passed which added fourteen Deputies to the assembly, the first election under the law being held the following year. Periodic sessions of the States were established in 1866 and the optional use of the English and French language was permitted in the assembly in 1900.

In Guernsey there was difficulty with regard to the office of Comptroller and changes in the composition of the States of Deliberation. After the reform of 1844 the States consisted of the bailiff, twelve jurats, eight rectors, the procureur, six deputies from St Peter Port and nine deputies from the other parishes, making a total of thirty-seven.

In 1851 the office of Queen's Comptroller had fallen vacant. A petition from the States to the Privy Council praying Her Majesty to fill the vacancy was dismissed by order of 6th July 1859. The States refused to accept this decision and made further representations which were successful in obtaining the re-establishment of the office of comptroller by order of 25th July 1861.

In 1899 the Privy Council approved a Guernsey Projet de Loi relating to the reform of the States of Deliberation whereby it would be composed of the bailiff, twelve jurats, ten rectors, two law officers, eleven deputies, four deputies from the four Cantonal Douzaines of St Peter Port, nine deputies elected by the heads of families of the whole island, making a total of forty-nine.

It was not only as a result of church building that the face of the islands had altered during the period. However, the changes were less considerable than those of the earlier years of the century. In St Helier the town hall was built in 1871; the market in Halkett Place was rebuilt in 1882; the Oddfellows Hall in Don Street was built in 1883; a new public library was opened in 1886; the Theatre Royal, Gloucester Street, was burnt down in 1899 and a new theatre, the Opera House, was built on the site in 1900. There were also changes in the countryside. In Guernsey there had also been changes in St Peter Port and especially in the countryside where a number of new greenhouses had been built for the rapidly expanding tomato industry.

During the reign there had been advances of all kinds in the Channel Islands, in addition to those already noticed, and many insular institutions and societies had been founded. In Jersey these included the Jersey Rifle Association (1861), the Jersey Swimming Club (1865), the Jersey Mutual Insurance Society (1869), La Société Jersiaise (1873), the Jersey Ladies College (now the Jersey College for Girls) (1880) and the Jersey Law Society (1899). In Guernsey they included the Guernsey Ladies College (1872), the Guille-Allès Library (1856—refounded 1882) and the Guernsey Society of Natural Science and Local Research (now La Société Guernesiaise) (1882). A register of births, deaths and marriages was established in Guernsey in 1840 and in Jersey in 1842. Telegraph communication between Jersey, Guernsey, Alderney and England was established in 1859, and between Jersey and France in 1860. After a break lasting some years direct telegraphic communication with England was re-established in 1870. The National Telephone Company started a telephone service in Jersey in 1896; the States of Guernsey established a telephone service in 1897. A piped water supply was established in both Jersey and Guernsey. La Société Jersiaise Museum at No 9 Pier Road, St Helier, was opened in 1894. The first motor-car was introduced into Jersey in 1899. A law regulating primary education was passed in Guernsey in 1893 and a compulsory education act was passed in Jersey in 1899.

Just over a year after the turn of the century, on 22nd January 1901 H.M. The Queen, Empress of India, died. It seemed unbelievable, after all the years during which she had reigned, that she was dead. To everyone the loss seemed personal. Her death marked the passing not only of a queen but of an age.

Although the Queen was dead she was not forgotten and so long as a Victorian remains she never will be, but even when the last Victorian has died and the Victorian Age has entirely receded into history the memory of Queen Victoria and the Victorians will be kept forever green by the tremendous achievements in every department of life which they have left behind them and will serve as their memorial.

The Queen's name is familiar to the present generation and will be to generations to come because of the many buildings, thoroughfares and places named after her—in Jersey Victoria Avenue, Victoria College, Victoria Cottage Homes, Victoria Crescent, Victoria Harbour, Victoria Marine Lake (West Park Bathing Pool), Victoria Road (Georgetown), Victoria Road (St Aubin), Victoria Street, Victoria Tower, Victoria Village, Queen's Farm, Queen's Road, Queen's Valley; in Guernsey Victoria Road, Victoria Tower and Queen's Road; in Alderney Victoria Street (formerly La Rue de Grosnez). In Jersey there is a statue of the Queen (1890—by G. Wallet) at the top of the harbour, which used to stand in the Weighbridge Gardens, before they were destroyed, and in Guernsey there is another statue of her which stands in the Candie Gardens, ironically not far from one of Victor Hugo.

CHAPTER FIFTEEN

Forty Years On—1901–40

Wars and rumours of wars.
Matthew XXIV, 6

With the accession of King Edward VII, whose consort was the beautiful Queen Alexandra, came an Indian Summer which was to last for thirteen short years during which the sun was to shine in all its glory on Great Britain and her Empire—including the Channel Islands, the oldest part of that empire. The British people were able to luxuriate in the knowledge that they were the masters of one-quarter of the population of the world and nearly one-quarter of the earth's land mass.

The new King was a man who enjoyed the good things of life and his zest for living permeated society. Perhaps his greatest personal achievement as sovereign was his visit to Paris in 1903 which paved the way for the *Entente Cordiale* and the Anglo-French Treaty of 1904.

What was to prove to be the first of many Battles of Flowers was organized in honour of the coronation of the new King. It was inspired by the Flower Carnival at Nice and was a great success. The press gave full coverage to this colourful occasion which took place on 9th August 1902 on Victoria Avenue, St Helier.

The event attracted large crowds and the stands bordering the southern side of the avenue were filled to capacity; the Lower Park was virtually hidden by thousands of spectators and many more covered the southern slopes of Wesmount (formerly called Mont Patibulaire). The double line of vehicles forming the procession passed along the avenue between lines of bright-hued bunting, stirred slightly by the light breeze, and beneath arches of gay lampions. Every kind of vehicle was pressed into service, from heavy trollies to the smallest pony carriage. "Veritable fairy bowers many of them were, the fair occupants being half hidden beneath the masses of beautiful flowers . . . Carnations and roses preponderated, but dahlias, hydrangeas, chrysanthemums, smilax, asparagus fern, sweet peas and many other products of the gardener's art were liberally represented . . ."

The signal for the start of the 'battle' was the firing of a gun from the bridge across the old quarry on Westmount. Those taking part in the procession were well supplied with ammunition in the form of tiny bunches of flowers with which they bombarded the spectators. Needless to say the fire was returned with energy and the battle raged along the whole length of the avenue for half an hour.

A Battle of Flowers was held until the outbreak of World War I. The event was revived between the wars at Springfield and continued to be held until the start of World War II. It was once again revived in 1951 since when it has been held each year along Victoria Avenue.

The Duke of Connaught visited Alderney in 1905 and Royal Connaught Square in St Anne was named after him.

In 1902, with the Second Boer War ended, peace, perfect peace, seemed to reign supreme. The pleasure-loving King and his equally pleasure-seeking subjects were able to give their undivided attention to the pursuit of happiness.

A memorial to Guernsey's dead in the South African War was erected in St Peter Port towards the top of the southern side of St Julien's Avenue. At Victoria College, Jersey, a brass framed in granite on the wall of the main staircase commemorates the Old Victorians who fell in the war.

Abadie was to remain Lieutenant-Governor of Jersey until 1904 when he was succeeded by Major-General Hugh Sutlej Gough. Major-General Saward was to remain lieutenant-governor of the sister island until 1903. One of his successors was General Sir Reginald C. Hart who was appointed in 1914 and held office throughout World War I.

Collings was still Lord of Sark.

Prince Blücher ceased to be Tenant of Herm on the outbreak of World War I and was interned. Despite the fact that the Prince was held in affection and regard by the people of Guernsey and was not a supporter of his country's warlike policy, he was not compensated for the loss of his tenancy of Herm. Sir Compton Mackenzie was the Tenant of Herm 1920–23. He described the Manor House as "the ugliest building in Europe". Mackenzie was also Tenant of Jethou 1920–34.

Vernon was still Bailiff of Jersey. Carey was succeeded as Bailiff of Guernsey in 1902 by Sir Henry Giffard, K.C., who himself was followed successively by William Carey in 1908 and Sir Edward Chepmell Ozanne in 1915.

Gough, the lieutenant-governor, sent a letter to Vernon, the bailiff, on 2nd January 1907 which ran:

Jersey Airways' aircraft on West Park beach, Jersey, in the 1930s—before the States built the airport at St Peter

(*above*) German troops marching past St Peter Port Parish Church in 1940

(*below*) German prisoners of war leaving Jersey in 1945

With reference to correspondence ending with your letter of 16th December, 1905, relative to the subject of the revision of the Admiralty Flag Book, I have the honour to inform you that the Secretary of State has recently submitted to His Majesty for decision, the question of the continued use by the Island of Jersey of the Arms at present claimed, and His Majesty has been graciously pleased to sanction their continued use.

A *Concours Musicale* was held in Jersey on 20th and 21st May 1907. It was announced that there would be 2,000 competitors, fifty-six competing bands and nine locales in use at the same time, and that there were concerts to suit all tastes with prices of admission designed to meet everybody's purse. Seven choral societies could be heard for 1s or seven brass bands or seven brass and reed bands for 6d. Coloured postcards symbolizing the *Entente Cordiale* were issued for the event. The handsome prizes were displayed at Messrs Le Riche's establishment in Beresford Street, St Helier, and attracted much attention.

On 6th May 1910 King Edward VII died and the Indian Summer was nearly over. Some idea of Great Britain's seemingly unassailable position as head of an immense Empire may be gained from this quotation from the Reverend W. Alexander Crist's address delivered at the memorial service for the late King held by the Free Churches at Grove Place Chapel (now Wesley-Grove), St Helier, on the 20th May:

Edward VII looked upon the throne as the symbol of national unity—the bond of Empire—linking the Motherland with vast Colonies and Dependencies over the seas. England is no longer what it was under the Tudors and Stuarts; we are not now a little island Kingdom, but an Empire formed by the federation of free States. Pass in swift review the widely-scattered parts of the British Empire: the vast Dominion of Canada, the West Indian Islands, a pacified and united South Africa, the mighty lands of Australia and New Zealand, the immense dependency of India, and the native States which look up to England as the paramount Power and, lastly, the protectorate of Egypt.

The late King's son, George, Prince of Wales, succeeded his father as King George V; his consort was Queen Mary. Almost from its outset the reign was difficult and sad. The political strife occasioned by the passing of the Parliament Act of 1911 was soon to be followed by strife between nations, which was to occasion death, destruction and misery on an unprecedented scale.

The first aircraft to arrive in the Channel Islands were four hydro-aeroplanes taking part in a race organized by the French-Commission Aéronautique from St Malo to Jersey and back which landed in St Aubin's Bay on 26th August 1912, where they were refuelled. There was tremendous interest in the event among the Jersey people and large crowds

14

gathered to see the arrival of the planes. The following week West's Pictures at the Royal Hall, Peter Street, St Helier, screened the hydro-aeroplane trials at St Malo of which the race had formed a part.

In August 1913 Winston Churchill who was to play a part, a somewhat controversial part, in the war that was soon to come, visited Jersey with Mrs Churchill. He played golf at the Royal Jersey Golf Club course at Grouville and she played tennis at Springfield. On 26th July 1886 when the young Churchill was at school at Brighton he had written a letter to his mother, Lady Randolph Churchill, in which he said that he would very much like to go to Jersey. The visit made in the summer of 1913 was to be the only one he was to make to that island or to any of the Channel Islands. However, when he was Home Secretary (1910–11), by virtue of that office, he had had responsibility for the islands.

A few months later and it was 1914. That summer the visitor season in the Channel Islands went on as it had done in previous years. Some of the holidaymakers may have been apprehensive of the dangers which threatened, but, no doubt, many were oblivious of the future. That year the concert party in Jersey was called *The Gaieties*. Performances were given in the Triangle Park (if wet, West Park Pavilion), St Helier, under the direction of Mr Wilson James, and the audiences sat watching the show while the sea lapped on the beach a few yards distant and the melodies were wafted over the waves and war seemed very far away. In fact, it was imminent. On 4th August Great Britain declared war on Germany and the Indian Summer was over and nothing would be quite the same again.

On the day war was declared an Order in Council was issued recalling to active service the Royal Militia Island of Jersey reserve as a whole in accordance with the terms of the Jersey Militia Act. The order was registered by the Royal Court two days later. The mobilization of the militia was proceeded with by the lieutenant-governor as G.O.C. the troops in the island. In Guernsey the militia, including reservists, was mobilized and an office opened for recruiting "men who do not at present belong to any branch of His Majesty's forces", a phrase which excluded those who were in the militia.

A Jersey Contingent was formed in December from volunteers of the Royal Militia, with the consent of the War Office. It consisted of six officers and 224 N.C.O.s and men and on 7th February 1915 was attached to the 7th Battalion Royal Irish Rifles. The contingent under the command of Major W. A. Stocker left the island on 2nd March 1915 to join the battalion at Buttevant, Ireland. While there it was joined by seventy-three men from Jersey bringing up its strength to 300. On 9th September 1915 the company left Ireland with the battalion for further training at Aldershot, where it was inspected by the Queen.

The company arrived in France in December and from the 27th of the month to 26th August 1916 they remained on the Loos Hullock front. They reached Albert on 1st September and during the attack on Guilliemont suffered heavy casualties. The attack on Ginchy was made on 9th September, resulting in its capture. From the Somme after a brief rest the company moved to Belgium on 26th September. On 31st July 1917 the company took part in the third battle of Yprès and after four days was withdrawn having suffered heavy casualties. They took part in further fighting and suffered more casualties.

During October 1917 the 7th Battalion was disbanded and amalgamated with the 2nd Battalion. The company took part in the Cambrai Battle. In December what remained of the company was ordered to join the 2nd Hants, with whom a number of Jerseymen were already serving. They remained with the battalion until the end of the war.

In March 1915 a Guernsey company joined the 6th Battalion Royal Irish Regiment. Shortly afterwards 156 men left Guernsey to serve with the Royal Artillery. They became the 9th Division Ammunition Column and preserved their identity throughout the war. Later another company of Guernseymen joined the 7th Battalion Royal Irish Fusiliers.

In 1916 the Royal Guernsey Militia was reformed as the Royal Guernsey Light Infantry, comprising two battalions, the 1st (Service) and the 2nd (Reserve). It was one of two new regiments formed in the British Isles during World War I, the other being the Welsh Guards in 1915. In September 1917 the 1st Battalion was sent to France on active service as part of the 29th Division, commanded by Major-General Sir Beauvoir de Lisle (1864–1955), who himself was a Guernseyman. Two months later at Cambrai the battalion lost 600 men and was mentioned in despatches. In April of the following year it suffered so many casualties at the Battle of Lys that less than one hundred men survived and as a consequence it was withdrawn from the front line. The remnant of the battalion carried out guard duties at General Headquarters until the end of the war. The names emblazoned on its colours tell its story: Yprès 1917, Cambrai 1917, Estaires, Passchendaele, Lys, Hazelbrouck—France and Flanders 1917–1918.

Two senior British naval officers who bore famous Guernsey names were Admiral Sir Reginald Godfrey Otway Tupper (1859–1945), successively Vice-Admiral Atlantic Blockade, Admiral Northern Patrol and Commander-in-Chief Western Approaches, and Admiral of the Fleet Sir Osmond Brock (1869–1947), who took part in the Battle of Jutland in 1916 and was Chief of Staff to the Commander-in-Chief, Grand Fleet, 1916–19.

During the war French seaplanes were based at Castle Cornet in Guernsey, and a camp for German prisoners of war was established at

Blanches Banques in Jersey. By 1917 the camp had been enlarged to accommodate 1,500 prisoners, as well as 150 guards and a staff of between twenty and thirty officers. It was closed in October 1919.

In 1918 there was an influenza epidemic; over 300 people died in Jersey alone in six weeks.

The States of Jersey contributed a total of £100,000 towards the expenses of the war; in 1918 the States of Guernsey made a similar contribution.

The States published *Jersey's Roll of Honour and Service*. In the foreword appears the following paragraph:

> The Roll of Honour contains 862 names—a touching record of death's toll of the Island's manhood. In that long list of heroes will be found a representative of nearly every Jersey patronymic. Jersey's sons have fallen in well nigh every battle on sea or land. They took up arms that we might live in peace. It behoves us to take care that their noble deeds be kept in lasting remembrance.

The Armistice marked the beginning of the troubled and uneasy years which were to end with the outbreak of World War II. The sailors, soldiers and airmen who had won victory at a terrible price returned home sickened by war and hoping for a new and better world. Their expectations were all too soon to be dashed. There were memorials in plenty for the dead, and for the living honours and medals and in many cases little else. A cenotaph to Jersey's dead was erected at the eastern end of the Parade Gardens in St Helier; a war memorial to Guernsey's dead was erected at the top of Smith Street, St Peter Port.

In 1918 Major-General Sir Alexander Wilson was Lieutenant-Governor of Jersey. Among his successors were the Honourable Sir Francis R. Bingham (1924–29), after whom Mount Bingham, St Helier, was named, and Major-General J. M. R. Harrison, who only held office for a few months in 1940. In 1918 General Sir Launcelot E. Kiggell was appointed Lieutenant-Governor of Guernsey in succession to Hart and held office until 1920. Major-General J. R. Minshull-Ford was appointed Lieutenant-Governor in 1940 and, like Harrison, only held office for a few months.

Vernon was still Bailiff of Jersey. He was succeeded on his retirement by Charles Edward Malet de Carteret in 1931, who in turn was succeeded by Alexander Moncrieff Coutanche in 1939.

Ozanne was still Bailiff of Guernsey. He was succeeded by Sir Havilland Walter de Sausmarez in 1922. He in turn was succeeded by Arthur William Bell in 1929, who died in 1935 and was succeeded by Victor Gosselin Carey.

Mellish was still Judge of Alderney and remained so until his death in 1938. He was succeeded by Frederick G. French.

William Frederick Collings remained Lord of Sark until he died in 1927; he was succeeded by his daughter Sybil Mary Beaumont (1884–   ). She married Dudley Beaumont in 1901—it was a runaway marriage. Beaumont died of Spanish influenza in November 1918. Mrs Beaumont married Robert Woodward Hathaway, an American who had become a naturalized British subject, in 1929.

Peace came to a changed world, very different from what it had been before the war. The twenties provided the strange contrast of carefree abandon on the one hand and depression on the other culminating in the General Strike of 1926. For the most part the Channel Islands fared well during the period although both the years 1920 and 1921 were marred for Jersey by industrial unrest. On 20th March 1920 there was a strike of store hands, necessitating the swearing in of special constables; this lasted until 26th April. The following year there was a much more serious strike which started on 1st October. It began to crumble on 19th November and was over in December. Originally only employees in the building and allied trades were involved, but later employees of the Jersey Gas Light Company Limited also came out on strike.

At the outbreak of the war the States of Guernsey formed an Island Police Force for the duration of hostilities. The force consisted of an inspector, two corporals and twenty-three constables, of whom twelve were the constables already employed by the parish of St Peter Port. In 1919 the States decided to establish the force on a permanent basis and to transfer to it all the police duties hitherto exercised by the parish constables.

In 1921 King George and Queen Mary, accompanied by the Princess Mary, visited the Channel Islands, the first visit of a reigning sovereign since those of Queen Victoria in 1859. The Royal Squadron comprised the Royal Yacht *Victoria and Albert*, the Royal Yacht *Alexandra*, H.M.S. *Cleopatra*, H.M.S. *Wryneck* and H.M.S. *Watchman*. The French Republic was represented by a light cruiser and two destroyers. The weather was sweltering and the visit must have been quite an ordeal for the royal visitors. In Jersey there was a sitting of the States at which the King was presented with a Loyal Address of Welcome. This was followed by a sitting of the Royal Court at which the Lords of the Manors owing suit of court at the Assize of Heritage paid homage to the King; the Lord of the Manor of Trinity presented His Majesty with two mallards in accordance with the terms of the tenure of his manor. The royal party visited the Royal Jersey Agricultural and Horticultural Society's show grounds at Springfield, Victoria College and Mont Orgueil Castle. In Guernsey the King reviewed ex-service men and women, presented decorations, received addresses and knighted Edward Ozanne, the bailiff. He visited Elizabeth College, attended a parade of schoolchildren and accepted a pedigree Guernsey cow from the Royal Guernsey Agricultural and Horticultural Society and fruit from the Guernsey Growers' Association. The ceremony of homage was performed by the Guernsey Lords of the Manor, as in Jersey.

The British Government decided to ask Jersey and Guernsey to make an annual contribution to the British Exchequer. This request was unprecedented and met with resistance from the insular administrations. After negotiations which lasted for some considerable time Jersey and Guernsey made once and for all contributions of £300,000 and £220,000 respectively to the British Exchequer towards the cost of the war which were accepted in 1927.

A Jerseyman famous in the world of the theatre of this period was Lionel Frederick Leonard, later known as Frederick Lonsdale (1881–1954), the playwright and librettist. His best-known plays are probably *The Last of Mrs Cheyney* (1925), *On Approval* (1927) and *Canaries Sometimes Sing* (1929). His light opera *The Maid of the Mountains* (1916), for which he wrote the libretto, ran for 1,352 performances at Daly's Theatre, London. He died suddenly while walking in a London Street. Lonsdale was almost certainly the only Jerseyman ever to have been received by a President of the United States—Franklin D. Roosevelt.

A famous Jerseywoman of the time was the novelist Elinor Glyn (1864–1943). The daughter of Douglas Sutherland, a civil engineer, she married Clayton Glyn, J.P., in 1892, Elinor Glyn was an extremely penetrating observer of the environment in which she lived, and her books, despite their imperfections, were read with avidity. In the Hollywood of 1920, where some of her stories were filmed, she began a new career, that of a scriptwriter. The well-known *Three Weeks* (1907) was regarded as naughty and as usual in such cases was widely read. *It* (1927), a short novel with an American setting, made the word 'it' synonymous with personal magnetism. Elinor Glyn was a prolific writer and enjoyed great international success. A popular edition of her books, issued in 1917, sold over one million copies.

Air travel was on the way. A flying-boat service (believed to have been the first in the British Empire) between Southampton and St Peter Port was started in 1923, but it did not prove successful and was discontinued. Nevertheless, flying had come to stay and regular Channel Islands' routes were soon to be established.

Jersey Airways Ltd was formed on 9th December 1933 and some nine days later the first aircraft took off from the beach at West Park, St Helier, bound for Portsmouth. Permission for the beach to be used as a landing strip was given by the receiver-general. During the company's first year of operation 20,000 passengers were carried. Originally the service was confined to Jersey–Portsmouth, but in January 1934 an alternative Jersey–London service was started, to be followed in March of the same year by a Jersey–Southampton service. In June a bi-weekly Jersey–Paris service was commenced, but ran into difficulty owing to colorado beetle control and had to be suspended in September. The number of passengers travelling by air to the islands steadily increased—24,717 were carried in 1935 and more than 30,000 the following year.

The first airport in the Channel Islands was opened in Alderney in 1935, the States of Jersey Airport at St Peter was opened in 1937 and the States of Guernsey Airport at La Villiaze, Forest, in 1939.

In 1935 the Channel Islands with the rest of the British Empire celebrated the Silver Jubilee of the King and Queen. The following year their son Edward, Prince of Wales, who was the darling of the nation, paid a visit to the islands. The same year the King died and was succeeded by the Prince as King Edward VIII. Before the year was out the new King had abdicated and been succeeded by his brother George, Duke of York, as King George VI, whose consort was Queen Elizabeth.

During his short reign King Edward approved the continued use by Guernsey of the Cross of St George as its flag. How long the island had used the flag before authorization is a matter for conjecture.

The principal exports from Jersey in 1939 were potatoes, tomatoes, granite and cattle; those from Guernsey were tomatoes, grapes, granite and cattle.

The tourism industry was continuing to grow in the Channel Islands and had increased greatly since the beginning of the century. Although air services had begun augmenting the shipping services, there was no decline in sea travel and new ships were built for the Channel Islands' services: G.W.R.—*St Helier, St Julien* and *St Patrick* and S.R.—*Isle of Jersey, Isle of Guernsey* and *Isle of Sark*, with the *Brittany* on the Jersey–St Malo route. More and bigger hotels were being built, especially in Jersey, to cater for the influx of visitors. Jersey's railways and Guernsey's tramway had succumbed to the competition of the motor-buses; the excursion cars had given way to motor char-à-bancs. Bathing machines had disappeared; bathing costumes were becoming briefer. Dancing was popular and West Park Pavilion in Jersey was rebuilt in the South African Dutch style (1931—by R. Blampied)—no longer was it the 'Tin House' providing cover for *The Gaieties* "if wet". The *thé dansant* was the rage; so were beach pyjamas. Tourism was becoming 'big business', especially in Jersey, and the Channel Islands were beginning to lose their old-world charm.

Since the end of the Great War the number of 'residents' in the Channel

Islands, principally Jersey, was increased by the arrival of a few 'rich residents' whose primary, if not only, object was to preserve their riches from the depredations of the British Inland Revenue and especially the British Estate Duty Office. Hitherto, generally 'the residents' had been retired people, many of them from the navy, army, Indian army and colonial service, who were attracted to the islands by the low cost of living, the temperate climate and the fact that they were able to find kindred spirits with whom to discuss the 'old days'.

The face of the islands had changed somewhat since the turn of the century, especially in Guernsey where greenhouses had been built in large numbers. In Jersey there was some ribbon development and many bungalows had been built, often little more than shacks, which disfigured the coastline along part of the Royal Bay of Grouville and also along St Ouen's Bay. Those concerned for the natural beauty of the island founded the National Trust for Jersey in 1936.

Life had undergone many changes since the beginning of the century. Electricity, radio and talking motion pictures had come to stay. The first electric cable for lighting and power was laid in St Helier in 1924. The first Jersey cinema was opened at the Cercle St Thomas, New Street, St Helier, by Messrs Langlois and Poulain in 1908; the first 'talkie' shown in the island was *The Perfect Alibi*, screened at the Picture House (formerly the Oddfellows' Hall), Don Street, St Helier, in 1929. The first licence to install and work wireless apparatus in Jersey was issued on 20th February 1920. The telephone system was transferred from the British Post Office to the States on 31st March 1923. It will be recalled that the States of Guernsey already ran their island's telephone system. Alderney had no telephones. The same year the British Government transferred Elizabeth Castle to the States of Jersey to be maintained as an historic monument. Mont Orgueil Castle had been handed over similarly in 1907. Income Tax was first introduced into Guernsey in 1920, although the principle of income tax had been adopted in 1918; income tax was introduced into Jersey in 1928; and in the same island women over thirty years of age were given the vote in 1919 and women over that age were permitted to become Deputies in the States in 1924.

The Channel Islands were linked to the Church Assembly (now the General Synod) by The Channel Islands (Church Legislation) Measure, 1931 and The Channel Islands (Representation) Measure, 1931.

As the fourth decade of the century drew towards its close the storm clouds were gathering. On 3rd September the storm broke which was to rage over Europe for nearly six years.

After the declaration of war there followed months of inactivity along the whole of the front. The air raids and the gas attacks did not materialize. There was a feeling of unreality about the whole situation. Matthew

Le Marinel, Dean of Jersey (1937–59), at the end of his Christmas message, published in *The Islander* of December 1939, wrote:

And so, even in war time, we can keep Christmas with joy and hope. God has already proved His love by sending his Son to be born into the world. We know that above all the trials and difficulties of life God reigns Supreme and just. We know too that in the end, right must always triumph over might. Therefore we look forward with confidence and hope, and joyfully keep the festival of the coming of God's Son into the world, who came to be our only stay and hope, our Saviour and Prince of Peace.

Suddenly in 1940 Germany sprang forward to the attack and the phoney war was over. The offensive bowled Germany's enemies off their feet and left France prostrate before her. By 17th June it was all over— France had surrendered and the battered remains of the British Expeditionary Force were by a miracle back in England. Members of the St Helier Yacht Club assisted in the evacuation from Dunkirk. In recognition of the fact the Admiralty gave permission in 1952 for the club to fly a defaced Red Ensign, the defacement taking the form of two crossed axes of gold on a blue ground (the badge of the Parish of St Helier) and an anchor. These emblems also feature on the club's burgee.

On 10th May Churchill had become Prime Minister and on the evening of 17th June he made his historic broadcast to the nation in which he growled defiance at the enemy; he said that the British nation would never surrender, and it never did. Alas, at this stage words, however fine, could not save the Channel Islands. On 19th June it was announced that the British Government had decided that the islands were to be demilitarized. From that moment their fate was sealed and their occupation by the enemy had become inevitable.

The lieutenant-governors had been instructed that in the event of their recall the bailiffs were to discharge their civil duties in their place and to remain at their posts; the Crown Officers were also instructed to remain. The lieutenant-governors and the British troops who had been sent to the islands were withdrawn; Harrison left on 21st June and Minshull-Ford on 20th June. The Royal Jersey Militia volunteered for overseas service and left in a body. The insular authorities began arranging their affairs to meet the difficult and unparalleled circumstances in which they found themselves. In Jersey a Superior Council or cabinet was established to direct the island's affairs; in Guernsey a similar body known as the Controlling Committee was set up with Ambrose Sherwill, the procureur, as its president.

As the Germans had advanced further through France, so more and more people decided to leave the Channel Islands. It was a big decision to make, particularly for those whose only experience of the outside world was of holidays spent in happier days. For all who evacuated it meant abandoning most of their worldly possessions; for those who remained it was to mean five dreary dangerous years of occupation. The people of Alderney were given little choice; they were totally evacuated in three ships on 23rd June. One-fifth of the population of Jersey and one-half of the population of Guernsey were evacuated. Most of the people of Sark decided to remain.

On 28th June the Germans carried out air raids on Jersey and Guernsey. Jersey suffered ten dead and a number wounded, and in the more severe attack of the two Guernsey had thirty-four dead, commemorated by a plaque on White Rock pier, and a number of wounded. The *Isle of Sark* had been in St Peter Port harbour during the raid on Guernsey. German military aircraft flew over the islands the following day but did not attack. The Occupation was imminent.

CHAPTER SIXTEEN

The German Occupation—1940-45

For strategic reasons it has been found necessary to
withdraw the armed forces from the Channel Islands.
I deeply regret this necessity . . .
                              King George VI (1895–1952)

Those who remained in the Channel Islands either intentionally or unin-
tentionally waited with heavy hearts for the Germans to arrive. If they
had been aware of the brutal enormities of which the Nazis were capable
fear and terror would have filled their hearts. As it was they were resigned
to enemy occupation and nothing more.

The Germans arrived in Guernsey on 30th June, Jersey on 1st July and
Sark on 3rd July and all communications with England ceased. It was the
first time for centuries that any of the islands had been in enemy hands. In
Guernsey the occupying forces were met by the inspector of the Island's
police force; in Jersey they were met by the bailiff, Lieutenant-Colonel
H. H. Hulton, the government secretary and C. W. Duret Aubin, the
attorney-general.

At this point it is worth recalling that Coutanche was Bailiff of Jersey,
Carey and Sherwill were respectively Bailiff and Procureur of Guernsey,
and Mrs Hathaway was Dame of Sark. The procureur was removed by
the Germans from both the office of procureur and president of the Controlling Committee, but was subsequently reinstated as procureur. The
Reverend John Leale was appointed president of the Controlling Committee in succession to Sherwill.

The legislatures and courts of the islands were allowed to continue. All
laws, ordinances, regulations and orders had to be submitted to the
German commandant before being enacted. The Bailiff of Jersey presided
over the Royal Court with the royal mace before him.

Members of the British forces on leave in the islands were taken prisoner and sent to Germany.

Freemasons, Oddfellows and the Salvation Army were forbidden to meet and their property was confiscated. In January 1941 the interior of the Temple in Stopford Road, St Helier, Jersey, was wrecked and the contents removed. Church services were allowed, as were prayers for the Royal Family and for the welfare of the British Empire. Church bells were allowed to be rung before service. Motion pictures, plays and other entertainments were also permitted, but were subject to censorship. The local newspapers continued publication, but were also subject to censorship. A curfew was imposed. Hotels and private residences were taken over to house German troops. Other troops were billeted on the civilian population.

The Germans commandeered cars and petrol was only allowed for essential services; horses took over from the internal combustion engine. Bicycles were at a premium. There was a run on the shops, both by the local population and the German troops and goods became steadily scarcer. Inevitably a black market developed. The islanders also bartered amongst themselves. Someone would offer, say, a pound of tea "for what?" and be offered in exchange another commodity in short supply. Prices rocketed, for example, a pound of tea cost anything between £18 and £25 and a pound of Jersey butter cost £2 2s 9d. Shortages taxed the islanders' initiative and, among other things, they produced substitutes for tea and tobacco; salt they obtained by evaporating sea water.

The Germans had an official newspaper in both Jersey and Guernsey. In the former island it was entitled *Deutsche Inzelzeitung* and in the latter *Deutsche Guernsey Zeitung*. They also produced two booklets on the Channel Islands, *Die Kanalinseln, Jersey, Guernsey, Sark* by Hans Auerbach and *Ein Bilderbogen von den Kanalinseln* by Baron von und Aufsess, who became Chief of Administration. Both publications were illustrated with excellent photographs. Colonel Graf von Schmettow, who was appointed Commander-in-Chief of the Channel Islands in September 1940, sent a copy of Auerbach's book to Hitler as a Christmas present.

Schmettow had his headquarters in Jersey. Major Bandelow was military commander in Guernsey. The islanders were fortunate in having Schmettow in command as he was more sympathetic to them than many other commanders might have been.

The Germans set about turning the Channel Islands into impregnable fortresses; bunkers, fire control towers and gun emplacements appeared everywhere. Slipways were blocked, anti-tank walls constructed and thousands of mines planted. The labour necessary for carrying out the work was supplied by foreign prisoners—French, Spanish, Polish and Russian, who were half-starved and brutally treated by their captors.

The insular authorities endeavoured to keep local labour fully occupied so as to avoid it being used by the Germans. With this object in view the States of Jersey built La Route du Nord during the Occupation. In addition to innumerable fortifications, the Germans built two large underground hospitals, one at St Lawrence in Jersey and one at La Vassalerie at St Andrew's in Guernsey, which are now preserved as tourist attractions. The Organization Todt was brought in to carry out the building works. Guernsey lost two well-known landmarks, the de Saumarez memorial at Delancey Park and the Doyle Column at Jerbourg, said by the Germans to have been in the way of their guns. The four bronze plaques from the base of the de Saumarez memorial which depict the Admiral's exploits are preserved at Castle Cornet; the Doyle Column was replaced by a new one in 1953.

The British Post Offices in the Channel Islands continued to operate. Originally the Germans had intended overprinting the stocks of British stamps held in the Channel Islands with the swastika and the words "Jersey 1940". As the result of protests on the ground that the overprinting defaced the head of a reigning sovereign the overprinted stamps were destroyed except for a small number. In Jersey a design for a local stamp similarly overprinted was produced, but it was never issued. Guernsey ran out of supplies of the British penny stamp by December 1940 and diagonally-bisected twopenny stamps were used as penny stamps.

In connection with their vast building works the Germans built railways in Jersey, Guernsey and Alderney. In January 1942 a railway was commenced in Jersey which was officially opened on 15th July. Ultimately lines ran from St Helier to Gorey, from St Helier to Corbière and from St Helier to Ronez. The line to Gorey had small branches towards its Gorey Pier end and the line to Ronez had two branches, the first to Tesson Mill and the second to St Ouen's Bay, connecting with a line running along the Bay from L'Etacq in the north to La Pulente in the south. At St Helier's harbour there was a network of lines linking the east and west lines and serving the Albert Pier and the New North Quay. The Germans' railway system in Guernsey was started in 1941. Ultimately lines ran from St Peter Port to St Sampson's, and then on to Les Vardes Quarry and down the west coast to L'Erée Bay. Branches ran northward from St Sampson's to Petils Bay and northwards from L'Islet Depôt. The railway also served the White Rock arm of St Peter Port Harbour. Although the Germans destroyed the old railway in Alderney, they eventually established their own, which ran from New Harbour to Platte Saline gravel works and also had branch lines.

Between 13th July 1940 and 28th December 1943 British Commandos carried out seven raids on the Channel Islands, one each on Jersey,

Guernsey, Herm, Burhou and the Casquets, and two on Sark. In the raid on the Casquets the seven Germans occupying the lighthouse were taken completely by surprise and were carried off to England as prisoners.

On 24th September 1940 R.A.F. planes carried out leaflet raids over the Channel Islands. Two differently worded leaflets were dropped containing messages. The first from the King, read:

The Queen and I desire to convey to you our heartfelt sympathy in the trials which you are now enduring. We earnestly pray for your liberation, knowing that it will surely come.

GEORGE RI

The second read:

All of you, His Majesty's loyal subjects on the Channel Islands, must keep asking yourselves two great questions: "How long must we put up with the German occupation?" and "How are our friends on the mainland?"

This news-sheet brings you the heartening answers. We on the mainland are in good heart. By subjecting our women and children to the wickedest forms of warfare known to history, Hitler has only stiffened our backs. And the events of the last three weeks have only served to confirm Mr Churchill's words on 21st August, that "the road to victory may not be so long as we expect". Nor may the day be so distant when we shall come to your relief. All our rapidly and enormously increasing strength is directed towards that day when the shadow of the bully will be lifted from you and from the whole of Europe. We shall continue to bring you the news from England as often and as regularly as we can.

In 1941 Guernsey issued her first postage stamps. They were designed by E. W. Vaudin of the Guernsey Press Company. Two denominations were issued, a 1d scarlet in February and a ½d emerald-green in April. A third denomination, a 2½d deep ultramarine, was issued in 1944. All denominations featured the same design, which incorporated the arms of the bailiwick, and were reprinted on a number of occasions. Jersey also issued her first postage stamp in 1941. It was designed by Major N. V. L. Rybot, a prominent member of La Société Jersiaise. A single denomination—1d scarlet—was issued in April. A further denomination—½d bright green—was issued in January 1942. Both denominations featured the same design which incorporated the arms of the bailiwick. In each corner of the 1d stamp there appeared the letter A which stood for *Ad Avernum Adolf Atrox* (To hell with you atrocious Adolf); in each of the top corners of the ½d stamp there appeared the letter A and in the bottom corners the letter B which respectively stood for Atrocious Adolf and Bloody Benito. In 1943 Jersey issued a pictorial set of six denominations designed by Edmund Blampied, a well-known local artist, engraved by Henri Cortot and printed by *Postes, Télégraphes et Téléphones* in Paris. Certain denominations were reprinted in 1943 and 1944.

In 1941 the States of Jersey issuing notes. The first to be issued was a 2s note which appeared on 31st May. It was followed by a series in denominations of £1, 10s, 2s, 1s and 6d, designed by Blampied, issued on 20th April 1942.

The Germans issued special currency called Reichskredit marks, which it was forbidden to circulate in Germany. There were notes representing Reichmarks 50, 20, 5, 2 and 1 and Reichspfennigs 50, and small zinc coins representing Reichspfennigs 10, 5, 2 and 1.

In January 1941 François Scornet, a young Frenchman, twenty years old, together with some friends younger than himself, attempted to reach England with a view to joining the Free French forces. They sailed from Brittany and on reaching Guernsey were under the mistaken impression that they had arrived at the Isle of Wight. They landed in high spirits singing the *Marseillaise* as they did so. Their happiness was short-lived because they were arrested by the Germans almost at once. They were taken to Jersey and lodged in prison. They were brave young men and in spite of being captured they were far from downhearted. The Germans tried Scornet and his companions on 3rd February. Scornet accepted full responsibility for the escape and was condemned to death. On the morning of 17th March he was taken to St Ouen's Manor where he was executed by a firing squad. As he fell the cry of *"Vive la France!"* was on his lips. Scornet's companions were sent to prison where they were so cruelly treated that four of them died.

At this point it is appropriate to mention that during the Occupation a number of islanders effected their escape.

On 8th June 1942 the Germans issued an order requiring all Channel Islanders to hand in their wireless receiving sets. The ban on wirelesses did not prevent the islanders from gaining news of the outside world and the progress of the war. Some people did not surrender their sets; others made crystal sets, "cat's whiskers" as they were called. Thus many were able to listen to British broadcasts, particularly news bulletins, and news was rapidly passed on to those who either had not the nerve or the opportunity to listen themselves. Churchill's speeches were a constant source of encouragement and hope to the islanders, as they were to those in Great Britain and elsewhere.

Great ingenuity was used in concealing radios of all kinds. Those who did have them ran the risk of imprisonment and a heavy fine. Fortunately the majority were not found out. However, some were. The consequences of being discovered were in most cases not serious; in a small number they were. Among the unfortunates was Canon Cohu, the Rector of St Saviour, Jersey, who was indiscreet in the use of the radio which he had installed in the organ-loft of his church. Despite a warning from the dean to be more careful, the canon made no secret of what he was doing. Inevitably the Germans took action against him, as well as others who were implicated. The canon was sentenced to four years' imprisonment. He died in the concentration camp at Spergau, having undergone brutal treatment.

There were other unfortunate victims of German brutality. Among them were Mrs Gould and her brother Harold Osmond Le Druillenec and sister Mrs Ivy Foster. Mrs Gould had hidden a young Russian prisoner-of-war who had escaped from the Germans and came to her door seeking help. All went well and it looked as though the Russian would never be discovered. It seems that someone informed against Mrs Gould and, although the Russian escaped, she was tried for harbouring him, and her brother and sister for having radios. Le Druillenec and Mrs Foster had had their houses searched following the tip-off against their sister, which is how it was that the radios had been discovered. Mrs Gould was sentenced to two years' imprisonment and both her brother and sister to five months' simple imprisonment. In the event Mrs Foster served her sentence in Jersey, but Mrs Gould and Le Druillenec were sent away and cast into concentration camps. Mrs Gould died in the hell of Ravensbrück; Le Druillenec miraculously survived the horrors of Belsen and was eventually restored to his family.

In May 1942 an underground news-sheet, entitled *Guernsey's Underground News Service*, but known as *GUNS* for short, began to be circulated in that island. It appeared almost every day except Sunday until February 1944. The news-sheet measured 13½ by 8 inches. At its head was its name *GUNS* and a V for victory. It was typewritten on tomato-packing paper and averaged 780 words daily. The news was obtained from the BBC's news bulletins. Those connected with the newspaper were denounced to the Germans by an informer, tried and sentenced to imprisonment—Charles Machon two years and four months; Cecil Duquemin one year and eleven months; Ernest Legg one year and ten months; Frank Falla one year and four months; and Joe Gillingham ten months. They were all sent to Germany and imprisoned. Machon and Gillingham died in prison, ironically enough after they had completed their sentences; Duquemin, Legg and Falla survived.

The Channel Islands had a champion in Britain throughout the Occupation in the person of Lord Portsea, formerly Sir Bertram Godfrey Falle, Bt (1860–1948), son of Joshua George Falle. He had been Member of Parliament for Portsmouth 1910–18 and for Portsmouth North 1918–34, and elevated to the peerage in 1934 as Baron Portsea of Portsmouth. He made a number of speeches in the House of Lords and elsewhere in the interests of the islanders, but although they were well intentioned and

The Bailiff and members
of the Royal Court of
Guernsey on their way to
the Market Place to hear the
reading of the Proclamation
of Accession in 1952

Princess Margaret accompanied by General Sir George Erskine, the
Lieutenant-Governor and Sir A. M. Coutanche, the Bailiff and their ladies
leaving the States Building, St Helier—1959

displayed extremely patriotic sentiments so far as the islands were concerned, they were couched in somewhat extravagant language and must have been a source of minor irritation to the British Government on whom they made very little impression.

More effective so far as the Channel Islands' refugees were concerned was the work of the Channel Islands Refugee Committee which during the five and a half years of its existence did excellent work on behalf of the refugees. A number of Channel Islands' Societies sprang up throughout the United Kingdom. A monthly magazine, *The Stockport Review*, kept the refugees in touch with each other and gave them the latest news from the islands. Red Cross messages, containing a few censored words, provided an inadequate, but, nevertheless welcome, link between those in the islands and those in Britain.

In September 1942 most of those living in the islands who had been born elsewhere in the British Isles were sent to Germany, where they lived in internment camps—Biberach, Laufen and Wurzach—until the end of the war. The procureur was among the deportees from Guernsey; Mrs Sherwill and her two sons remained in Guernsey.

On 6th June 1944 began the allied invasion of Europe. The whole might of Great Britain and the United States of America and others who espoused the cause of Freedom was hurled against Hitler's western wall. Indeed this was the beginning of the end. The drooping spirits of the Channel Islanders were buoyed up by the hope of speedy liberation, but nearly a year, possibly the grimmest period of the Occupation, was to elapse, before they were freed.

The Germans issued a proclamation asking the people to keep their heads, to remain calm and to refrain from any acts of sabotage and threatening those who attacked the German Forces with death.

On 27th December the International Red Cross ship *Vega* arrived in Guernsey with much needed supplies. She arrived in Jersey three days later and was to make a number of further visits to the islands before the Liberation.

Schmettow was replaced in his command by Vice-Admiral Hüffmeier in February 1945. In announcing his appointment to the German troops he declared:

> I have only one aim: to hold out until final victory.
> I believe in the mission of our Führer and of our people.
> I shall serve them with immutable loyalty.
> Hail our beloved Führer.

The regular army officer aristocrat had been replaced by the 'dyed in the wool' Nazi.

15

Prior to the Liberation there was unrest among the German troops. Subversive literature was circulated among them. On 7th March 1945 fire broke out at the Palace Hotel at St Saviour in Jersey and spread to an ammunition dump. There was a violent explosion which caused damage to buildings in the vicinity. On the same day a Todt depôt at Georgetown in the same parish was burnt out. The Germans suspected sabotage in both cases.

During the night of 8th–9th March somewhat surprisingly the Germans in Jersey carried out a successful raid on Granville. They came back with a ship, the *Eskwood* and thirty prisoners, the majority American. They also released fifty-five of their own men.

The Channel Islanders were aware of each new allied victory and knew that their liberation was daily growing closer. Eventually, in May 1945 it was realized by the islanders and the Germans alike that the war would only last for a few more days. The islanders' ordeal was nearly over.

No one who did not endure those five long years of the Occupation can ever fully understand what it was like to live under German domination. The islanders settled down after the upheaval of the evacuation and the arrival of the Germans and resumed their daily round. The good behaviour of the occupying forces allayed their initial fears. However, once the days had slipped on into months and the months into years, life got steadily more monotonous and more difficult. Furthermore, there was an ever growing realization of the wickedness of which the Germans were capable, although, on the whole, the actual occupying forces behaved themselves extremely well. Gradually food became scarcer, as did all the everyday necessities of life which are taken so much for granted. The civil authorities did as much as they could to organize food supplies and to distribute what there was fairly among the population. However, during the last year of the Occupation shortages of practically everything became acute and it was only the arrival of Red Cross supplies which saved the situation from becoming very grim. It must be placed on record that the Germans, who were themselves very short of food, made no attempt to divert the food parcels from reaching the civilian population.

A few more days and the ordeal was over and the events of the past five years merely a grim nightmare best forgotten in the dawn of liberation.

CHAPTER SEVENTEEN

History in the Making—1945-73

... and our dear Channel Islands are also to be freed
today.
                    Winston S. Churchill (1874-1965)

"Our dear Channel Islands are also to be freed today." These words
spoken by Winston Churchill on 8th May 1945 in his VE-Day speech
were heard by the people of Jersey, not only over the loudspeakers in
the Royal Square in St Helier, but also on many a wireless set which had
been hidden away from the Germans. The large crowd in the Square
heard the reference to the Channel Islands with joy in their hearts and
tears in their eyes at this the end of their long ordeal. The Prime Minister's
speech was also heard in Guernsey and Sark; it was heard by the evacuees,
by Channel Islanders serving in the forces, by Major Sherwill at Laufen.
Wherever Channel Islanders heard the Prime Minister's reference to their
homeland they were deeply moved.

Churchill's words were being put into effect by the men of 'Operation
Nest Egg'—the liberation of the Channel Islands. At 10 am on Tuesday,
8th May, the destroyer *Bulldog*, escorted by the destroyer *Beagle*, sailed
from Plymouth for a rendezvous with the Germans four miles off
Guernsey. The Germans arrived at the appointed hour in a rusty mine-
sweeper flying a swastika. A young German naval officer, Lieutenant-
Commander Arnim Zimmerman, went aboard *Bulldog* with a paper
authorizing him to receive armistice terms and convey them to Vice-
Admiral Hüffmeier. Brigadier Alfred Ernest Snow, in command of
Operation Nest Egg gave Zimmerman an instrument providing for
immediate surrender, and the time for a further rendezvous. Zimmerman
said that Hüffmeier had ordered him to state that if the British ships did
not move away from the island he would consider their continued

presence as an act of provocation. At midnight, the time appointed for the next rendezvous, Major-General Heine, Hüffmeier's military adviser, arrived aboard an armed trawler at the place appointed with authority to sign an unconditional surrender. Early on the morning of Wednesday, 9th May, Heine signed the surrender. Within a short time the first British troops landed in Guernsey, where they received a tremendous welcome.

The Bailiff of Jersey was growing impatient at the delay. All he knew was that the *Beagle* was on its way. At last the telephone rang and the bailiff was requested to meet General Wolfe and accompany him to the *Beagle*. The bailiff went to the Pomme d'Or Hotel to meet Wolfe. There was then a delay until the attorney-general and the solicitor-general were fetched. At last all was ready and Wolfe, two staff officers, the bailiff and the two crown officers went out in a launch to the *Beagle*, where the surrender was soon signed. The bailiff then sent a signal to the King:

With my humble duty I send to Your Majesty this assurance of the devotion of the States and People of Jersey to Your Majesty's Throne and Person.

We have kept ourselves informed of the Armed Forces of Your Majesty and of Your Majesty's Allies and of the ceaseless efforts of the workers behind them, and on this day of our liberation we rejoice that we can once more take our place and play our part within Your Majesty's Empire.

and another to the Prime Minister:

The People of Jersey assembled yesterday, Tuesday, 8th May, in the Royal Square to listen to your broadcast will ever remember your affectionate reference to "Our dear Channel Islands," and on this day of liberation I address to you, in the name of the States and People of Jersey our undying gratitude for your inspired leadership of the British Commonwealth of Nations, which has led to the victory of the Allied cause in Europe, and to the liberation of the Channel Islands.

The liberation of Sark did not take place until Thursday, 10th May, but that did not worry the indomitable Dame who had effected her own liberation on 8th May and hoisted the Union Jack and the Stars and Stripes at La Seigneurie. British troops landed in Alderney on 16th May, but it was not until 2nd December that the first group of islanders returned home.

In May, Herbert Morrison, the Home Secretary, visited the Channel Islands accompanied by Lord Munster, Parliamentary Under-Secretary. He praised the local authorities, expressed the belief that it would have been folly for the British Government to have attempted to defend the islands, and gave assurances that the Government would do all in its power to restore the islands to their former position. In June the King and Queen paid a visit to the islands and received a rapturous welcome. The King and Queen presented a silver chalice and paten to Guernsey and Sark and the Queen presented a silver crucifix and candlesticks to Jersey. In 1947 the King handed over Castle Cornet to the people of Guernsey as a token of their loyalty during two world wars. Their Majesties were the first of many members of the Royal Family to visit the islands—the Duchess of Kent (1948), Princess Elizabeth and Prince Philip (1949), the Duke and Duchess of Gloucester (1952), Queen Elizabeth II and Prince Philip (1957), Princess Margaret (1959), Queen Elizabeth the Queen Mother (1963), Prince Charles (1968), Princess Alexandra and the Hon. Angus Ogilvy (1968) and Princess Anne (1972). The visit by Princess Elizabeth and Prince Philip to Sark in 1949 was the first official royal visit ever made to that island. The visit of Princess Victoria, a sister of King George V, in 1902 was unofficial.

In 1945 Lieutenant-General Sir Edward Grasett was appointed Lieutenant-Governor of Jersey, and Lieutenant-General Sir Philip Neame was appointed Lieutenant-Governor of Guernsey. Admiral Nicholson who was appointed Lieutenant-Governor of Jersey in 1953 was the first naval man to hold the office since Sir George Carteret. The first airman to hold the office of lieutenant-governor in either island was Air Marshal Sir Thomas Elmhirst who was appointed Lieutenant-Governor of Guernsey in 1953. Grasett gave his name to Grasett Park (formerly Clifton Park Estate) and Nicholson to Nicholson Park, both in Jersey.

In 1947 each bailiwick assumed the responsibility for its lieutenant-governor's salary and establishment in return for the British Treasury's paying the insular exchequers a sum equivalent to that received on each island from the hereditary revenues of the Crown, the whole in accordance with the Jersey and Guernsey (Financial Provisions) Act 1947.

In December 1945 the King conferred honours on a number of Channel Islanders for their services during the Occupation. Coutanche, the Bailiff of Jersey, Carey, the Bailiff of Guernsey, and the Reverend John Leale, Jurat of the Royal Court of Guernsey and President of the Controlling Committee of the States of Guernsey, each received a knighthood. C. W. Duret Aubin, Attorney-General for Jersey, E. A. Dorey, Jurat of the Royal Court of Jersey, President of the Department of Finance and Economics and Member of the Superior Council of Jersey and Ambrose J. Sherwill, Procureur of Guernsey, were made Commanders of the British Empire. Others were made O.B.E. or M.B.E., or received the B.E.M. The Dame of Sark did not receive an honour at that time. However, in 1965 she was made a Dame of the British Empire.

Coutanche continued as Bailiff of Jersey. Carey retired as Bailiff of Guernsey in 1946 and was succeeded by Sherwill, who was knighted in

1949. Sherwill retired in 1960 and was succeeded as bailiff by William Henry Arnold, who had been procureur since 1946. Mr Arnold was knighted in 1963 and remained bailiff until his death in July 1973, when he was succeeded by Mr John Henry Loveridge, C.B.E., who had been deputy bailiff since that office was created in 1969.

The first ecstasy of liberation having subsided there was time to take stock of the Occupation, particularly of the attitude of the civil authorities towards the Germans. Most islanders were satisfied with the way in which the authorities had acted; others, a minority, were far from satisfied. The critics felt that there had been too much co-operation with the Germans. Some criticism was unmerited. If the authorities had been less co-operative than they were the local populations would have suffered. If the authorities had either indulged in or encouraged active resistance inevitably appalling consequences would have resulted, as so often was the case in occupied Europe. In any event, acts of resistance or sabotage committed in the islands would have had no effect on the course of the war. Nevertheless, it is possible to appreciate the views of those who wished to strike a blow, however small, for freedom.

The first task which faced the insular authorities after the Liberation was the rebuilding of their economies. The export of potatoes and tomatoes was revived, the tourism industry was re-started and 'the residents' began returning, their numbers being considerably augmented by many new 'residents', some rich and some very rich, refugees from the penal taxation obtaining in the United Kingdom. In addition, there were a number of immigrants from Britain who were more interested in escaping from the frustrations imposed by socialist policies and controls than from taxation, however burdensome.

Between 1901 and the outbreak of war in 1939 there had been very little political activity in the Channel Islands and during the Occupation political activity was not possible. However, during that time islanders, both living in the islands and in the United Kingdom, started thinking about the changes they would like to see made in the islands when the war was over. In the United Kingdom islanders calling themselves the Channel Islands Study Group were thinking along the same lines and published a booklet entitled *Nos Iles* in 1944 setting out their ideas. After the Liberation a number of political parties emerged in Jersey—the Jersey Democratic Movement, the Jersey Labour Party and the Jersey Progressive Party.

Soon after the Liberation the politicians were hard at work endeavouring to carry reforms into effect. In January 1946 the States of Guernsey adopted proposals relating to their own reform; in March the States of Jersey followed suit. Proposals in relation to judicial reform were under discussion between the States and the Royal Court of Guernsey; proposals of a similar kind were also under discussion between the States and the Royal Court of Jersey. The insular authorities submitted their proposals for constitutional and judicial reform to His Majesty so that his pleasure concerning them might be ascertained. An Order in Council was made on 4th June appointing a Committee of the Council to be sent to the islands to take evidence from all the interested parties on the proposals for constitutional and judicial reforms. The committee visited the islands in September and evidence was taken in public for four days in both Jersey and Guernsey. The report of the committee was presented by the Home Secretary to Parliament in 1947. In the result legislation providing for the reform of the insular constitutions and legal systems, which, although making radical changes, nevertheless, in large measure preserved the traditional form of the legislatures and the courts, was enacted and received the Royal Assent.

The British Labour Party had been swept to power by a tremendous wave of popular support, resulting in Clement Attlee and his government commanding a substantial majority in the House of Commons. The Labour government was thus enabled to implement its policies without any risk of defeat in the lobbies. Hitherto, generally speaking, the political colour of the British government of the day had little effect on the Channel Islands. Now things were to be different and the results of the nationalization of the railway companies and their cross-channel services, and of the British airlines was to be felt in the islands. The insular authorities opposed the extension to the Channel Islands of the Civil Aviation Act, 1946, but their protestations were in vain against a Government ruthlessly pursuing its predetermined doctrinaire policy of nationalization. The States of Jersey felt that they had no alternative but to submit to the registration of the Order in Council extending the Act to the Channel Islands, but nevertheless they placed on record their regret that the Government had not agreed to meet the wishes of the island as set out in the resolution adopted by the States on 25th February 1947, and more amply detailed by the delegation of the States at the Conference held at the Home Office on 10th March 1947. Considering the successes which the island had had against the British authorities in the high noon of Great Britain's imperial power this was indeed a humiliating defeat in the days of its imperial eclipse.

It was with very genuine regret that islanders viewed the passing of the Great Western Railway and the Southern Railway which, with their predecessors, had had so long a connection with the islands; it was with similar feelings that islanders viewed the passing of Channel Islands Airways which during their few years of existence had served them so well.

The British Nationality Act 1948 recognizes the special status of the

Channel Islands by providing that "a citizen of the United Kingdom and Colonies may, if on the ground of his connection with the Channel Islands or the Isle of Man he so desires, be known as a citizen of the United Kingdom, Islands and Colonies". The inclusion of this provision in the Act was attributable largely to the efforts of Lord du Parcq (1880–1949), a Jerseyman and a Lord of Appeal in Ordinary, who pressed for it during the bill's passage through the House of Lords. Herbert du Parcq had a brilliant scholastic and university career. He was secretary, treasurer and in 1902 President of the Oxford Union. He was called to the English Bar in 1906 and admitted to the Jersey Bar later the same year and took silk in 1926. He appeared for the defendant in Attorney-General *v* Brown before the Jersey Assizes in 1931, which is believed to have been the first occasion on which a King's Counsel had pleaded in the island. The same year du Parcq was raised to the bench as a Judge of the High Court, King's Bench Division. In 1938 he was appointed a Lord Justice of Appeal and a Privy Councillor. During World War II du Parcq devoted himself to the work of the Channel Islands Refugees Committee. In 1946 he was appointed a Lord of Appeal in Ordinary, created a Life Peer and made a member of the Judicial Committee of the Privy Council.

In September 1950 C. T. Le Quesne, Q.C. (1885–1954), a distinguished son of Jersey, who had been President of the Baptist Union of Great Britain and Ireland (1946–47), was appointed lieutenant-bailiff solely for judicial duties.

In 1951 the Jersey Paid Police Force was constituted to be available for duty throughout the island. The new force was in addition to and not in replacement of the Honorary Police who continued and still continue to function. However, it did absorb the existing Paid Police Force which was small in number and operated only in the town of St Helier. In Guernsey further legislation was passed regulating the Island Police Force and in 1949 a law was passed which authorized the States to determine the establishment of the force by resolution.

If any Jerseyman had been asked in 1951 whether the Minquiers and Ecréhous were British unhesitatingly he would have answered "Yes". He might also have added that they formed part of Jersey, the Minquiers being considered part of the Parish of Grouville and the Ecréhous part of the Parish of St Martin. However, differences arose between the British and French Governments regarding the sovereignty of the islands and late in 1951 they submitted their dispute to the International Court of Justice. The case was heard at The Hague between 17th September and 8th October 1953 and not unexpectedly the judgement was in favour of the British. For his part in the presentation of the British case C. S. Harrison, the Attorney-General for Jersey, was awarded the C.M.G.

In 1960 Jersey celebrated Coutanche's Silver Jubilee as bailiff. He had attained high office at an early age; he had borne a considerable burden during the Occupation; he had played a leading rôle in the post-war years. There were a number of celebrations to mark his twenty-five years as civil head of the island. There were ceremonies in the Royal Court and States. A splendid portrait of the bailiff by James Gunn was unveiled in the Court Room. A thanksgiving service was held in the Town Church and another at St Mary's and St Peter's Roman Catholic Church. There was also a banquet in the bailiff's honour, attended by R. A. Butler, the Home Secretary. The following year Coutanche was created a life peer taking the title of Baron Coutanche of St Brelade in the Island of Jersey and of the City of Westminster. The following year he retired.

Lord Coutanche was succeeded as bailiff by Harrison who had been since 1958 deputy bailiff and before that attorney-general. Unfortunately he died in office in 1962. Harrison was succeeded by Robert Hugh Le Masurier, the attorney-general. Mr Le Masurier was knighted in 1966.

King George VI died in 1952. The new Queen was proclaimed in the Channel Islands as her predecessors had been. In Jersey the proclamation was read by the acting viscount from a raised platform in the Royal Square, St Helier, in the presence of the lieutenant-governor, bailiff, jurats, Crown officers, advocates and members of the States. In Guernsey the proclamation was read three times, firstly in the Royal Court Room, secondly from a platform draped with the Guernsey flag at the north end of the terrace in front of the Royal Court House and thirdly from the balcony in the Market Place. The ceremonial in Guernsey was far more elaborate and picturesque than in Jersey. The bailiff wore his ermine-trimmed robe, the jurats wore their robes, and the members of the bar wore their black gowns and head-dresses. After the second reading of the Proclamation the guard of honour moved off headed by the Guernsey Brass Band followed by the Court Usher, then came H. M. Sheriff and H. M. Sergeant, in a black robe with tricorn hat and chain of office, walking together. Next came the lieutenant-governor and bailiff followed by Major-General Colwill and Captain M. H. T. Mellish, A.D.C. to His Excellency, the jurats, H. M. Procureur and H. M. Comptroller, the advocates, the rectors, clergy and more official guests all walking in pairs. When the procession reached La Barrière de la Ville in Smith Street it was met by the Constables and Douzaine of St Peter Port who acceded to a request for the procession to proceed through the town and then formed an escort, walking in pairs in front of the procession with the Chief Inspector at their head. The procession proceeded to the Market Place by way of Smith Street, High Street and Commercial Arcade.

In Alderney the proclamation was read by the president in front of the Court House in St Anne in the presence of the members of the Court and States. It is said that proclamations used to be read in Le Huret, near the back of the vicarage, and someone objected to the Proclamation of Accession being read elsewhere.

In Sark the proclamation was read by the prévôt outside the Boys' School which serves as the Court House.

When the Queen visited Jersey in 1957 the ceremony of homage was held in the Royal Court Room as it had been in 1921. The jurats, greffier, advocates and solicitors, the lords and ladies of the manor who were to make homage, as well as a number of spectators, were all assembled when the Queen entered the court room from the judges' room escorted by the bailiff and the lieutenant-governor and followed by the royal suite. The bailiff explained that certain lords and ladies who held manors and attended twice a year at the Chief Pleas of the Court of Heritage desired to pay homage and asked for permission for them to do so. The Queen having assented, the roll was called by the attorney-general and the lords and ladies of the manor answered to their names, bowing or curtseying as they did so. When all their names had been called they clasped their hands and together with bowed heads recited the words of homage: "I am your liege man to bear you faith and homage against all." The Lord of St Ouen, being the senior of those paying homage, stood in front of the Queen and had his hands clasped by hers. At the conclusion of this part of the ceremony the Lord of the Manor of Trinity came forward bearing two mallards on a silver dish, which he offered to the Queen, and when she had signified her acceptance, he handed the dish to the receiver-general. This concluded a most interesting occasion. All the formal words in the ceremony were spoken in French.

In passing, it should be mentioned that on her arrival at St Helier's Harbour the Queen was met by the Lord of Rozel Manor and the Lord of Augrès Manor, in accordance with ancient custom. The Lord of Rozel Manor is one of the Sovereign's hereditary butlers in the island, but the present holder was not called upon to carry out the duties of that office as his predecessor was in 1921; the Lord of Augrès is also an hereditary butler.

In Guernsey the ceremony of homage was held in 1957 at St George's Hall (now a timber store) and was far more impressive than the Jersey ceremony. The bailiff's procession, which entered the hall preceded by the usher of the Royal Court, consisted of the constables carrying their bâtons, the advocates, the greffier, the procureur, the comptroller, the jurats (all walking two by two), the sergeant and lastly the bailiff in his ceremonial robes. After a fanfare of trumpets, the Queen's procession, which consisted of Her Majesty and Prince Philip and the royal suite, entered the hall preceded by the sheriff with drawn sword. As Her Majesty entered the sheriff cried out, "Her Majesty and His Royal Highness". After the greffier had said the Lord's Prayer, he read the roll and each member of the Court of Chief Pleas answered to his or her name, rising and bowing as they did so. The bailiff then read the loyal address and presented it on bended knee to the Queen, who then rose and replied. The Lord of the Manor of Sausmarez was then called by the greffier and he mounted the platform, escorted by the lieutenant-governor and the bailiff, and approached the Queen. He then bowed and knelt in front of her and all the lords and ladies who owed homage stood up in their places. With his hands held between those of the Queen the Lord of Sausmarez then spoke the words of homage to which she gave reply. The greffier then called the Lord of the Manor of Les Eperons (the Spurs), and he ascended the platform carrying a crimson and gold cushion on which were the pair of silver-gilt spurs owed by him as his feudal due. The lord of the manor then addressed the Queen stating that he wished to discharge his service and to offer the spurs which he owed for his manor. Then on bended knee he offered the spurs to the Queen, who touched them as a token of acceptance. The lord of the manor then rose and withdrew. The proceedings closed by the greffier reading the grace.

The Lord of the Manor of Sausmarez is hereditary Third Butler to the Sovereign, a service performed by the holder of the manor in 1921.

The year 1966 saw the nine hundredth anniversary of the Battle of Hastings. Nine centuries had passed since the Channel Islands had first become linked with England through the fact that their Duke William II had by conquest become the King of that fair land. Except for brief periods, the link had not been broken, and if during the Great Rebellion some islanders had sided with Parliament against King Charles I, it was no more than many true-blooded Englishmen and Scotsmen had done. The loyalty of the Channel Islands' Parliamentarians to England was unswerving. The islanders irrespective of their own internal differences had always been loyal to her and even the constitutional and ecclesiastical disputes which had arisen on numerous occasions had done nothing to shake this loyalty. Down the years the islanders because of their determination, tenacity and skill had retained and extended their constitutional independence. Resolution on the part of the islanders and restraint on the part of the British authorities produced the happy relations which existed between them.

As the years passed so the islanders' Norman heritage of language and law, of custom and tradition, steadily declined and the islanders ties with Britain ever grew closer and by 1966 the Channel Islands were very largely anglicized.

When the islands were first linked with England she was a kingdom on her own. Since then she became part of the United Kingdom which took to itself a mighty empire. That empire came of age as the Commonwealth and by 1966 had largely melted away leaving the United Kingdom bereft of dominions beyond the seas. However, after 900 years the Channel Islands were part of what remained and happy and proud to be so.

The islands had changed out of all recognition during those years. Each century had made its contribution towards what they had become both physically and otherwise by 1966. Many old buildings had disappeared, but many remained, including churches, chapels, castles, houses, water mills and windmills. The people had also changed, but many of the old families remained, some of which had been established in the islands five, six, seven, eight or even nine centuries before. The de Sausmarezs still occupied their manor house in Guernsey, as did the Lemprière-Robins Rozel Manor and the Malet de Carterets St Ouen's Manor in Jersey. As the face of the islands and the islanders had changed so had their language, laws and way of life. The ancient and picturesque piece of legal procedure which had survived the passing of the years, *Le Clameur de Haro*, provided a link between the native islanders and their Norman ancestors, for in making *Le Clameur* they were both using the same method to obtain justice from their sovereign. The cry "Haro! Haro!" echoed across a thousand years.

In 1966 Jersey issued a 5s piece, a 3d piece and 1d piece and Guernsey issued a 10s piece, square in shape, but with rounded corners, a 3d piece, heavier than that issued in 1956, an eight-double (1d) piece and a four-double (½d) piece to mark the anniversary. During the year Guernsey held *La Chevauchée de St Michel* for the first time since 1837.

The Bailiwicks of Jersey and Guernsey each set up its own postal administration in 1969 which issued their first stamps on 1st October. Since then they have produced a number of issues of the first quality.

The Royal Commissioners appointed to consider the constitutional relationship between the various parts of the United Kingdom (including the Channel Islands and the Isle of Man) and the government at Westminster visited the islands in 1970 and took evidence.

During the past few years the Channel Islanders have been very much concerned about their future in the event of the United Kingdom going into the European Economic Community. At last the British Government concluded its negotiations for entering the Community. In November 1971, the islands, through the British Government, obtained special terms, which means that they will be exempted from E.E.C. legislation and fiscal regulations and yet will enjoy free trade with Great Britain and the other Market countries. These were the best conditions that the islands could reasonably have expected to obtain in the circumstances.

In 1972 the Channel Islands celebrated the Silver Wedding of Queen Elizabeth II and Prince Philip. Both insular postal administrations produced commemorative sets of stamps. Jersey issued a set of nine gold and silver coins ranging from £50 to 50p. A profile of the Queen appears on the obverse of all the coins and on the reverse appear from the £50 piece downwards—the arms of the bailiwick, the royal arms from Elizabeth Castle, an ormer shell, the gold torque, the Jersey shrew, a lobster, a Jersey-built sailing ship, the *Alexandra*, a Jersey Lily and the royal mace superimposed on an outline map of the island. Guernsey issued a 25p piece with the arms of the bailiwick on the obverse and Eros on the reverse.

In the years since the liberation the islands have undergone great changes. The legislatures and judicatures have been reformed and measures of social security initiated and extended. Hospitals and schools have been built and the essential services extended and improved. The airports have been enlarged and their equipment improved to keep pace with ever more exacting safety requirements. Many wealthy immigrants from Great Britain have taken up residence in the islands in order to reduce their liability to British income tax and surtax and to prevent their estates from having to bear estate duty at their death. Many companies have been formed and numerous banking houses have been opened in the islands with the result that the islands have become recognized as international banking centres. The tourist industry has increased considerably and continues to grow. Many islanders enjoy a high standard of living and throughout the islands there is a very apparent air of prosperity. Naturally, there are problems, shortage of housing being one of the most serious. However, despite these the people have on the whole every reason to be content, and those dark days of the Occupation over a quarter of a century ago seem very far away. The effects on the islands of British entry into the E.E.C. and of their special relationship with the Community will not be fully felt for some time. The future presents, as always, a challenge, particularly for the islands' agricultural industries. There is little doubt that the islanders will accept the challenge and adapt themselves to the changed circumstances, as always has been the case during their long history. So far as the present is concerned, those who live in the Channel Islands may indeed regard themselves as fortunate and each might well re-echo the words written by Sir Amias Poulett, Governor of Jersey, nearly four hundred years ago:

> . . . I can now tell you by experience that it is a blessed life to live in those little Isles. When I consider the course of things in this worlde I persuade myself that God loveth those Isles and careth for them.

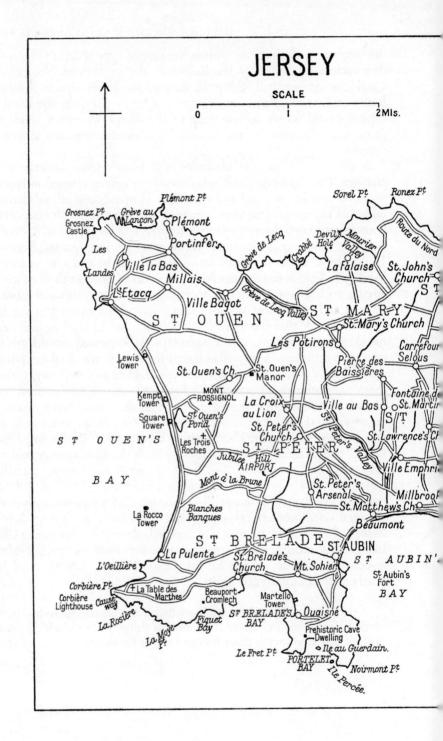

JERSEY

SCALE

0   1   2 Mls.

Plémont Pt

Sorel Pt

Ronez Pt

Grosnez Pt
Grosnez Castle

Grève au Lançon

Plémont

Route du Nord

Devil's Hole

Mourier Valley

Les Landes

Portinfer

Grève de Lecq

Crabbé Hole

La Falaise

St. John's Church

Ville la Bas

Grève de Lecq Valley

St.

Millais

St. MARY

Ville Bagot

ST OUEN

St. Mary's Church

L'Etacq

Les Potirons

Carrefour Selous

Lewis Tower

St. Ouen's Ch.

St. Ouen's Manor

Pierre des Baissières

Fontaine de St. Martin

Kempt Tower

MONT ROSSIGNOL

La Croix au Lion

Ville au Bas

ST

Square Tower

St. Ouen's Pond

St. Peter's Church

St. Lawrence's Ch

ST OUEN'S

Les Trois Roches

Jubilee Hill

ST PETER

Ville Emphri

Millbrook

BAY

AIRPORT

Mont à la Brune

St. Peter's Arsenal

St. Matthew's Ch

La Rocco Tower

Blanches Banques

Beaumont

ST BRELADE

St. Aubin

L'Oeillière

La Pulente

St. Brelade's Church

Mt. Sohier

ST AUBIN'S

Corbière Pt
Corbière Lighthouse

Causeway

La Table des Marthes

Beauport Cromlech

Martello Tower

St. Aubin's Fort

BAY

La Rosière

Ouaisné

La Moye Pt

Figuet Bay

ST BRELADE'S BAY

Prehistoric Cave Dwelling

Ile au Guerdain

Le Fret Pt

PORTELET BAY

Noirmont Pt

Ile Percée

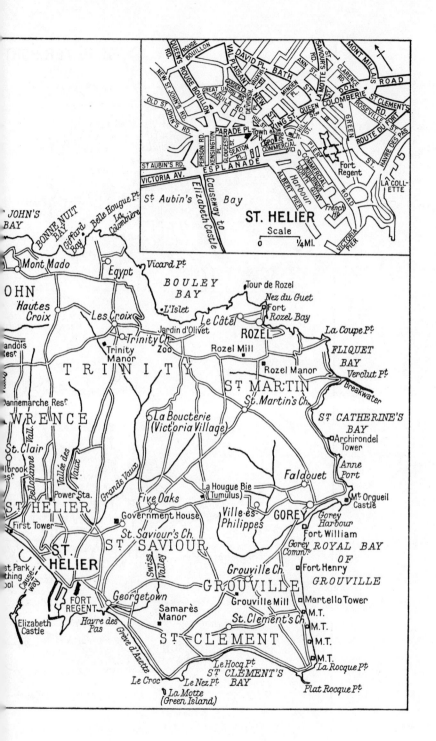

Inset map:

ST. HELIER

ROUGE BOUILLON RD.
QUEENS RD.
NEW ST. JOHN'S RD.
ROUGE BOUILLON
OLD ST. JOHN'S RD.
VAL PLAISANT
DAVID PL.
BATH
MONT MILLAIS ROAD
GREAT UNION RD.
AQUILA
ST. JOHN'S RD.
DEVONSHIRE
CLARENCE
DON RD.
ST. CLEMENT'S RD.
ROSEVILLE
ROUTE DU FORT
HAVRE DES PAS
CLARENCE
PARADE PL.
KENSINGTON PL.
GLOUCESTER PL.
SEATON PL.
ST AUBIN'S RD.
VICTORIA AV.
PERSIAN RD.
ESPLANADE
PARADE PL.
Town
KING ST.
QUEEN ST.
COMMERCIAL
COLOMBERIE
GREEN ST.
HILL ST.
COMMERCIAL BUILDINGS
NORTH QUAY
PIER
Harbour
ALBERT PIER
French Hd.
Fort Regent
LA COLLETTE
VICTORIA PIER
ANN ST.
MINDEN PL.
HUE ST.
BROAD ST.
SAVIOUR'S RD.
LA MOTTE ST.
Elizabeth Castle
Causeway to
St. Aubin's Bay

Scale
0   ¼ MI.

Main map:

ST JOHN'S BAY
BONNE NUIT BAY
Gifford Bay
Belle Hougue Pt
La Colombière
Mont Mado
Egypt
Vicard Pt
BOULEY BAY
Tour de Rozel
Nez du Guet
Fort Rozel Bay
La Coupe Pt
ST JOHN
Hautes Croix
Les Croix
L'Islet
Le Câtel
ROZEL
FLIQUET BAY
Verclut Pt
Breakwater
Jardin d'Olivet
Jandois Resʳ
Trinity Ch.
Zoo
Rozel Mill
Trinity Manor
Rozel Manor
ST MARTIN
T R I N I T Y
St. Martin's Ch.
ST CATHERINE'S BAY
Archirondel Tower
Dannemarche Resʳ
LAWRENCE
La Boucterie (Victoria Village)
St. Clair
Vallée des Vaux
Anne Port
Ilbrook
Bellozanne Vall.
Power Sta.
Grands Vaux
La Hougue Bie (Tumulus)
Faldouet
Mᵗ Orgueil Castle
ST HELIER
First Tower
Five Oaks
Government House
Ville-es-Philippes
GOREY
Gorey Harbour
Fort William
Gorey Commᶯ
ROYAL BAY OF GROUVILLE
st Park
thing ool
ST SAVIOUR
St. Saviour's Ch.
Swiss Valley
Grouville Ch.
Fort Henry
ST. HELIER
FORT REGENT
Georgetown
Samarès Manor
Havre des Pas
Grève d'Azette
GROUVILLE
Grouville Mill
St. Clement's Ch.
Martello Tower
M.T.
M.T.
M.T.
Elizabeth Castle
Causeway
ST CLEMENT
Le Hocq Pt
ST CLEMENT'S BAY
La Rocque Pt
M.T.
Le Croc
Le Nez Pt
Plat Rocque Pt
La Motte (Green Island)

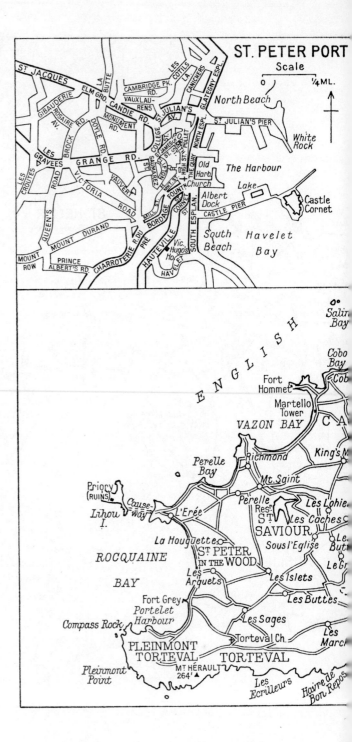

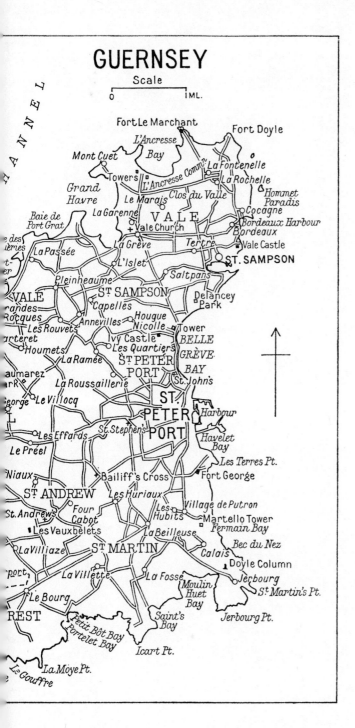

Select Bibliography

Ahier, P., *The Governorship of Sir Walter Raleigh in Jersey 1600–1603*, Bigwood Printers Ltd (Jersey, 1971)

Alderney Society & Museum, *Bulletin* (Alderney, 1966–   )

Balleine, G. R., *A Biographical Dictionary of Jersey*, Staples Press (London, 1948)

Chevalier, J., *Journal*, Société Jersiaise (Jersey, 1906)

de Gruchy, G. F. B., *Medieval Land Tenures in Jersey*, published privately (Jersey, 1957)

Eagleston, A. J., *The Channel Islands under Tudor Government*, published for the Guernsey Society at the University Press (Cambridge, 1949)

Ewen, A. H., and de Carteret, A. R., *The Fief of Sark*, The Guernsey Press Co. Ltd (Guernsey, 1969)

Falla, F., *The Silent War*, Leslie Frewin (London, 1967)

Guernsey Society, *The Quarterly Review* (London, 1944–   )

Kendrick, T. D., & Hawkes, A., *The Archaeology of the Channel Islands*, Methuen & Co. Ltd, London, Vol. I, *The Bailiwick of Guernsey* (Kendrick), 1928, and Vol. II *The Bailiwick of Jersey* (Hawkes), 1939

Le Patourel, J. H., *Medieval Administration of the Channel Islands 1199–1399*, Oxford University Press (London, 1937)

Le Quesne, C., *A Constitutional History of Jersey*, Longman, Brown, Green and Longmans (London, 1856)

Sinel, L. P., *The German Occupation of Jersey*, Corgi Books (Transworld Publishers Ltd.) (London, 1969)

Société Guernesiaise (formerly The Guernsey Society of Natural Science and Local Research), *Report and Transactions* (Guernsey, 1882–   )

Société Jersiaise, *Bulletin Annuel* (Jersey, 1875–   )

—— *Actes des Etats*, 1524–1800 (Jersey, 1897–1917)

—— *Cartulaire des Iles Normandes* (Jersey, 1924)

States of Guernsey, *Actes des Etats de l'Ile de Guernesey 1605–1829*, (Guernsey, n.d.—1932)

—— *Recueil d'Ordres en Conseil* 1800–   (Guernsey, 1903–)

States of Jersey, *Ordres du Conseil et Pièces Analogues Enregistrés a Jersey 1536–1867* (Jersey, 1897–1906)

—— *Recueil des Lois de Jersey* 1771–   (Jersey, 1939–)

Tupper, F. B., *The History of Guernsey and its Bailiwick*, Le Lièvre and Simpkin, Marshall & Co. (Guernsey and London, 1876)

Wood, A. & M., *Islands in Danger*, Four Square Books (The New English Library Ltd.) (London, 1967)